MISSING LINKS

John Reader was born in South London in 1937 and is a grateful beneficiary of the British post-war educational reform that introduced him to subjects he might otherwise have missed while at the same time permitting him to pursue a passion for photography and writing. From this happy conjunction he developed a career in photo-journalism, with particular interest in the life sciences. He contributes to major international publications and is the author of *Pyramids of Life* (with Harvey Croze, 1977), *Kilimanjaro* (1982), *The Rise of Life* (1986) and *Man on Earth* (1988).

JOHN READER

MISSING LINKS

THE HUNT FOR EARLIEST MAN

Foreword by David Pilbeam

With sixteen pages of photographs by the author

PENGUIN BOOKS

PENGUIN BOOKS

Published by the Penguin Group
27 Wrights Lane, London w8 5TZ, England
Viking Penguin Inc., 40 West 23rd Street, New York, New York 10010, USA
Penguin Books Australia Ltd, Ringwood, Victoria, Australia
Penguin Books Canada Ltd, 2801 John Street, Markham, Ontario, Canada L3R 1B4
Penguin Books (NZ) Ltd, 182–190 Wairau Road, Auckland 10, New Zealand

Penguin Books Ltd, Registered Offices: Harmondsworth, Middlesex, England

First published by William Collins Sons & Co. 1981
Second edition published in Pelican Books 1988
3 5 7 9 10 8 6 4 2

Made and printed in Great Britain by
Richard Clay Ltd, Bungay, Suffolk
Filmset in Monophoto Sabon

CONTENTS

HOMO nosce te ipsum.

Carolus Linnaeus
Systema Naturae, 1735

FOREWORD

by David Pilbeam

Missing Links is a substantial and solid piece of work, and also a very timely one. In a field that is beginning to overflow with new texts, its unique approach fills what ecologists would call an 'empty niche'. The book is a fascinating account of the history of palaeoanthropology which brings new information and insights to the early phases of the story, and in addition gives us detailed coverage of the contemporary history of palaeoanthropology. Contemporary history is always the most difficult kind to write, and inevitably more controversial. I think this is a successful attempt, demonstrating as it does the continuity of palaeoanthropological discourse over more than a century and the extent to which many apparently quite new problems are not in fact new. I do not agree with everything in the book; on balance, though, the contemporary events I know about seem accurately and soundly recorded.

The story told is a fascinating one. The book concentrates throughout on the stars of the field – the anthropologists who made or first interpreted major discoveries – and on the objects – the fossils. As the story comes closer to the present we see that scientists pay more attention to context: how old a fossil is and how accurate is its dating; what kind of environment existed at the time; and what part of the habitat a particular human ancestor might have exploited.

Early on the accounts of human evolution were fossil-free, or essentially so. They had to be, because Darwin, Haeckel, Huxley and the other mid-nineteenth-century theorizers had either no or few fossils. Yet they still managed to devise plausible schemes, plausible both to many of their contemporaries and as judged in the light of a century of subsequent fossil discoveries. I suppose the crux of the subject and of this book is, why have the schemes been so durable, so robust? Is it because those nineteenth-century great men were so prescient, because the story really was rather simple and straightforward? Or is something more subtle and unexpected going on? Could we be partly

because it helps explain how discoveries were made, both the finding of the fossils and, infinitely more important, the invention of the concepts which are built upon, or sometimes exist in spite of, the fossils. The book tells us what happened, not only in the past but up to the present too, and it tells us a little of why things happened: through a blend of 'ideas in the air at the time', a little sociology, a dash of ideology, a touch of individual psychology and some good or bad luck.

There are some surprises for the reader in the book. A new hero, or rather, perhaps, a forgotten one, emerges: Robert Broom, who did more than any man to establish the australopithecines as hominids and therefore as creatures central to our understanding of human evolution. I think there were some surprises for the author too. He has stumbled on the fact that scientists (or at least palaeo-anthropologists) don't behave as scientists are supposed to behave: as fact-grinding, theory-generating, objective automata. 'Science' is often subjective and untidy. Nowhere is the dependence of fact on theory, or the existence of preconceptions, or the importance of emotional commitment, more clearly demonstrated than the case of Piltdown; or in the controversy over the KBS tuff; or in the debate over *Australopithecus afarensis*. They are 'sloppy', 'untidy', 'personal', yes. But that is because they involve scientists who are also people, and because much is at stake, for there are glittering prizes in the form of fame and publicity. And there is more general pressure too for answers to cosmic questions, a hunger that sometimes makes palaeo-anthropologists priests of a new kind of secular theology.

Yet we should not despair. Progress has been made. Out of the KBS tuff-dating debate came general advances in methodology and approach, and a much deeper understanding of the chronology of that time-period. Although the human evolutionary story remains ambiguous, we now have many more data – fossils and contextual information – than we did even ten years ago. There is a new realism enabling us to narrow our quest to answerable problems, and to devise ingenious new ways of re-opening apparently unanswerable questions. Despite our obsession with methodology, our science is becoming more mature. As far as explanations can go, it is beginning to look as though the old story of human evolution, one dominated by a brain expanding in response to elaboration of culture and tools,

tions, and then by searching for the data to answer those questions. Fossil hominids are, of course, still the main objects of the quest, but rather as the bearers of information than as objects in their own right. At least, this is how the current generation of practitioners likes to view its work!

Yet the fossils remain glamorous, the centre of attention certainly for the non-professional public, frequently for those palaeo-anthropologists who are not the actual 'hunters', and often – perhaps not surprisingly – for the hunters themselves. So the point is worth emphasizing that the fossils are important not in themselves but because of what they tell us: yet what they tell us is highly ambiguous. Interpretations, schemes and stories vary from one authority to the other, and evolve and re-emerge through time. Why? Because inferences, or conclusions, or speculations, are derived in a complicated way, depending on one's theoretical stance, implicit and explicit assumptions, and on the way in which particular items are selected to be 'facts' (for example, a tooth length is considered a useful fact while colour usually isn't). The inferential process itself is affected by assumptions, theoretical frameworks, the particular facts collected and so forth. The facts chosen, and the inferences drawn, are heavily dependent upon theoretical background assumptions, many of which are either not acknowledged or not even recognized.

If you read technical papers on human evolution today you will often find them full of quantitative techniques and the jargon of hypothesis testing: formalism, objectivity, quantification and rigour have finally come to the field. More and more of our students spend time learning methodology, reading about it and writing about it: learning to behave like 'real' scientists. Our science, we learn, is empirical and involves the collection of facts; when enough are collected we should be able to derive, by a process of induction, theories to explain the facts. From the theories we then invent hypotheses, which are tested experimentally or observationally by collecting more facts, enabling us to reject or modify those hypotheses.

Actually, just as palaeoanthropology has hit its 'philosophical' phase, the emphasis elsewhere in science has begun to shift, or expand, to look more closely at the history of science, to see what actually did happen in the development of an idea rather than what ideally ought to have happened. Hence the timeliness of John Reader's book,

fooling ourselves in letting an incomplete and ambiguous record be moulded by theoretical assumptions that have remained essentially unaffected by the actual fossil record? Careful historical research can help answer that question.

Human fossils were found infrequently in the early days, but by the early twentieth century enough were known to flesh out the evolutionary stories with real characters: *Pithecanthropus*, Neanderthal, Piltdown. Most authorities agreed that the human brain and its tremendous growth were of great importance in understanding the apparently inexorable rise of modern humans. There were differences of opinion about the speed of the process, how old modern humans were, exactly how many extinct side branches there had been, and so forth. But there was general agreement that the brain was important, had led the way, and that aberrant branches of the human evolutionary tree represented failed attempts at becoming human. (Of course, there were always minority opinions, and Haeckel's theoretical proposal of the 1860s that bipedalism preceded brain expansion remained 'available' as a potential evolutionary framework.)

A relatively minor controversy erupted in 1925 over the first australopithecine from Taung in South Africa, only to die down when these strange small-brained creatures could be explained away as odd apes. The 1930s and 1940s provided a major injection of new fossils, mainly from China and South Africa. Those from Asia clarified the nature of *Pithecanthropus*, or *Homo erectus* as it became known. The African fossils revived and then resolved one of the major controversies of human origins: they greatly expanded our knowledge of the australopithecines and established virtually beyond doubt that upright walking preceded brain expansion in human evolution. With that clarified, the basic outlines of the human evolutionary story as most of us now see it were cast. Since the 1950s we have added many more fossils, but our basic schemes have hardly changed.

Along with the new fossils of the last two decades came new kinds of sophisticated evolutionary and ecological thinking, and new kinds of data, made possible by our asking new questions. We now actively seek information about context – time and habitat – when planning an expedition. Perhaps 'planning' is the key word here. Along with the growth of multidisciplinary projects has come, slowly, a different way of approaching research, by defining problems and asking ques-

tells only a fraction of the story. Upright stance came long before brain enlargement, probably in response to changes in mainly vegetable foods that were being eaten. Food and how it is obtained and eaten are now considered of prime importance in the evolution of other kinds of animals, and these seem now increasingly important in telling the story of human evolution. This realigns us with 'nature', by involving the same determining factors in both human and non-human evolution.

Missing Links describes some of what has gone into the process of understanding our past, and demonstrates that what is said about that past can reveal much of how we perceive ourselves today. It shows the humanism of the science of human evolution, and does it with skill, care and beauty.

INTRODUCTION

to the First Edition

On the morning of 2 August 1978 Mary Leakey joined her research team clearing the surface of a solidified volcanic ash-bed at Laetoli Site G, in north-eastern Tanzania. Assistants were deployed around the perimeter while Mary Leakey worked for three hours on a small patch near the centre. She used a dental pick, a soft brush and great care. Time passed slowly; there was little conversation or apparent purpose and the uninitiated might have been struck by the incongruity of the scene – seven adults on their knees tediously sweeping back a tiny patch of wilderness in the company of giraffes and antelopes.

Then, at 10.45, Mary Leakey straightened up abruptly. She lit a cigar, leant forward again, scrutinized the excavation before her and announced: 'Now, this really is something to put on the mantelpiece.' She had uncovered a human-like footprint fossilized in the ash. It was not the first to be found that season, but it was certainly the clearest so far – heel, toes and arch were all well defined. 'This *must* be Homo,' said Mary Leakey. In 1976 geochronologists had reported that the Laetoli ash surface was 3·6 million years old, so the footprint Mary Leakey had found was, in effect, the earliest indisputable evidence of mankind's bipedal gait – an outstanding discovery. While she knelt, the rest of the team gathered round to congratulate her and admire the discovery. But for everyone it was a private moment whose import was not easily shared. The sight of footprints left by an ancestor so long ago combines the commonplace and the miraculous in a manner that language cannot accommodate. It strikes a chord that words distort – especially superlatives.

As the assistants returned to their own work in search of their own discoveries, Mary Leakey, still on her knees, still puffing at her cigar and still gazing at the footprint, said quietly: 'Ah, it is pretty.'

It should be noted that mantelpieces are more a part of Mary Leakey's cultural heritage than of her present lifestyle, and the footprints will *never* be removed from Laetoli. But even so, the Laetoli

expedition in itself and the moment of discovery that morning demonstrate very well both the fascination and the frustration that attend
the study of fossil man. The evidence is rarer than diamonds, and the
study is therefore an intriguing mixture of science and treasure hunt.

The study aspires to discover the origins of mankind and define the
course of human evolution. But these objectives are concealed by a
breadth of time we can barely comprehend. The Laetoli evidence
shows that more than 3·6 million years ago some ape-like creature
must have stumbled on to the evolutionary path that has led to modern
man, but we know very little of the events that determined the route
and we have not identified the ancestor who predetermined the result.
Yet the mystery intrigues everyone. Where did we come from, how
and why? For many generations religious explanations of one sort or
another sufficed to answer these questions, but during the latter half
of the nineteenth century the theory of evolution added a biological
dimension to the mystery. And ever since, scientists have endeavoured
to explain the origins of mankind in evolutionary terms.

The best evidence of human evolution, they believed, would be
found in fossils linking modern man and extinct ancestor. Accordingly,
scientists have scoured the globe for such 'missing links' during the
past 120 years. Some remarkable finds have been unearthed, strange
and fragile relics that evoke fascinating images of the men who lived
long ago but leave the story of human evolution tantalizingly incomplete. The trouble is that the evolutionary significance of the
fossils found so far is not easily determined, and the specimens are
pitifully few. One modern scientist describes attempts to decipher the
course of human evolution from the fossil evidence presently available
as 'rather like trying to follow the story of *War and Peace* from twelve
pages torn at random from the book'.

The ideal fossil evidence would be a sequence of complete fossil
skeletons spanning a known period of time: this would enable scientists to trace evolutionary development with exemplary precision. But
the arbitrary nature of the fossilization process virtually eliminates all
chance that such an ideal could ever be achieved or even approached.
Far from the ideal, the study of fossil man has been restricted to a
slowly accumulating collection of diverse specimens. In the first fifty
years only five were discovered, another twenty-five years passed
before a dozen were known, and even today the significant specimens

could all be accommodated on a billiard table. The fossils have come from Europe, the Far East and Africa; they span over 3 million years, but their clues to the mystery of human evolution represent a minute fraction of mankind's potential ancestry during that time. It has been calculated that ten skulls from East Turkana in Kenya (an exceptional collection covering over 1 million years), for example, represent only one individual in every 100 million – which means that their evidence is no more valid than any two living Americans are today representative of the entire population of the United States (Walker and Leakey 1978: 62).

Such severe shortage of evidence is problematic enough, but there are other difficulties too. Uncertain geological age, for instance, means that differing features cannot be placed in chronological order, and, most important of all, the fragmentary condition of many fossils means that unequivocal interpretation of their significance is rarely possible. Fossils are often so broken, distorted or incomplete that different authorities may stress different features with equal validity, and the points distinguishing their interpretations may be so slight or unclear that each depends as much upon the proponent's preconceived notions as upon the evidence of the fossil.

Preconceived notions have played a fundamental role in the study of fossil man. Indeed, the science itself was not founded upon the evidence of fossils that needed explanation but upon the notion that if mankind had evolved then fossils would provide the evidence of links between modern and ancestral forms. Thus scientists have sought evidence to prove an idea. But fossil evidence is rare, and a variety of ideas about human evolution has developed in the long gaps between discoveries, when interpretative speculation inevitably became a predominant activity of the science. Different theories about the origin of mankind were formulated, theories that accommodated the existing evidence and created a preconceived notion of what fossils ought to be found next. And it is remarkable how often the first interpretations of new evidence have confirmed the preconceptions of its discoverer.

Throughout the study of fossil man, the related elements of interpretation, theory and preconception have always been firmly connected with the personality and persuasive ability of their proposer. Thus the science has been dominated by ambitious individuals and has advanced as much by the force of argument as by the strength of the evidence, and as much by the lure of the treasure hunt as by the discipline of science.

Knowledge is the ultimate goal of all science, though evidence occasionally has its own intrinsic appeal. In the study of fossil man, however, both knowledge and evidence are uniquely appealing. The knowledge sought is the ancestry of a supremely important animal: *Homo sapiens*. The evidence consists of rare and mysterious fossils.

Fossils are objects of inestimable value because they are so few, and of highest promise because of the secrets they may reveal. Some are objects of beauty as well, but above all each is an object of wonder. They are the tangible evidence of our ancestors' existence and they affirm mankind's ancient presence on earth. Scientists say fossils can help us define the course of human evolution, but everyone – including scientists – is subject to a more emotive response while handling, or even just looking at, a fossil. And the discovery of a fossil is the epitome of this sensation, a sublime moment that quite transcends any knowledge the fossil may afford.

'You must love the fossils,' said Ralph von Koenigswald, who found some important specimens in Java. 'If you love them,' he said, 'then they will come to you.'

The footprints at Laetoli are the latest discovery in a saga that blends the discipline of science with the romance of a treasure hunt and the vagaries of human nature. The saga is far from finished, but it began over 120 years ago when the discovery of Neanderthal Man coincided with the publication of Darwin's theory of evolution.

Richmond, March 1980

INTRODUCTION

to the Second Edition

Palaeoanthropology has advanced considerably since I began work on the first edition of *Missing Links* in 1977 and this second edition provides a very welcome opportunity to bring the book up to date and make it a fuller account of the science.

The first edition of *Missing Links* was very closely allied with the romance and treasure-hunt aspects of palaeoanthropology, simply because the book was composed around a new set of photographs of the original fossils. To take those photographs, I spent many hours and days with the fossils. They were magical times, combining the privilege of handling such precious objects with the challenge of producing photographs that would bring something of their intrinsic appeal to the printed page.

With fossils as its central theme, the book was concerned primarily with the historical sequence of specimens whose discovery had actually added something new to the developing science of palaeo-anthropology, and with how these discoveries had come about, and how they had been greeted and initially interpreted. This structure left little opportunity for dealing with the development of ideas among people who did not find fossils; nor did it allow me to follow the study of particular aspects of the science up to the present day in anything but the most cursory manner.

The exigencies of publishing economics make it impossible for this edition to be fully illustrated in colour, but the absence of photographs integrated with the text also removes the editorial and structural constraints of the first edition – and on balance, I am very pleased about that. A selection of the original photographs is reproduced in black and white, still giving, I hope, some sense of the fossils' appeal. The extended text covers more fully the work of people who were not, or are not, principally concerned with the discovery of fossils, and follows advances in the science up to the present day. My hope now is that the wonder of the fossils which inspired the first edition, and the rigour of science which has impressed me while researching the second, will combine in these pages to provide an interesting and satisfyingly full account of a science which has become a great deal more than just a treasure hunt in the last few decades.

Richmond, March 1988

NEANDERTHAL MAN

(1857)

The theory of evolution published by Charles Darwin in 1859 implied that man was simply a product of life on earth, not its ultimate purpose; it suggested that his origins were shared by the animals of the jungle. An outrageous idea. But if it were true, then the proof would be found in the fossilized remains of early man, which would link man to an earlier form. And since the theory of evolution proposed that man and the apes shared a common ancestor, then the link could be expected to bear some attributes of both. So began the search for the 'Missing Link', keenly followed by evolutionist and anti-evolutionist alike – the former seeking the incontrovertible evidence that would establish the theory as fact, the latter anxious to prove that the link was indeed missing, thus reconfirming the belief that the human form had remained unchanged since the day of creation.

It soon became apparent that conclusive evidence one way or the other was exceptionally hard to find. A fossilized vertebral column and other parts which the Swiss naturalist Johann Scheuchzer (1672–1733) had claimed were the remains of a man who lived before the time of the Flood were shown by the French comparative anatomist Georges Cuvier (1769–1832) to be those of a large salamander (Eiseley 1958: 86–7). A skeleton from Guadaloupe, found aboard a French ship captured by a British naval vessel in the early nineteenth century and described as 'the first known example of the bones of man in a fossil state' (British Museum 1814) later proved to be less than 200 years old and not fossil at all. This is obviously a crucial distinction for the palaeontologist.

The effect of the fossilization process is that instead of breaking down into their chemical components, bones of dead creatures (or plants, or insects) are buried away from the agents of decomposition, and infiltrated by minerals which replace them, molecule by molecule, until, where organic material existed before, stone remains, exactly preserving the form of the original.

The fossil remains of marine creatures, extinct elephants and so forth are unmistakable. Human fossils, on the other hand, are found only in geologically recent – and therefore comparatively shallow – deposits, where they may easily be confused with historically recent burials. So how can fossilized and unfossilized bone be distinguished one from the other? In the early nineteenth century the 'tongue test' was a method commonly used, the idea being that bone or fossil adhered to the tongue to a greater or lesser extent depending upon the amount of collagen it contained. However, the tongue test was occasionally contradicted by the hydrochloric acid test, which sometimes revealed large quantities of collagen where the tongue test had suggested it was absent (Blake 1862: 207). In view of these factors, geological circumstances were always the best indication of antiquity: were the remains found above, below or among the bones of extinct animals? But even where such indications existed, the evidence of early man was often ignored.

The first fossil human remains known to have been discovered, a skull fragment found at Cannstadt in southern Germany in about the year 1700, lay in the Stuttgart Museum for 135 years before they were scientifically described (see Quatrefages and Hamy 1882) and received little attention thereafter. Fossil human remains found by Baron von Schlottheim in 1820 near Koestritz, Upper Saxony, nearly two metres below the remains of extinct hyenas and rhinoceros, also were largely ignored, although he insisted that 'these human bones from the nature of the soil could not have been buried there, nor have fallen into fissures during battles of ancient times' (Anon. 1864: 71). And a similar lack of reaction greeted the discoveries and publications of Paul Schmerling (1791–1836), a founder of palaeontology in Belgium, who excavated artefacts and seven human skulls recovered from the Engis caves near Liège, some in clear association with rhinoceros and mammoth bones. 'There can be no doubt that the human bones were buried at the same time and by the same cause as the other extinct species,' he wrote (1833–4: 59). Schmerling's claims were dismissed by most experts of the day, but the English geologist Charles Lyell subsequently commended their significance in his book *The Antiquity of Man*, published in 1863, with a vivid account of Schmerling's efforts and tribulations:

To be let down, as Schmerling was, day after day, by a rope tied to a tree so as to slide to the foot of the first opening of the Engis cave, where the best-preserved human skulls were found; and, after thus gaining access to the first subterranean gallery, to creep on all fours through a contracted passage leading to larger chambers, there to superintend by torchlight, week after week and year after year, the workmen who were breaking through the stalagmite underlaying bone breccia nearly as hard; to stand for hours with one's feet in the mud and with water dripping from the roof on one's head, in order to mark the position and guard against the loss of each single bone of a skeleton, and at length after finding leisure, strength and courage for all these operations, to look forward, as the fruits of one's labour, to the publication of unwelcome intelligence, opposed to the prepossessions of the scientific and as well as the unscientific public – when these circumstances are taken into account, we need scarcely wonder, not only that a passing traveller failed to stop and scrutinise the evidence, but that a quarter of a century should have elapsed before even the neighbouring professors of the University of Liège came forth to vindicate the truthfulness of their indefatigable and clear-sighted countryman (Lyell 1863: 68–9).

(Modern views of the Engis fossils are summarized by Stringer *et al.* 1984: 111–12.)

And it was not only in continental Europe that the early evidence of man's prehistoric existence was passed over; in England too it received scant attention. Kent's Cavern, near Torquay, supplied evidence of flint tools together with extinct animals in 1829 but did not attract scientific attention (Pengelly 1869). The significance of a skull found in Gibraltar some time before 1848 was similarly overlooked (see p. 11).

And then again, as the concept of evolution filtered from the confines of science into the public consciousness during the nineteenth century, there were some who deliberately sought to hide evidence accidentally encountered. In 1852, for instance, a man chasing rabbits on a French hillside near Aurignac thrust his arm down a hole after his prey and, instead of a rabbit, drew out a large bone. He dug deeper and eventually discovered a cave filled with human remains. Local curiosity attracted the mayor, Dr Amiel, to the scene, and once that learned gentleman had satisfied his curiosity to the extent of establishing that the bones had belonged to seventeen individuals of both sexes and all ages, he arranged for their prompt Christian burial

in the parish cemetery. Eight years later the sexton professed complete
ignorance of the burial site when the palaeontologist Edouard Lartet
inquired after it in the hope of adding something to the study of
human evolution (Lyell 1863: 183).

The idea of evolution probably did not reach many people in any
comprehensive, or even comprehensible, form during the first part
of the nineteenth century; but in 1844 it appeared in a form that
was available to all, in a book called *Vestiges of the Natural History
of Creation*, written by Robert Chambers (1802–71), a journalist of
scientific bent. The book was very successful, selling out four edi-
tions in seven months and more than 20,000 copies by the time
Darwin's *The Origin of Species* appeared, fifteen years later (Eiseley
1958: 133).

Vestiges was published anonymously to protect Chambers's business interests and thus, writing for a popular audience and free from
the constraints of precise scientific presentation, he could afford to be
bold in presenting what he called 'the first attempt to connect the
natural sciences into a history of creation'. He drew together all available scientific evidence and hypothesis to describe how the universe is
arranged, and how the earth is composed of matter condensed from
'vaporiform chaos'. Calling upon (and occasionally misinterpreting)
the evidence of biology and palaeontology, he told how organic
creation and the proliferation of life was the result of natural law
rather than divine intent. 'The simplest and the most primitive type
. . . gave birth to the type next above it, . . . this again produced the
next higher, and so on to the very highest' (Chambers 1844: 231).
There was a principle of *development* involved, he said, that had
operated over a vast span of time. All animals were variations of the
same basic skeletal plan; they were, in fact, 'merely modifications of
that plan to suit particular conditions' and 'the whole train of
animated beings, from the simplest and oldest, up to the highest and
most recent [should] be regarded as a series of advances of the principle
of development' (Chambers 1844: 208).

Chambers did not stress the point, but his development hypothesis
clearly made man an immediate descendant of the apes (albeit fossil
apes then still undiscovered), retaining a 'strong affinity' to the preceding form, just like every other animal. And, of course, 'the development hypothesis would demand . . . that the original seat of the

human race should be in a region where the quadrumana [that is, apes and monkeys] are rife' (Chambers 1844: 281).

It is tempting to think of *Vestiges* as a brilliant forerunner of Darwin's evolutionary theory, lacking only the principle of natural selection to make the hypothesis complete. But it lacked other elements too. Darwin himself remarked that the book displayed 'little accurate knowledge and a great want of scientific caution'; even so, he praised the 'powerful and brilliant style', and considered that the book had 'done excellent service ... in calling attention to the subject, in removing prejudice, and in thus preparing the ground for the reception of analogous views' (Darwin 1888: xviii).

A charitable thought. It is possible that with *Vestiges* having drawn the fire, so to speak, the attack on Darwin's work was less fierce than it might have been. But it is equally possible that *Vestiges* awakened a broader spectrum of prejudice than would otherwise have been the case and, furthermore, that the book was regarded as a popular version of evolutionary theory upon the basis of which Darwin's work could be attacked without the necessity of reading his more knowledgeable and cautiously scientific book.

As public opinion gradually became aware of the evolutionary theory, most anxiety was caused by the proposition that man was an animal who shared a common ancestor with the apes. This anxiety occasionally turned to angry debate wherein science appeared to oppose religion. But serious debate is rarely as straightforward as that. Although the pulpit may have been the source of some outspoken and inflammatory opposition, there were also scientists who disagreed with the theory of evolution. Scientists were obliged to call upon science to support their arguments – whatever their religious beliefs – and at this level the debate inspired a great deal of earnest endeavour as scientists who opposed Darwin's theory attempted to reconcile the new facts their colleagues had glimpsed with the old truths in which they still believed.

In Britain the scientific opposition was led by the distinguished anatomist and palaeontologist Richard Owen (1804–92), who energetically applied his indisputable talents to the search for an alternative explanation of the evolutionary phenomena. In 1849 Owen published his concept of an archetypal vertebrate skeleton. The skeleton did not represent a creature that had ever existed; it was a

structural idea, he said, of which all actual vertebrates were functionally diverse embodiments which had arisen without any direct
evolutionary association (Owen 1849). And later, in 1855, Owen used
his anatomical expertise in an attempt to disprove the theory of evolution at its most controversial point – man's link with the apes.

The occasion was an evening meeting of the Royal Institution of
Great Britain. Owen discussed the structure of the apes as compared
to man, referring in particular to 'the last link in the chain of changes
– from Quadrumana to Bimana [four-handed to two-handed]
proposed in the hypothesis that specific characters can be so far
modified by external influences, operating on successive generations,
as to produce a new and higher species of animal, and that thus there
had been a gradual progression from the monad up to man' (Owen
1855: 26–41).

Beginning and ending with disparaging remarks on those who
supported the evolutionary theory, Owen endeavoured to show that
although ape and man are structurally very similar, the differences
between them are much more relevant. He mentioned especially the
differences that are not subject to external influences, and therefore
should be passed from generation to generation without modification,
appearing exactly alike in ancestor and descendant. Owen cited the
gorilla's prominent eyebrow ridge as an example of such a feature.
There is no muscle attached to it, he pointed out, nor is there any
aspect of the gorilla's behaviour which suggests that the prominent
ridge could be lost or gained by external causes operating on successive
generations. Therefore the ridges must have occurred in the gorilla's
ancestors, said Owen, and should occur in all that ancestor's descendants. It followed that if man and gorilla shared a common ancestor, they should also share the prominent eyebrow ridge. But ridges
rarely – and then only feebly – occur in man, he pointed out; therefore
man and gorilla could not have an ancestor in common. Thus, Owen
concluded, the notion that man had evolved from the apes was disproved.

The gorilla's eyebrow ridges were not the only evidence Owen
offered in support of his contentions that evening, nor was it the only
occasion on which he argued against the common ancestry of man
and ape. None the less, it is an extraordinary coincidence that the first
fossil to be accepted as evidence of early man's physical form,

Neanderthal Man, should have presented prominent eyebrow ridges as its most distinctive feature. Since 1857, when the Neanderthal remains were found, the prominent ridges above its eyes, which Owen claimed were an exclusively ape-like feature, have become symbolic of early man.

Neanderthal Man was found by limestone quarrymen clearing a cave in the deep and narrow ravine known as the Neander valley, through which the Düssel river flows, a short distance from its confluence with the Rhine at Düsseldorf. The cave was quite large but could be entered only with difficulty, the entrance being just a metre or so high and situated twenty metres up a precipitous cliff. The bones were found among the one and a half metres of mud that was dug from the cave floor. It is quite likely that the entire skeleton was present, but the bones were not immediately recognized as human and were unceremoniously dumped with the quarry debris. Several weeks passed before they came to the attention of J. K. Fuhlrott, a teacher from Elberfeld, some six or seven kilometres distant, and by then only the skullcap and some limb bones could be found. No faunal fossils, extinct or otherwise, were found with the remains; and because they were in a cave deposit, no stratigraphic position of any relevance could be determined. Consequently, Neanderthal Man could not be placed on the geological scale of relative ages, and the evidence of the fossil's antiquity lay solely in its physical appearance.

Fuhlrott promptly showed the remains to Hermann Schaaffhausen, Professor of Anatomy at the University of Bonn, who presented them to the world of science at a meeting of the Lower Rhine Medical and Natural History Society held in Bonn on 4 February 1857, nearly three years before the publication of Darwin's *The Origin of Species* in November 1859. Schaaffhausen was convinced that the remains were ancient and human; but the limb bones were exceptionally thick, he remarked, with pronounced muscle attachments, denoting an extremely powerful individual. The strange shape of the skull was due to natural conformation, said Schaaffhausen, but was quite unlike any modern race, even the most barbarous. The prominent eyebrow ridges – 'characteristic of the facial conformation of the large apes' – must have been typical of the Neanderthal race, he suggested, giving them a savage and brutal aspect. He concluded that the remains must

have belonged to one of the original wild races of north-western
Europe, a barbarous lot whose 'aspect and flashing of their eyes' had
terrified even the Roman armies (Schaaffhausen 1858, 1861).

Some listeners challenged Schaaffhausen's views (mostly contending
that the remains were not human at all), but controversy did not
assume significant proportions until his paper appeared in English in
the *Natural History Review* of April 1861. It was translated by George
Busk (1807–86), then Professor of Anatomy at the Royal College of
Surgeons, who appended some remarks of his own, drawing particular
attention to the Neanderthal skull's overall resemblance to that of the
gorilla and chimpanzee. Shortly thereafter, the recently knighted geologist Sir Charles Lyell acquired a plaster cast and some photographs
of the original specimen, which were examined and described by the
biologist Thomas Huxley (1825–95), and before very long Neanderthal
Man became the nub of an argument that was distinguished by its
vigour, imagination and unintended humour.

Broadly speaking, there were two points of view. The physical
peculiarities of Neanderthal Man represented either an early stage of
human evolution, linking man to an ape-like ancestor, or pathological
deformities of modern man more gross than any that medical science
had ever encountered. Because their antiquity could be neither proved
nor disproved, the fossils themselves were the only evidence and, as
was to be expected, interpretation of the evidence was decidedly
coloured by preconceptions concerning the theory of evolution in
general. Those willing to accept the theory believed the remains were
very old and freely discussed their primitive, 'barbarous' and ape-like
characteristics in evolutionary terms. Those opposed to the theory of
evolution, on the other hand, believed the remains were of modern
man and sought a modern, medical explanation for their peculiarities.

As it happened, the first thorough descriptions of the fossils were
compiled by evolutionists and, so long as the fossils and casts remained
unavailable for general inspection, these reports constituted the
evidence itself – which no doubt added the suspicion of bias and
misrepresentation to any anti-evolutionist stance. Add the clashing
personalities of very ambitious individuals to this already volatile
mixture of inconclusive evidence and preconceived belief, and the
result is a very lively brew. The protagonists were 'in danger of allowing the wanderings of imagination to take the place of scientific

deduction, and to lead us far away from sober fact', as the *Medical Times and Gazette*, Britain's leading medical journal of the day, commented in an editorial reviewing the evidence of '*Homo Antiquus*', (Anon. 1862).

Taken out of context, this remark seems the essence of moderation and good sense, but the context reveals how preconceptions may rule in the absence of conclusive evidence. Schaaffhausen's description of the Neanderthal fossils 'strongly reminds one of Sir Walter Scott's Black Dwarf,' wrote the editors; 'a theory of rickets and idiocy would ... go some way towards unravelling the mystery,' they said, and concluded that '... this skull belonged to some poor idiotic hermit whose remains were found in the cave where he died.'

There is a salutary observation to be made here, which applies to virtually every discovery that has added new knowledge to the story of human evolution. Where the evidence is not sufficient to prove interpretations based on current beliefs right or wrong, any speculation is permissible. Furthermore, the acceptance that speculation achieves is more a measure of the proposer's standing than of its validity. Some speculation, of course, turns out to be correct, but corroborative evidence is always required and, until that evidence is forthcoming, speculative argument continues.

For many years idiocy and rickets remained the anti-evolutionists' best explanation of Neanderthal Man's physical peculiarities (Schaaffhausen 1858, 1861; Blake 1864: 139–57). The theme was developed and expounded most forcefully by F. Mayer, Professor of Anatomy at Bonn University. Mayer had the advantage of having examined the original fossils. He dismissed the significance of the prominent eyebrow ridges and remarked instead upon the absence of a sagittal crest (that is, the ridge of bone running along the top of an ape's skull to which the chewing muscles are affixed). 'Show me a human fossil skull with a sagittal crest, and I will acknowledge the descent of man from an ape-like ancestor,' he said (Mayer 1864: 1–26).

Mayer was convinced that the remains had belonged to a modern individual. In the skull he saw similarities with some Mongolian and even some Caucasian specimens that he had examined. Nevertheless, Neanderthal Man had been a degraded creature in his view, and one who had probably suffered from rickets as a child, the disease being common, he pointed out, among those who lived in wet houses and

ate nothing but potatoes. Thus rickets might explain the distinctly
bent legs of Neanderthal Man. But bow-legs are also common among
those who spend a lifetime in the saddle, Mayer observed. And so,
turning to the evidence of history, the anatomist offered his interpretation of Neanderthal Man: a Cossack army under General
Tchernitcheff had camped in the vicinity prior to their advance across
the Rhine on 14 January 1814, and he believed that the bones in the
Neanderthal cave must have belonged to an ailing Cossack deserter
who had hidden and died there.

Thomas Huxley, the evolutionists' most ardent champion, dismissed Mayer's conclusions as a work 'laden with numerous jocosities
of small size, but great ponderosity, directed against Mr Darwin and
his doctrine . . .' He also noted that Professor Mayer had failed to
explain how the dying man had managed to climb a precipice twenty
metres high and bury himself after death; and wondered why the man
who would have removed all his clothes and equipment before performing these wonderful feats (Huxley 1864: 429–46).

On a more serious level, Huxley meanwhile had defined the evolutionist view concisely in three essays published together under the
title *Man's Place in Nature* in 1863. Here he described the natural
history of the apes, defined man's relationship with the lower animals
and presented the first thorough and detailed comparative description
of the Neanderthal remains. Huxley concluded that although the skull
was the most ape-like yet known, it did not represent a being that was
intermediate between the apes and man; at most it showed some
reversion from the modern human skull towards that of an ape-like
ancestor. The determining factor, Huxley said, was the size of the
brain. The cranial capacity of the Neanderthal skull was well within
the modern human range and twice that of the largest ape. And so,
with these remarks, Huxley effectively set brain size as the definitive
characteristic of the genus *Homo* – a status that has been central to
interpretations of the fossil evidence of human evolution ever since.

The assessment of Neanderthal Man's brain size raised the interesting question of his mental abilities. Could a creature of such ape-like
appearance think like a man? The anti-evolutionists, of course, said
no, he had been an idiot; and even some evolutionists were unwilling to
accept the creature as sapient man. William King, for instance, Professor of Geology at Queen's College, Galway, believed that Nean-

derthal Man had stood next to 'benightedness' with 'thoughts and desires . . . which never soared beyond those of the brute'. In fact, King felt so strongly about Neanderthal Man's mental deficiencies that he proposed his exclusion from the human species (*Homo sapiens*). He would have liked to exclude him from the genus *Homo* altogether, he said, but in the absence of facial bones and the base of the skull he appreciated that this 'would be clearly overstepping the limits of inductive reasoning'. So King settled for a new species: *Homo neanderthalensis* (King 1864: 88–97). This was a startling development, suggesting that formal zoological distinction could be given to the fossils of ancestral man. Since then, naming new species on man's evolutionary path has become common practice, as we shall see.

Given the liveliness of the Neanderthal debate it was inevitable that corroborative, or dismissive, evidence would eventually be found. It arrived just a matter of weeks after King had created the new species: a skull that, though missing some parts, possessed everything the Neanderthal skull had lacked: the entire face, the upper jaw and most of the teeth. Furthermore, it was strikingly similar to the Neanderthal specimen, especially in respect of the eyebrow ridges. In short, the new skull was just what King had required to complete his inductive reasoning. But it would not have helped him relegate Neanderthal from the genus *Homo*. On the contrary, it might well have persuaded him that the specimen did not deserve specific distinction, for its general aspect confirmed Huxley's assessment.

The new skull had been found during the construction of military fortifications in Gibraltar. When and by whom is not known. The first mention of the relic appears in the minutes of the Gibraltar Scientific Society for 3 March 1848, where it is recorded that the secretary 'presented a human skull from the Forbes Quarry, North front'. In other words, the discovery predated Neanderthal by at least eight years, but the Gibraltar specimen did not attract attention until much later. It was consigned to the 'small museum of natural curiosities which at one time existed in Gibraltar', where it languished while the museum was 'allowed to fall into a state of confusion and neglect' until 1863, when 'its extraordinary peculiarities fortunately struck the notice of Dr Hodgkin', an ethnologist on a visit to Gibraltar, who then arranged for its dispatch to George Busk (Busk 1864a).

Busk, of course, was the man who had translated Schaaffhausen's Neanderthal paper, and he immediately recognized the importance of the new and more complete specimen, not only in its own right but also for the corroborative evidence it brought to the Neanderthal case. The Gibraltar skull 'adds immensely to the scientific value of the Neanderthal specimen,' he wrote in the *Reader* a few days after receiving the skull, 'showing that the latter does not represent ... a mere individual peculiarity, but that it may have been characteristic of a race extending from the Rhine to the Pillars of Hercules; for ... even Professor Mayer will hardly suppose that a rickety Cossack engaged in the campaign of 1814 had crept into a sealed fissure in the Rock of Gibraltar' (Busk 1864b).

Busk exhibited the skull at the meeting of the British Association for the Advancement of Science held in Bath during September 1864. He spoke of its general appearance and compared it with the skulls of modern races, but primarily stressed how it matched and complemented the Neanderthal specimen (1864a). In a letter discussing the forthcoming meeting, the palaeontologist Hugh Falconer had suggested that Busk should name the fossil *Homo calpicus*, from Calpe, the ancient name for the Rock of Gibraltar. Falconer also composed an advertisement that would introduce the new species to science: 'Walk up: and see Professor Busk's Grand Priscan, Pithecoid, Mesocephalous, Prognathous, Agrioblemmatous, Platycnemic, wild *Homo calpicus* of Gibraltar.' Falconer was particularly pleased with Agrioblemmatous, feeling that the Greek combination happily united 'the truculence of the eye and the savagery of the face' which he was certain must have characterized the man on the Rock of Gibraltar (Falconer 1864: 313).

But the Gibraltar skull inspired little or no comment, despite its undoubted significance. After its formal description (Busk and Falconer 1865) the specimen virtually disappeared from the literature, and its corroborative evidence was ignored by the pathologist Rudolf Virchow in 1872, when he added his views to the Neanderthal debate.

Virchow (1821–1902) was a highly respected medical academician. He had been the first to describe the breakdown of the cell that marks the onset of disease, and the science of pathology was built upon his discoveries. He was also the founder and president of Germany's Institute of Anthropology; and, while his fierce opposition to the theory of evolution predicated his conclusions on the Neanderthal remains, his twin interests – pathology and anthropology – characterized their substance.

On the evidence of pathology Virchow decided that the bones had belonged to a very old man who had suffered from rickets as a child, from severe head injuries in middle age and from crippling arthritis for many years before he died. Thus the physical peculiarities were accounted for. To show that Neanderthal Man had died in the recent past and was not, therefore, an ancestor of man, Virchow called upon the evidence of anthropology. Such an ill and crippled individual could not have survived to old age in one of the nomadic hunter-gatherer groups that characterized the earliest stages of human social development, he said; therefore the man must have lived in an agricultural society of much more recent times, when people were settled and able to care for their sick and aged relatives (Virchow 1872: 157– 65).

Virchow's pronouncements on the Neanderthal remains were the last to be made by an eminent scientist reared and educated in the years before Darwin presented his comprehensive theory of evolution; in effect, they were the last words of the pre-evolutionists, and they present yet another example of a scientist struggling to reconcile new evidence with the old beliefs. But, of course, the debate concerning human evolution did not end with Virchow. Subsequently the search for more conclusive fossil evidence became intense and some spectacular discoveries were made. Two complete skeletons were found in a cave near Spy in Belgium during 1887; another was found near La Chapelle-aux-Saints in France during 1908 and several more came from La Ferrassie in 1909 and from La Quina in 1911. The most striking feature of these remarkably complete finds was their overall similarity to the original Neanderthal specimens; clearly, they all represented a race that had populated Europe from Belgium to Gibraltar.

Had he seen the new evidence, Virchow might have felt obliged to revise his diagnosis of head injuries and arthritis. But now the discoveries were examined by a new generation of investigators, a generation born and educated in the post-Darwinian era but one which was none the less subject to preconceptions of its own. And it is ironic that although fundamental beliefs had changed so radically, the conclusions of Virchow and the new investigators were essentially the same: both excluded Neanderthal from the ancestry of modern man.

Marcellin Boule (1861–1942) was perhaps the most authoritative of the post-Darwinian investigators. He eventually became Director of Human Palaeontology at the French National Museum of Natural History, and for more than fifty years commanded the respect of both science and the interested public, especially after the First World War had cast German science into disfavour and disarray. Boule wrote extensively on the fossils of early man (Boule 1921). His views and preconceptions are largely responsible for the image – which is still with us today – of Neanderthal Man as a shambling, frowning brute of low intelligence.

By the turn of the century, most scientists accepted the great antiquity of the earth, .the theory of evolution and the inevitable conclusion that man had evolved from an ancestor in common with the apes. There was no question that Neanderthal Man *had* evolved from some primitive stock, but could such a creature represent the ancestor of modern man? This was a question that Boule and his fellow thinkers barely deigned to contemplate.

Boule's judgement was based on his extremely thorough studies of the skeleton from La Chapelle-aux-Saints (Boule 1911–13). Neanderthal Man, he pointed out, was quite different from modern man in physical form, yet very close in time; and he concluded that the process of evolution could not have effected so much change in so few generations. Neanderthal Man had divergent toes like the apes, Boule said; he had walked on the outer edges of his feet like the orang-utan; he could not have straightened his knees; he lacked the convex spine essential for upright posture; he had the head slung forward with jutting jaw; and possessed only the most rudimentary psychic nature and articulate language.

Of those who endorsed Boule's conclusions, Grafton Elliot Smith (1871–1937), Professor of Anatomy at the University of London, was among the most influential. In his book *The Evolution of Man*, Elliot Smith described Boule's reconstruction of the La Chapelle-aux-Saints skeletons as:

a clear-cut picture of the uncouth and repellent Neanderthal Man. His short, thick-set and coarsely built body was carried in a half-stooping slouch upon short, powerful and half-flexed legs of peculiarly ungraceful form. His thick neck sloped forward from the broad shoulders to support the massive flattened head, which protruded forward, so as to form an unbroken curve of neck and back, in place of the alternation of curves which is one of the graces of the truly erect *Homo sapiens*. The heavy overhanging eyebrow-ridges and retreating forehead, the great coarse face with its large eye-sockets, broad nose, and receding chin, combined to complete the picture of unattractiveness, which it is more probable than not was still further emphasized by a shaggy covering of hair over most of the body. The arms were relatively short, and the exceptionally large hands lacked the delicacy and the nicely balanced co-operation of thumb and fingers which is regarded as one of the most distinctive of human characteristics ... The contemplation of all these features emphasizes the reality of the fact that the Neanderthal Man belongs to some other species than *Homo sapiens* (Smith 1927: 109).

The views of Boule and Elliot Smith are a mirror image of those expressed fifty years before; the same evidence called to support diametrically opposed conclusions. Mayer and Virchow had claimed that the Neanderthal fossils were of a modern man who was not related to the apes; now Boule and Elliot Smith claimed that Neanderthal Man was a descendant of the apes who was not related to modern man. In both cases the evidence lay in the physical peculiarities of the fossils and, in the interpretation of this evidence, Boule and Elliot Smith were no less guilty than their predecessors of allowing preconception to cloud conclusion. Mayer and Virchow had stressed the pathological aspects that supported the conclusions they preferred; Boule and Elliot Smith ignored the pathological aspects that would have refuted their conclusions.

In fact, the pathological evidence was the same in both cases: severe arthritis. This was first noted by Camille Arambourg in 1955 and precisely defined by Cave and Straus (1957: 348–63). These critical reassessments questioned Boule's reconstruction of the La Chapelle-aux-Saints skeleton (the centre of gravity was placed so far forward that the man was likely to have fallen flat on his face before taking a step). Cave and Straus expressed surprise that Boule had not noticed the 'severity of the osteo-arthritis deformens affecting the vertebral column'. In conclusion, they found 'no valid reason for assuming that the posture of Neanderthal Man differed significantly from that of present day man'. Given a bath, a collar and tie, he would have passed unnoticed in a New York subway, they said.

2

NEANDERTHAL
AND MODERN MAN

The suggestion that prehistoric Neanderthal Man, appropriately attired and properly behaved, could mingle unnoticed among a group of twentieth-century commuters emphasizes the importance of context in palaeoanthropology: fossils cannot be placed accurately in the story of human evolution without sound information on where they have come from, on when the people they represent had lived and, ideally, on how they had lived.

Palaeoanthropologists depend very heavily upon the evidence of other disciplines for this information. Foremost among the contributing disciplines are: geology, palaeontology, archaeology and anthropology. Briefly, geology establishes a context of relative age, according to the strata from which fossils are recovered (and these days, sophisticated dating techniques enable geochronologists to establish the *absolute* age); palaeontology sets the environmental and climatic context, as determined by the nature and variety of other fossil organisms found in the same deposit; archaeology sets the context of cultural status by providing indications of what technical expertise had been achieved (toolmaking and dwelling construction, for instance); and anthropology provides information on people in historical times which gives palaeoanthropologists some idea of how the people represented by the fossils might be expected to have lived.

The basic features of geology which palaeoanthropologists depend upon were established when Giovanni Arduino (1713–95) divided the stratigraphic succession he observed in the rocks into a temporal sequence of primary, secondary and tertiary rocks. In 1841 John Phillips added an organic dimension to the picture by applying the terms Palaeozoic (meaning early life), Mesozoic (middle life) and Cainozoic (now often spelt Cenozoic; recent life) to the fossil-bearing deposits. Charles Lyell (1797–1875) then established geology as a science with his meticulously detailed reviews of the evidence confirming the earth's great antiquity and man's prehistoric existence, published as *Principles of Geology* in three volumes between 1830 and 1834 and *The Antiquity of Man* in 1863.

The foundations of modern palaeontology were laid down in the late eighteenth and early nineteenth centuries, principally by the work of the French anatomist Georges Cuvier (1769–1832) and the English surveyor William Smith (1769–1839). Cuvier defined the principles of comparative anatomy which enabled him to reconstruct the physical form of strange extinct animals whose fossil bones were found in the neighbourhood of Paris (Cuvier 1808, 1812), while Smith established the principles of stratigraphical palaeontology with his observation that geological strata could be identified by the distinctive fossils they contained (Smith 1816, 1817).

The archaeological framework to which palaeoanthropologists refer was established early in the nineteenth century by collectors and curators of antiquities in Denmark, who, lacking the succession of Celtic, Anglo-Saxon and Roman influence that dominated so much of European history, were obliged to find other terms under which to classify and describe their numerous pre-Christian artefacts (Daniel 1975: 52). In 1819 Christian Jurgensen Thomsen, first curator of Denmark's National Museum, displayed the National collection under three main groupings, each named according to the level of technological sophistication that distinguished it: the Stone Age, the Bronze Age and the Iron Age.

Thomsen's three-age system appeared in print in 1836 (National Museum, Copenhagen), was translated into other languages (Ellesmere 1849) and spread gradually through Europe to become the fundamental system of classification of prehistoric man. Stone Age, Bronze Age, Iron Age: a chronological succession of increasing sophistication and, it implied, improvement.

By the 1860s, however, it was clear that the term Stone Age was too narrow a classification for all the numerous and varied stone artefacts that archaeologists were discovering, particularly in France. A division into the *période de la pierre taillée* and the *période de la pierre polie* was proposed by the French and given an air of scientific respectability by the English archaeologist John Lubbock (also known as Lord Avebury) in 1865 with the Latin terms *palaeolithic* – the Old Stone Age, 'when man shared the possession of Europe with the Mammoth, the Cave Bear, the Woolly-haired rhinoceros, and other extinct animals' – and *neolithic* – the New Stone Age, 'the later or polished stone age; a period characterized by beautiful weapons and instruments of flint and other kinds of stone' (Lubbock 1865).

Stone Age archaeology received its greatest impetus during this time from the work of Edouard Lartet (1801–71), a magistrate who gave up law to pursue palaeontology. After investigating sites at Aurignac (see p. 4) and in the Pyrenees, Lartet moved to the Dordogne in 1863, where, financed and helped by an English banker, Henry Christy, he began excavations at a number of now-famous sites along the valley of the River Vézère: Les Eyzies, Le Moustier, La Madeleine and Gorge d'Enfer among others.

Among the artefacts they uncovered in the caves of the Dordogne, Lartet and Christy found carved bone and images of animals engraved on stone. These were the earliest-known manifestations of art in the history of man and, as such, represented the culmination of what Lartet and Christy saw as a succession of cultural phases through time. In their *Reliquiae Aquitanicae* (1866–75), Lartet set the chronological sequence of successive cultural phases during the Palaeolithic in an ecological context, according to the species of animal remains most prevalent in each. Refined in the light of subsequent discoveries, he named the phases: the Age of the Hippopotamus, the Age of Cave Bear and Mammoth, and the Age of the Reindeer.

In palaeontological terms, Lartet's three ecological phases represented the Lower, Middle and Upper levels of the Palaeolithic Age, and an archaeological correlation was added in 1869 by Lartet's pupil and admirer Gabriel de Mortillet (1821–98), who proposed a system of classification which named the successive phases of human cultural endeavour according to the sites at which the various stone industries proliferated (Mortillet 1869, 1883). In this archaeological scheme of things, the Age of the Hippopotamus became the Chellean epoch, named for the simple chipped-flint tools found at Chelles, near Paris, and the Age of the Cave Bear and Mammoth was divided into two parts, the lower and older portion called the Mousterian, after the rock shelter at Le Moustier, where flaked-flint tools (but no worked bone) had been found, and the upper portion the Aurignacian, characterized by the worked bone and staghorn found together with flint tools at Aurignac and similar sites. The Age of the Reindeer was similarly divided into two parts: the Laugerian and the Magdalenian, the latter characterized by a profusion of worked bone and the development of artistic endeavour. ,

While these systems of Stone Age classifications were discussed (and sometimes dismissed) by the authorities of the day, the evidence of Stone Age man was expanded considerably in 1868, when Edouard Lartet's son, Louis, uncovered the remains of five people in a rock shelter at Cro-Magnon, also in the Vézère valley in the Dordogne. Flint tools and ornaments were also found in the shelter and the bodies appeared to have been deliberately buried (Lartet 1869; Lartet and Chaplain-Duparc 1874). Four years later, a skeleton covered with red ochre and decorated with pierced seashells and the canine teeth of red deer was excavated from the Grimaldi caves, near Menton. Later, the skeletons of two children were found in another cave at Grimaldi, both wearing belts of perforated seashells (Rivière 1887).

The human remains at Cro-Magnon and Grimaldi were the first to be recovered from sites of the Upper Palaeolithic, or Aurignacian, period. Anatomically, the remains were virtually indistinguishable from modern *Homo sapiens*: their flint tool technology was well established, they also used tools of bone, their artistry was beautifully expressed and the deliberate manner of their burial indicated, as Glyn Daniel implied in his review of these developments, that Upper Palaeolithic man was not merely a sophisticated toolmaker and an artist but also a man with an awareness of death and, if not the concept of an afterlife, certainly a primitive philosophy of life (Daniel 1975: 96–7).

Thus archaeology suggested that Upper Palaeolithic man had lived in a manner which any modern civilized person might find acceptable – quite different from the seemingly more crude lifestyle of the Neanderthals. While the people of the Upper Palaeolithic had produced fine flint and bone tools of the Aurignacian industry and displayed a sense of artistry, the Neanderthals had employed only Mousterian stone-tool technology, with no bone tools and no sign of any artistic endeavour. Subsequent discoveries (and the re-examination of earlier finds) only confirmed the distinction between the two groups. Remains from Engis, Gibraltar, Neanderthal itself, Spy, Krapina, Le Moustier, La Chapelle-aux-Saints, La Quina, Ehringsdorf and La Ferrassie all showed that although the Neanderthals had populated Europe widely, and for a considerable period of time (from about 130,000 to 35,000 years ago, according to modern dating techniques), they remained essentially different from the people of later times, both physically and culturally.

And yet the Neanderthals had been a successful group of hunters and gatherers who moved across Europe with the advance and retreat of the Ice Age glaciers. The evidence of their bone structure indicates that they were strong and heavily built people; their average brain size was well over 1,400 cubic centimetres, (and exceeding 1,700 cubic centimetres in some large males), 10 per cent larger, relative to body size, than is average in modern humans (Bunney 1986). Unquestionably, the Neanderthals were well adapted to their environment and survived successfully for 100,000 years. But between 30,000 and 35,000 years ago they disappeared. Only the remains of people anatomically indistinguishable from modern man have been recovered from more recent sites.

This transition from Neanderthal to modern man poses what has become known as the 'Neanderthal Problem'. What happened to the Neanderthals in Europe? There are only three possible explanations: either the Neanderthals themselves were transformed into modern humans by a process of rapid evolution, or they were overrun and replaced by modern humans who moved into Europe from some other point of origination, or they interbred with modern human immigrants, losing their distinctive Neanderthal characteristics in the process. All three explanations have had their advocates. Arguments and counter-arguments have been pursued at length, and occasionally with some heat, since the turn of the century, but mostly in an academic context where language and verbosity have often obscured the original problem from non-specialist eyes and strengthened a suspicion that the volume and longevity of arguments in palaeoanthropology usually indicate a lack of evidence strong enough to settle the case one way or the other.

Following the dramatic pronouncements of Professor Schaaffhausen, the 'numerous jocosities' of Professor Mayer and the solemn appraisal of Virchow among others, the first serious attempts to set Neanderthal in the context of human evoluton were undertaken by K. Gorjanovic-Kramberger and Gustav Schwalbe in the early 1900s. Both believed that human evolution had proceeded through distinct stages of development, with the Neanderthals representing the immediate ancestors of modern man. Gorjanovic-Kramberger's views developed from the evidence of Neanderthal remains he had dug personally from a rock shelter near the small town of Krapina in Yugoslavia (Gorjanovic-Kramberger 1906), but Schwalbe's experience was less direct (Spencer 1984: 14), his views inspired primarily by the renewed interest in human evolution which greeted Eugene Dubois's discovery of a so-called 'Missing Link', *Pithecanthropus* (meaning 'ape-man'), in 1891 (see Chapter 3).

Over a period of years, Schwalbe made a thorough study of all the then known Neanderthal remains, enumerating a series of anatomical features which he described as intermediate between those of *Pithec- anthropus* and modern man, and concluding that Neanderthal Man was the penultimate stage in a progression of human evolution that led stage by stage from an ape-like ancestor to modern man (Schwalbe 1906).

Schwalbe's scheme reduced the entire history of human evolution to a single line of development, along which were arranged the three or four types of fossil man then known. This satisfyingly simple idea found support in some quarters, but the ancestral status it bestowed on Neanderthal Man was firmly contradicted by Marcellin Boule (see p. 14), whose studies of the remains unearthed at La Chapelle-aux-Saints in 1908 concluded that the Neanderthals were a degenerate and archaic race which had diverged from the line leading to modern man and then disappeared without issue. 'This species is fossil in a double sense,' he wrote (quoted in Boule and Vallois 1957: 256), 'because it dates from a geological period prior to the present day, and because we are aware of no descendants.'

The first decades of the twentieth century were a time when France was becoming established as 'the mother-country of physical anthro- pology' (Hrdlicka 1919). Boule was a major part of that develop- ment, and his pronouncements on the Neanderthals, occupying extensive portions of the *Annales de Paléontologie* and published as a large monograph in 1913, were weighty enough to convert many authorities to his point of view. But, as Frank Spencer points out in a detailed summary of the Neanderthal debate (Spencer 1984: 21), removing the Neanderthals from Schwalbe's single-line view of human evolution raised another problem: if the Neanderthals were not the ancestors of modern man, who was? Boule could only acknowledge the absence of a candidate for the position when he summarized his views of human evolution at a congress held in 1912, but, just two months later, the announcement that alleged fossil human remains had been found near the small village of Piltdown in England (see Chapter 4) provided a large-brained, ape-jawed specimen that allegedly predated the Neanderthals and thus filled the gap perfectly. 'The Piltdown race seems to us the probable ancestor in the direct line of recent species of man, *Homo sapiens*,' he wrote (Boule 1913: 245–6, quoted in Spencer 1984: 21).

The consensus of opinion turned against the single-line view of human evolution incorporating Neanderthal Man as the immediate ancestor of modern man (a change of opinion that was encouraged, no doubt, by a widespread lack of sympathy for most things German in the aftermath of the First World War) and promoted the idea that two races of man had existed in Stone Age times, one which became extinct with the Neanderthals and was probably descended from earlier forms represented by Dubois's *Pithecanthropus* and remains found at Heidelberg in 1907, and another descended from Piltdown which had overwhelmed the Neanderthals and became the immediate ancestors of modern man. By the 1920s, this view of human evolution was firmly entrenched (even Schwalbe had been partially converted) and had become the accepted academic consensus underlying every argument and discussion on the subject.

Ales Hrdlicka (1869–1943), a founder of palaeoanthropology in the United States, was one of a small minority which did not accept the consensus view. Hrdlicka was of Czech and German origin and had studied anthropology in Paris under Léonce Manouvier (1850–1927), who promoted a rather more gradualist view of evolution than that of Boule. Manouvier preferred to see human evolution in terms of a progressive transformation to the modern form, and from this background Hrdlicka developed the idea of the Neanderthals as a distinct *phase* in the evolution of modern humans rather than a *species* standing apart from it. 'My conviction that the Neanderthal type is merely one phase in the more or less gradual process of evolution of man to his present form, is steadily growing stronger,' he wrote in 1916 (quoted in Spencer 1984: 25).

By 1927 the conviction was strong enough to form the basis of the Huxley Memorial Lecture that the Royal Anthropological Institute had invited him to deliver. Entitling his talk 'The Neanderthal Phase of Man', Hrdlicka described the highly variable morphology of Neanderthal anatomy as an indication of 'instability, evidently, of evolutionary nature, leading from old forms to more modern' (Hrdlicka 1927: 267). Moving from the anatomy of the Neanderthals to the environment of the Mousterian period, he pointed out that the Neanderthals had lived towards the end of a warm phase in the global climate, when Ice Age glaciers were advancing south again. Increasingly severe winters would have demanded more shelter, more clothing, more food, more fire, more storage of provisions, he said. Such demands intensified natural selection; populations declined as the less able perished, and from among the highly variable, evolutionarily unstable Neanderthals, modern man emerged. 'Here seems to be a relatively simple, natural explanation of the progressive evolution of Neanderthal Man, and such evolution would inevitably carry his most advanced forms to those of primitive *H. sapiens*' (Hrdlicka 1927: 272).

Though Hrdlicka's Huxley lecture has often been quoted as a definitive attempt to establish the Neanderthal ancestry of modern man, it made little impact in its day – or, indeed, for many years thereafter. Two notable German authorities, Hans Weinert (1887–1967) and Franz Weidenreich (1873–1948) – Weidenreich had studied under Schwalbe – subsequently supported the single-line hypothesis of human evolution in their publications, but even they had reservations about the Neanderthal ancestry of modern Europeans (see Vallois 1954: 113), and the influence of Hrdlicka's Neanderthal Phase hypothesis may be judged from the fact that it was hardly deemed worthy of refutation until 1954, by which time Hrdlicka had been dead for eleven years and further discoveries had expanded the evidence of early man.

Much had changed by 1954, when Henri Vallois was invited to give the Royal Anthropological Institute's Huxley Memorial Lecture and used the occasion to argue against the assertions of a Neanderthal phase in human evolution that Hrdlicka had made at the same venue twenty-seven years before. The discovery of partial skulls at Swanscombe in England (Marston 1936, 1937; Stringer *et al.* 1984) and Fontéchevade in France (Vallois 1949; Stringer *et al.* 1984) presented new evidence of early man in Europe. Fossil remains found in caves on Mount Carmel, near Haifa, in what is now Israel by a joint British–American archaeological expedition included some specimens with Neanderthal affinities, and others more similar to modern man – although how they were related to their European counterparts was unclear (Garrod and Bate 1937; Trinkaus 1984). Discoveries in the Far East (see Chapters 3, 6) had established *Homo erectus* as a candidate for the ancestry of *Homo sapiens* who appeared to predate both the Neanderthal and the anatomically modern remains from Europe. In Africa, Raymond Dart had discovered and described *Australopithecus* (see Chapter 5) and Robert Broom had found enough specimens to make the australopithecines prime candidates for a position close to the beginning of the human line, with Africa its cradle of origin (see Chapter 7).

Marcellin Boule had died in 1942 and Henri Vallois was the successor, both in spirit and status, of the position that Boule had held in the French study of early man. In his 1954 Huxley Memorial Lecture Vallois brought Boule's views up to date and argued against Hrdlicka's Neanderthal phase of human evolution with the proposition that a group he termed the Praesapiens were the true ancestors of modern man, while the Neanderthals were 'a retarded form extinguished without issue' (Vallois 1954: 112). There was no evidence of continuity between the Neanderthals and modern man, he claimed: the Neanderthals were a highly specialized group which even the selective pressures of severe climatic change could not have transformed into a modern human form in the relatively short period of time available. On the other hand, the Praesapiens were represented by fossils from Swanscombe and Fontéchevade (the latter discovered and described by Vallois himself) which predated the Neanderthals and bore strong affinities to modern humans. Vallois concluded his lecture: 'One fact at all events seems now to be established: the European *Homo sapiens* is not derived from the Neandertal men who preceded him. His stock was long distinct from, and, under the name of Praesapiens, had evolved in a parallel direction to, theirs. Long-debated, the Praesapiens forms are thus not a myth. They did exist.

The few remains of them we possess are the tangible evidence of the great antiquity of the phylum that culminates in modern man' (Vallois 1954: 128).

Vallois's 1954 Huxley lecture became a classic statement of the belief that the Neanderthals were not the ancestors of modern man, just as Hrdlicka's 1927 Huxley lecture stood as a definitive statement of the belief that they were. These two opposing hypotheses – Neanderthal Phase and Praesapiens – have set the framework for a good deal of academic argument over the last thirty years.

The presapiens (as it is spelt nowadays) hypothesis was challenged in 1955 and 1957 by observations that Boule had made some serious errors of interpretation in his reconstructions of the Neanderthals from La Chapelle-aux-Saints (see p. 15); correction of these errors (though some might say it was an over-correction) turned Neanderthal Man into a New York commuter. This work rekindled interest in the Neanderthals as possible ancestors of modern man. In the 1950s Ralph Solecki of the Smithsonian Institution recovered Neanderthal remains from caves at Shanidar in northern Iraq; subsequent studies showed that some remains dating from about 60,000 years ago may have been buried with bunches of wild flowers collected from the surrounding grassland (the flowers were identified by pollen analysis, Leroi-Gourhan 1975). This information evoked poignant images of spiritual awareness denied the Neanderthals until then (Solecki 1957, 1960, 1975), though this interpretation is open to question (see Chase and Dibble 1987: 275; Mann 1988). Meanwhile, the torch that Hrdlicka had held aloft in 1927 has been taken up by a number of academics since the early 1960s, foremost among them C. Loring Brace and Milford Wolpoff, who have continued to argue strongly in favour of a unilineal scheme of human evolution that includes the Neanderthals (Brace 1964; Wolpoff 1971, 1980).

By the 1970s the concept of a Neanderthal Phase in human evolution had spilled over into popular knowledge: 'it now seems unlikely that the outcome [of further research] will ever demote the Neanderthals from the mainstream of human evolution . . . We stand on their burly shoulders,' a Time–Life book, *The Neanderthals*, entoned (Constable 1973: 28).

But argument persisted among academics, becoming lengthier and more convoluted as point and counterpoint were raised and disputed. In 1976 it drew what amounted to an appeal for moderation from William Howells of Harvard University, who called attention to a question too often neglected by those participating in a protracted argument of interpretation, though it may be obvious to bystanders: is the available evidence capable of settling the argument one way or the other?

Howells published a paper which stripped the arguments to their basic contentions: 'My interest here lies not in elegance of data or analysis but in the actual contribution to solving the main problem' (Howells 1976: 479). He defined the Neanderthal Phase hypothesis as one which derives modern humans directly from archaic Neanderthals already present in the area, and the presapiens hypothesis (renaming it the Noah's Ark hypothesis) as one which assumes a single origin, with populations migrating outward and diverging genetically. 'The two hypotheses are irreconcilable,' he stated at the outset and, having reviewed the available fossil and genetic evidence, concluded that both were faulty and neither could be proved right. Nor could either be proved wrong, he added. 'Paucity of fossils and infirmity of dates remains a central problem,' Howells wrote at the conclusion of his paper; 'the base for most attempts at reconstructing recent human history is weaker than we like to recognize' (1976: 493).

In the 1960s and 1970s, the main thrust of palaeoanthropological research shifted to Africa, with a series of outstanding discoveries which pushed the origins of man back to putative ancestors who lived 1, 2 and more than 3 million years ago (see Chapters 8, 10–13). Furthermore, with this wealth of new evidence, advances in analytical techniques shifted the emphasis of the science from field to laboratory, from discovery to analysis, thereby calling for a greater degree of intellectual rigour in the process of interpretation. A new breed of palaeoanthropologists emerged during the golden years of discovery in Africa, and when their attention turned back to Europe and the origin of modern humans, the standards they applied were more demanding than those of their predecessors.

Meanwhile, the evidence of early man in Europe had been extended too. Neanderthal remains recovered from a deep rock shelter at Saint-Césaire in the Charente-Maritime region of France in 1979 (Léveque and Vandermeersch 1980) were found in association with tools of an early Upper Palaeolithic industry (previously thought to be associated only with anatomically modern man) and were proclaimed to date from between 31,000 and 34,000 years ago (ApSimon 1980). Any date in this range would make the Saint-Césaire Neanderthal the most recent known, as recent as the first evidence of modern humans in an area which appears to have been densely populated during the Middle and Upper Palaeolithic.

'The discovery of a Neandertal with an Upper Palaeolithic industry has considerably modified our ideas about the extinction of Neandertals in western Europe and their replacement by anatomically modern hominids,' reports one commentary on the development (Stringer *et al.* 1984). The Neanderthals did not completely disappear in the Mousterian period at the end of the Middle Palaeolithic. Some groups persisted into the beginnings of the Upper Palaeolithic, it seems.

The evidence from Saint-Césaire, indicating that populations of Neanderthals and modern humans had existed in the same place at the same time, rules out any possibility that modern humans evolved from Neanderthals in that area (Stringer and Kruszynski 1981: 824), leaving only the certainty that the Neanderthals were either absorbed into or overrun by an immigrant population of modern humans. Supporters of the Neanderthal Phase hypothesis continued to argue for the evolutionary transformation of Neanderthals into modern humans in Europe or Asia (Wolpoff 1981: 823), but they were lone voices. More central to recent discussions have been the intriguing questions of where the Neanderthal and modern human populations had come from, and when? The most probable answer now seems to be Africa.

The fossils collected during more than a century of scouring the world for evidence of early man's existence are now sufficiently numerous, and interpretative techniques sufficiently advanced, to permit the conclusion that the Neanderthals emerged in Europe and the Middle East between 300,000 and 35,000 years ago (Andrews 1986: 426) from stock as yet undefined. Fragmentary remains of what could be modern humans have been recovered from a cave site in Bulgaria and are thought to be approximately 43,000 years old, but of all the other specimens recovered from sites in Europe, Asia, the Far East and the Americas, only the skeletal remains from Qafzeh in the Middle East have been given an older date – 90,000 to 100,000 years (Valladas *et al*. 1988; Stringer 1988; Bower 1988). All the rest appear to date from 40,000 years ago or later. Thus the world outside of Africa appears to have been devoid of modern humans until 100,000 years ago at the very earliest, and only widely populated by them since about 35,000 years ago. But in Africa the picture is very different.

Beginning in the 1920s and continuing through to the present day, a host of fossils with predominantly modern anatomical characteristics have been discovered at thirty-one sites spanning Africa from north to south: Libya, Morocco, Algeria, Sudan, Ethiopia, Kenya, Tanzania, Zambia, South Africa (Brauer 1984a: 338). The specimens are numerous and date from between 500,000 and 30,000 years ago. Some retain features of an archaic nature; others are entirely modern. One of the latter, from the mouth of the Klasies river in South Africa, dates from between 100,000 and 70,000 years ago, thus making it the oldest-known example of modern man. Extensive analysis of the African evidence has persuaded Gunter Brauer of the University of Hamburg to formulate what he has called the Afro-European *sapiens* hypothesis.

'There are no longer any real reasons to assume the existence of two parallel lines in Europe, one leading to the Neanderthals, and one via Fontéchevade, to Cro-Magnon Man,' says Brauer (1984b: 145). Anatomically modern man evolved in eastern and southern Africa during the late Middle and/or early Upper Pleistocene, he concludes, from hominid stock which had probably given rise to a number of diverging early human populations (one of whom migrated from Africa around 700,000 years ago to found the populations from which Neanderthals of Europe and western Asia emerged). According to Brauer's hypothesis, the ancestors of modern man spread from their cradle of origin in eastern and southern Africa to range across the continent from north to south by about 50,000 years ago and then moved into the Near East and Europe, replacing and absorbing the indigenous Neanderthals over a period of several thousand years (Brauer 1984a: 395).

While the fossil evidence of modern man's African origin was accumulating in museums and university departments, awaiting a synthesis such as Brauer has supplied, evidence of a more immediate and intimate nature existed in the cells of every living human being: the DNA molecules that carry the code of life itself.

Evolution leaves a record of its progression in the genetic structure of every living organism. The modifications that create new species from existing forms of life arise in the DNA sequence which directs the assembly of every individual. With each generation a reshuffling of the DNA sequence occurs, and as evolution carries diverging species away from their common ancestor, the degree of difference separating them can be measured in their DNA, thus giving an indication of the number of generations that have passed. The basis of this knowledge was established in 1901 by George Nuttall, a Professor of Biology at Cambridge University, whose analysis of blood proteins from a wide variety of different species demonstrated the close affinity of man and the African apes (Nuttall 1904). Proteins differ only because the DNA ordering their assembly differs, and thus Nuttall's work touched on a fundamental fact of life, even though DNA and its function were unknown at the time, and would remain so for another forty years.

A timescale was applied to the evolutionary divergence of apes and man in the 1960s by Vincent Sarich and Allan Wilson, anthropologist and biochemist respectively, at the University of California, Berkeley. Noting that the degree of difference found in the proteins of different species must be directly related to the period of time that has passed since the species split from a common stock, Sarich and Wilson established what has become known as the molecular clock (Sarich and Wilson 1967a, 1967b).

The molecular clock set the time of man's divergence from the African apes at 5 million years ago, which in the 1960s pointedly contradicted current interpretations of the fossil evidence and was largely dismissed. Such a timescale could not accommodate *Ramapithecus* or *Kenyapithecus*, hominoid species based on fragmentary fossils found in deposits of the Miocene period (7 to 27 million years ago) in Pakistan and Kenya and proposed as the link between early forms of man (hominids) and the ancestor of man and ape which was believed to have existed about 30 million years ago (Simons 1965).

Developments during the 1970s and 1980s have resolved the contradiction between the molecular clock and palaeoanthropology, however. Fossils discovered in Turkey and Pakistan dismissed *Ramapithecus* from the hominid line (Pilbeam 1982; Andrews and Cronin 1982), and an extensive collection of new fossils, described in

1979 as *Australopithecus afarensis* (see Chapters 12, 13) firmly established the existence of a distinctly ape-like hominid between 3 and 4 million years ago. And as the new fossil evidence brought palaeoanthropology in line with the broad outline of human evolution as delineated by the molecular clock, research into the genetic structure of the mitochondria in living cells was producing evidence capable of resolving the detail of its final stages. It seemed that where proteins had enabled geneticists to establish the evolutionary distance *between* species, the mitochondria would now enable them to measure the evolutionary distance *within* species and *between* populations. This in turn would throw light on the recent origin and dispersal of modern humans, the question at the root of the Neanderthal Phase versus Presapiens controversy that the fossil evidence had been unable to resolve.

The mitochondria are discrete parts of the cell which play a vital role in the energy-production systems of living organisms. In effect, mitochondria are the 'powerhouses' of the cell, and such a basic function has endowed them with a very stable basic structure. Throughout the animal kingdom, the DNA which orders their function (mitochondrial DNA, usually abbreviated to mtDNA) is remarkably uniform: the same thirty-seven genes specify the same sets of molecules in all multicellular animals so far tested and the genes themselves are arranged along the mtDNA strand in a very consistent manner. Furthermore, the mtDNA molecules are identical in every cell of an individual; they themselves are reproduced in the cell by cloning, that is, asexually, by division, but are inherited only from the female parent because the mitochondria in sperm cells disintegrate at fertilization (Wilson *et al.* 1985).

Clonal reproduction and female inheritance leave mtDNA unaffected by the recombination of genes which occurs in the reproduction of nuclear DNA, and this means that mtDNA mutations pass intact from generation to generation. 'Each mtDNA molecule carries in its sequence the history of its lineage, not complicated by recombination' (Wilson *et al.* 1985: 379), which makes mtDNA a wonderful tool for determining the evolutionary distance between closely related species and populations.

Studies of the mtDNA of people in Papua New Guinea, who are known (from archaeological evidence) to have been isolated since the previously unpopulated island was first colonized by man between

40,000 and 50,000 years ago, have enabled researchers to measure the rate at which mtDNA mutations accumulated in the population (Stoneking *et al.* 1986). From these data, they have calculated that the average rate of evolutionary divergence in human populations is about 3 per cent per million years.

Subsequent analysis of mutations in the mtDNA of 147 people from different populations around the world (Cann *et al.* 1987) revealed a very low degree of variation among them (only a fraction of that found in the great apes and other vertebrates), which can only mean that these populations diverged recently (in evolutionary terms). The greatest degree of mtDNA variation was found among indigenous people in Africa, which implies that modern humans have existed there longest. Significantly less mtDNA variation is found among non-African populations around the world, and this means that they must all be the descendants of a relatively small group of people who left Africa quite recently and spread rapidly around the world.

Setting these data against the timescale of divergence, the geneticists put the origin of all modern humans at between 140,000 and 290,000 years ago, in Africa. Furthermore, the scientists conclude that every human being alive today carries the mtDNA of just one African mother who lived more than 10,000 generations ago. This does not mean that Eve was the only woman alive at that time (along with Adam, as the Creationists might like to believe). On the contrary, she may have been one of thousands, but the fact is that *her* mtDNA has become dominant. How could this happen? Allan Wilson explains:

Imagine a human population containing 10,000 mothers, with each mother contributing an average of two children to the next generation. The size of the population remains stable through time. In each succeeding generation, however, some maternal lineages disappear, simply because not every mother produces a daughter. The mathematics of random walks indicate that after about 10,000 generations, all but one of the founding maternal lineages will have become extinct. Hence, all the descendants will bear mtDNA derived from only one of the 10,000 mothers who founded the population (Wilson *et al.* 1986: 3).

'Our common mother', the geneticists have dubbed this ancestor, though she is becoming more popularly known as 'the African Eve' (Poulton 1987; *Newsweek* 1988).

The evidence of mtDNA suggests that the founders of the world's non-African population left the continent between 90,000 and 180,000 years ago, reaching Asia by 53,000 years ago, Australasia by 33,000 years ago and Europe by between 55,000 and 28,000 years ago (Stringer in prep.). Thus the genetic evidence of African origins for modern man accords well with the fossil evidence, and its suggestion that modern man arrived in Europe around the time of the most recent known European Neanderthal seems to settle the 'Neanderthal Problem'. The study of human population genetics has added another dimension to the context of studies of early man. In future, 'palaeo-anthropologists who ignore the increasing wealth of genetic data on human population relationships will do so at their peril,' a review of the genetic and fossil evidence of modern human origins boldly concluded in 1988 (Stringer and Andrews 1988: 1268).

3
JAVA MAN

(1891)

In 1865, six years after *The Origin of Species* first appeared, and six years before Darwin published *The Descent of Man*, the eminent German zoologist Ernst Haeckel (1834–1919) published a book called *Generelle Morphologie*. In it he treated the theory of evolution as established fact and ventured to speculate upon the yet deeper mysteries of life and natural order to which Darwin's theory might be applied. Haeckel subsequently expanded and developed his ideas in *The History of Creation*, an extremely popular book which caused Darwin to write: '. . . if *History of Creation* had appeared before my essay [*The Descent of Man*] had been written, I should probably never have completed it. Almost all the conclusions at which I have arrived I find confirmed by the naturalist, whose knowledge of many points is much fuller than mine' (Darwin 1871: 3).

Ernst Haeckel was a perceptive and energetic scientist who created several of the words and images now central to the natural sciences ('ecology' is one worthy of mention). He constructed the first of the now commonplace ancestral trees (1879 (2): 188), describing the evolution of life from 'living creatures of the simplest kind imaginable, organisms without organs' (Haeckel 1868; 1876 (2): 278), through twenty-one stages of development to modern man, the twenty-second and final stage. Within this general scheme of things, Haeckel created the concept of the 'Phylum', that is, the 'stem', to accommodate all organisms descended from a common form, and the word 'Phylogeny' to describe their evolutionary development from common form to distinct species. Within each species, Haeckel suggested that 'Ontogeny' should describe the development of the individual from conception to maturity and, recognizing the parallels that exist between the evolution of a species and the development of an individual, proposed his fundamental biogenetic law: ontogeny recapitulates phylogeny (1876 (2): 33).

In principle, Haeckel's law synthesized the observation that an organism seemed to pass through all the stages of its species's evolution as it grew from egg to mature individual. During nine months in the womb the human embryo could be said to recapitulate man's entire evolutionary history, and as it grew the important stages of development could be recognized. To begin with, the foetus had only the internal organs of the simplest creatures. Later the gill-arches of the fish appeared (and subsequently disappeared), followed by the backbone of the vertebrates and finally the placenta of the mammals. An important corollary of Haeckel's observation was that, at certain stages, the embryos of quite different creatures should reveal the identical form of their common ancestor. And, indeed, in *The History of Creation* Haeckel presented illustrations which he believed showed that at four weeks, for example, there was little to choose between the embryos of man, dog and tortoise; differentiation between the embryos of man and ape came very much later (Haeckel 1876 (1): 307).

Thus Haeckel found the theory of evolution proved to his satisfaction in the science of embryology. There were several awkward anomalies, it is true: some organs appeared in the embryo out of the evolutionary sequence, for instance, and some vestigial features were retained while other, once important, features scarcely showed at all. But Haeckel created a new term for each anomaly – caenogenesis, dysteleology, heterochronism – and regarded them as mysterious puzzles rather than negative evidence. A similarly creative attitude characterized much of his work. Where no scientific evidence was available he used his own persuasive logic to fill the gap. The 'Chain of the Animal Ancestors of Man' he devised is a case in point, particularly relevant here because its twenty-first link is believed to have inspired the discovery of some important fossil human remains.

Haeckel's chain began with 'structureless and formless little lumps of mucous or albuminous matter' – that is, protoplasm, spontaneously generated – and proceeded via the sack worms (eighth stage), the mud fish (twelfth stage) and the tailed amphibians (fourteenth stage) to the tailed ape (nineteenth stage). The twentieth stage in the chain comprised the man-like apes (Anthropoides): the orang-utan, gibbon, chimpanzee and gorilla. But were the man-like apes the ancestors of man? 'There do not exist direct human ancestors among the Anthropoides of the present day,' reasoned Haeckel, 'but they certainly existed among the unknown extinct Human Apes of the miocene period.' And how did he know? 'The certain proof of their former existence is furnished by the comparative anatomy of Manlike Apes and Man,' he wrote (Haeckel 1876 (2): 293).

In fact, Haeckel considered the man-like apes to be so much like man that his chain hardly required an intermediate stage connecting the two. But there was one behavioural characteristic that merited distinction in Haeckel's opinion: articulate speech. This important human attribute was not shared by the apes, and could not have been acquired in just one stage of the chain, he reasoned, so there must have been some sort of speechless primeval man between the apes and Genuine Man. He proposed the Ape-like Man (*Pithecanthropi*) as this intermediate link and twenty-first stage of his Chain of the Animal Ancestors of Man. 'The certain proof that such Primeval Man without the power of speech, or Ape-like Man, must have preceded men possessing speech is the result arrived at by an inquiring mind,' he wrote (Haeckel 1876 (2): 294).

We as yet know of no fossil remains of the hypothetical primeval man who developed out of the anthropoid apes, but considering the extraordinary resemblance between the lowest woolly-haired men, and the highest man-like apes, which still exists at the present day it requires but a slight stretch of the imagination to conceive an intermediate form connecting the two, and to see it in an approximate likeness to the supposed primeval men, or ape-like men. The form of their skull was probably very long, with slanting teeth . . . their arms comparatively longer and stronger . . . their legs, on the other hand, knock-kneed, shorter and thinner, with entirely undeveloped calves; their walk but half erect (Haeckel 1876 (2): 326–7).

And where might this chain of man's ancestry have been wrought? Haeckel said a continent now sunk below the Indian Ocean was the most likely place. Such a landmass had been postulated by other scientists on the basis of plant and animal distributions; it was called Lemuria, after the ancestral primates (the lemurs) that would have characterized the fauna of the ancient continent. In Haeckel's scheme, Lemuria embraced what is now Madagascar and India, and extended from Africa across the Indian Ocean to Indonesia and the Philippines. From this 'so-called Paradise, the cradle of the human race' (Haeckel 1876 (2): 325), the ancestor Haeckel called *Pithecanthropus alalus* ('speechless ape-man') would have spread and populated the world:

westward to Africa, north-westward to the Middle East and Europe, northward to Asia and over the landbridge to the Americas, eastward via Java to Australasia and Polynesia.

Of course, the best proof of Haeckel's contentions would be a series of fossils representing each of the links in his chain, but Haeckel was fully aware that fossil collecting was an imprecise affair: it is 'ridiculous to expect paleontology to furnish an unbroken series of positive data,' he once wrote (Haeckel 1906: 77). And besides, for Haeckel, logic and reason supplied ample proof of evolutionary theory. 'The descent of man from an extinct series of primates is not a vague hypothesis' to be proved, he had written, 'but an historical fact', and therefore as incapable of exact scientific proof as the fact that Aristotle, Caesar and King Alfred once lived (Haeckel 1899: 77).

The History of Creation was translated into a dozen languages and remained in print for many years. Haeckel's ideas were well known among students of the immediate post-Darwinian era, and among those whom they inspired was Eugene Dubois (1858–1940), the eldest son of a devout Dutch Catholic family, who collected fossils as a boy and entered medical school in 1877 at the age of nineteen.

The impressionable, formative years of Dubois's generation of medical students coincided with the period during which evolutionary thinking suffused the biological sciences with new vigour. Scientists were exploring the new horizons revealed by Darwin's work, formulating new hypotheses to answer old questions, creating new beliefs. It was a period of unhesitating consolidation, but while medical school introduced Dubois to the persuasive excitement of a revolutionary discipline, at home he was subject to the intractability of the old faith. And from these irreconcilable influences of his youth, Dubois emerged as an ambitious, determined and intractable believer in evolution.

Dubois completed his medical studies in 1884 and seemed poised for a successful academic career. He taught anatomy at the University of Amsterdam and might have succeeded Max Furbringer as professor of the department had he not angered the gentleman excessively in 1886 by publishing, under his own name, a paper on the larynx of the platypus which Furbringer thought should have carried *his* name. This may have been only a contributory factor, but in any event, the matter of his status became the subject of increasingly heated conversa-

tions with senior colleagues thereafter, and Dubois finally decided
that he would much rather look for fossils of early man than become
a professor of anatomy. In 1887 he resigned his lectureship, leaving
behind only the rumour that he had promised to return with the
'Missing Link'.

As an anatomist acquainted with both geology and palaeontology,
Dubois was well equipped for the search. And, indeed, the circumstances of the day were especially auspicious: Darwin's theory was
established; Huxley and Haeckel had shown that man's ancestry lay
among the extinct apes; Haeckel had proposed *Pithecanthropus* as a
likely link and the East Indies as an early stage in man's dispersal from
Lemuria, 'the cradle of mankind'. Furthermore, Emil Selenka had
recently described certain features of the human embryo as closer to
those of the orang-utan and gibbon than to those of the African apes.
This suggested an evolutionary connection between man and orang or
gibbon. The orang and gibbon live only in the East Indies, and the
East Indies were a colony of Holland. Where better could a Dutchman
search for the fossil evidence of early man? Getting there, however,
was another matter. Attempts to raise finance for a private expedition
failed completely, so as a last resort, we are told, Eugene Dubois
signed on for eight years in the Medical Corps of the Dutch East
Indian Army. With wife and infant daughter, he sailed for Sumatra in
the autumn of 1887.

Such a long spell of military service might seem a desperate choice
for a medical man in search of man's ancestors, but if Dubois had not
arranged a degree of official connivance at his real ambition before
leaving Holland, he certainly managed to do so within a few months
of arriving in the East Indies. First his immediate colleagues, then his
commanding officer, then some senior administrators were all persuaded to lighten his duties and allow him to explore the fossil-
bearing deposits as often as possible. Later, Dubois honoured two of
the gentlemen concerned by naming a fossil antelope and a fossil tiger
after them.

Finally, Dubois won the support of the Dutch East Indian
Government itself. During 1889 he persuaded the relevant officials
that a comprehensive palaeontological survey should be conducted
under his full-time supervision. Second Lieutenant Eugene Dubois
was placed on active reserve, inactive duty with instructions to pursue

scientific investigations as he saw fit, and in March 1890 he moved to
Java, where convict labour awaited his deployment under the direction
of sergeants Kriele and de Winter.

Dubois made his base at Tulungagang, in the south of eastern Java.
Immediately to the north stood Mount Willis, one of the many volcanoes that form the spine of the Malay Archipelago (another is
Krakatoa, which had killed 36,417 people seven years before). The
region was well endowed with promising limestone caves and volcanic
sedimentary deposits. Dubois had a predilection for the former, not
only because of boyhood discoveries in such places but also because
all the remains of early man known in Europe had been found in caves
and rock shelters. So his Java search began near Wadjak, where, in
fact, some fossil human skullbones had been found the previous year
by a Dutchman looking for workable marble deposits. By May 1890
Dubois's team had recovered a skull, some teeth and other fragments
from the same site, but, like the earlier find, they all proved to be of
recent origin. Soon thereafter Dubois abandoned the caves and turned
to the sediments.

Dubois's proposal to the government had called for a systematic,
widespread survey, and he did indeed travel extensively on his preliminary explorations, but before long his attention was almost exclusively devoted to the Kendeng deposits at the foot of Mount Lawu,
an occasionally active volcano standing about thirty-two kilometres
west of Mount Willis. In trial excavations throughout the Kendeng
deposits his workmen found many vertebrate fossils, some in quite
large accumulations. This led Dubois to believe that the animals had
been killed simultaneously by volcanic action and that their bodies
and bones had been swept together by flood waters down ancient
rivers, to be deposited in calm pools and on sharp bends. The quantity
and variety of the fossil fauna Dubois's expedition recovered from the
Kendeng is most impressive. It includes fish and reptiles, elephants,
rhinoceros, hippopotamus and tapir, deer, cats and a giant pangolin.
In all, more than 12,000 fossils were collected, filling more than 400
cases when they were shipped back to Holland and holding a wealth
of information on the fauna and environment of prehistoric Java. But
Dubois's consuming interest was fossils that would shed light on the
ancestry of man and these remains were very few.

The first appeared in November 1890. It was a fragment of a

primate's chin unearthed at Kedung Brubus. The first right pre-molar was still in place and the socket of the canine tooth next to it could be seen. Dubois mentioned the specimen in his regular quarterly report (Dubois 1891). It was man-like, he said, but 'of another and probably lower type than those existing and the extinct diluvial species'. His judgement was based on the manner by which the digastric muscle appeared to have been attached to the bone: Dubois felt the attachment was incompatible with the functioning of the tongue for normal articulate speech.

The Kendeng deposits are transected by the Solo river. On a bend in the river near a village called Trinil, a sequence of sandstone and volcanic deposits fifteen metres thick attracted Dubois's attention. He decided to concentrate his efforts there for a while, and began excavations in August 1891, less than three months before the seasonal rains would flood the Solo. Once Dubois had outlined how excavations should proceed, he left day-to-day management to Kriele and de Winter while he continued to reconnoitre or returned to Tulungagang. Every few weeks the sergeants packed the newly found fossils in teak leaves and sent them to Dubois, together with progress reports, which were frequently little more than complaints about the weather and the workmen. The fossils accumulated on Dubois's verandah as he endeavoured to discover their affinities to fossils from other parts of the world. Ultimately he concluded that the Kendeng fauna corresponded in age with some from the Siwalik deposits in India. While not exactly confirming the existence of Lemuria, this certainly affirmed the existence of a landbridge between India and Java across which animals could have moved and mingled.

The Trinil excavation was roughly circular, about twelve metres in diameter. Up to fifty convicts laboured in the pit, each of them assigned a specific portion of the deposit to remove each day. Fossils characteristic of the Kendeng fauna were frequently encountered as the excavation floor progressed below the high-water mark. Within a month the workers had reached the low-water mark, fifteen metres below the surface, and here they struck a lapilli formation – a bed of compacted tuff containing numerous fragments of volcanic rock. The lapilli bed was a metre or so thick; beneath it was a layer of conglomerate and beneath that a bedrock of marine origin extending beneath the river itself. Fossils were most numerous in the lapilli bed and removing them from the hard material was arduous, especially as the approaching monsoon heightened humidity. The rains finally brought excavations to a halt some time around the end of October.

During the course of these excavations, two very important fossils were discovered. It is generally assumed that Dubois personally witnessed the discoveries, but there is no evidence of this. Indeed, the absence of any such assertion from his reports on the discoveries, and the lack of dates and precise detail, make it seem more likely that he first encountered the fossils on his verandah at Tulungagang. This point was to be very important when the position of one fossil in relation to another became crucial to its interpretation. Then Dubois found himself most embarrassed: if he had been present at the time of discovery, he was guilty of not recording the details carefully enough; if he had not been present, then he had to admit that the sergeants' reports were open to question.

The fossils were a tooth, found in September, and a skull cap, found in October. It was immediately clear that both specimens had belonged to a primate, but which genus and species of primate was far from clear, and Eugene Dubois was the first to demonstrate the uncertainty of their affinities. He did so not by indecision, nor by emphasizing the ambiguous and inconclusive nature of the evidence they offered; on the contrary, Dubois consistently expressed the most confident opinions on his discoveries; but they changed with his needs. In the beginning Dubois decided that the tooth and skullcap had both belonged to a chimpanzee. In the *Mining Bulletin* for the fourth quarter of 1891 he wrote, 'The Pleistocene fauna of Java which in September of this year was augmented by a molar of a chimpanzee, was much further enriched a month later. Close to the site on the left bank where the molar had been found, a beautiful skullcap was excavated which without any doubt, like the molar belongs to the genus *Anthropopithecus* (troglodytes)' (Dubois 1891: 13). (Anthropopithecus was the scientific name of the chimpanzee then in use and means 'man-like ape'.) However, a fossil found the following year caused him to revise this assessment.

Weather and water level did not permit the resumption of excavations at Trinil until May 1892. Then the convicts began digging a trench twenty-four metres long and eight metres wide upstream from the 1891 excavations. In August a fossil thighbone was discovered, man-like in every respect. The fossil was found in the same lapilli bed that had held the 'chimpanzee' tooth and skullcap, but some distance away. No accurate record was made at the time, but on various occasions Dubois later asserted that the femur had been found ten, twelve and fifteen metres away from the skull. In any event, Dubois was convinced that thighbone, skullcap and tooth had all belonged to the same individual. But was it a chimpanzee? The thighbone suggested not, because it quite obviously had belonged to a creature with an habitual upright stance. But Dubois resolved that problem by blending his evidence into a new species of upright chimpanzee which he called *Anthropopithecus erectus* ('upright man-like ape'). The creature was announced in the *Mining Bulletin* for the third quarter of 1892, where Dubois claimed 'through each of the three recovered skeletal parts, and especially by the thighbone, the *Anthropopithecus erectus* (Eugene Dubois) approaches closer to man than any other anthropoid' (Dubois 1892: 11).

In October 1892, another tooth was picked up two or three metres from the spot where the skullcap had been found. No more primate remains were discovered that year, nor during 1893 when the excavations were doubled, nor during subsequent years when more than 10,000 cubic metres of sediments were removed from around the site of the original discoveries. With the exception of a few thighbone fragments found among the 400 cases of vertebrate fossils when they were examined during 1932, Dubois's collection was complete at the end of the 1892 season: a scrap of jawbone, two teeth, one skullcap and one thighbone.

While preparing a monograph (Dubois 1894) on the fossils during 1893, Dubois revised their attribution once again. In this he was entirely justified, for *Anthropopithecus erectus* would have been very difficult to support with the inconclusive evidence he held. The thighbone was too human and the skullcap too large for an ape, even a fossil man-like ape. So what could the creature have been? In truth, the evidence was too scanty and the current state of knowledge too slight for any specific attribution at all. But not for the first (or last) time in the story of the hunt for early man, an absence of evidence encouraged speculation; and Dubois was free to reach the conclusion which became a point of faith (and argument) dominating the rest of his life. He decided the bones had belonged to an ape-like man. In other words, he reversed the earlier attribution and *Anthropopithecus* (meaning 'man-like ape') became *Pithecanthropus* ('ape-like man'), though he retained the species name: *Pithecanthropus erectus*, upright ape-man. The generic name *Pithecanthropus* acknowledges the hypo-thetical form Haeckel had created for the twenty-first stage on the Chain of the Animal Ancestors of Man. On the basis of the chin fragment, which Dubois had earlier described as having belonged to a 'speechless lower type of man', we may ask why Dubois did not call the Trinil fossils *Pithecanthropus alalus*, the speechless ape-man that Haeckel had proposed. But, of course, the chin fragment afforded only weak evidence of an inability to speak, while the thighbone presented strong evidence of an erect posture, and Dubois needed to emphasize the stronger elements of his evidence rather than draw attention to the less substantial. Later he wrote: 'this was the man-like animal which clearly forms such a link between man and his nearest known mammalian relatives as the theory of development supposes ... the transition form which in accordance with the teachings of evolution must have existed between man and the anthropoids' (Dubois, J. M. F. Unpub. ms: 65).

Dubois believed he had discovered the 'Missing Link' and tele-graphed the news to Holland. He followed in August 1895, eight years of military service completed. *Pithecanthropus erectus* was presented at the Third International Congress of Zoology, held in Leiden that same year, at a meeting presided over by Rudolf Virchow. The fossils were greeted with unanimous recognition of their great importance, but Dubois's interpretation was questioned. Virchow did not believe the fossils had belonged to one individual; others felt they were more ape than man, while another group said they were more man than ape. Only a minority shared Dubois's view that the creature rep-resented an intermediate stage. Among them was Ernst Haeckel, cer-tain that the fossils confirmed his prediction of a 'Missing Link', but astute enough to remark: 'Unfortunately, the fossil remains of the creature are very scanty: the skullcap, a femur, and two teeth. It is obviously impossible to form from these scanty remains a complete and satisfactory reconstruction of this remarkable Pliocene Primate' (Haeckel 1899: 22).

The reaction at Leiden was repeated at meetings in Liège, Brussels,

Paris, London, Dublin, Edinburgh, Berlin and Jena. Everywhere, Dubois's discoveries were applauded and his interpretations doubted. Dubois became increasingly impatient and angry with his critics. As Arthur Keith wrote: 'he attributed their opposition to ignorance, or to personal animosity, rather than to a desire to reach the truth' (Keith 1942).

The points of contention were quite straightforward. If the remains had belonged to one individual, as Dubois claimed, then they represented an ape, a man or the intermediate ape-man that Dubois proposed. But not everyone agreed that the fossils had belonged to one individual, which considerably increased the number of interpretations; and the question could never be proved one way or the other. It was more a matter of probability than of fact, and in considering it, the protagonists were free to choose the facts they thought more probable. Dubois, for example, ignored his own assertion that the Kendeng fossil accumulations were the jumbled remains of many volcano victims, while his critics ignored the observation that the four fossils were the only primate remains among thousands of fossils recovered from the lapilli bed, which Dubois felt was enough to prove their association. But while the question of provenance could never be proved, Dubois was certain that the proof of status lay on the fossils themselves, and he thoroughly re-examined the scanty evidence they presented. He compared the thighbone with more than 1,000 modern specimens. He removed the compacted sediment from the interior of the skullcap, made a cast of the brain-case thus revealed and estimated the cranial capacity. He could do no more, but from this limited amount of information he drew conclusions he believed should convince everyone that *Pithecanthropus erectus* was the 'Missing Link'.

Presenting his conclusions at the Fourth International Congress of Zoology, held at Cambridge in August 1898, Dubois announced that the thighbone was significantly different from that of modern man, suggesting that although *Pithecanthropus* had stood erect and walked on two legs, it retained some ape-like characteristics. And turning to the evidence of the brain-cast, Dubois produced an 'index of cephalization' and attempted to prove the intermediate, ape-man status of *Pithecanthropus* by disproving the contentions that it was either ape or man. Applying the brain size/body weight ratio of modern apes to the fossils, Dubois pointed out that an ape with *Pithecanthropus*'s cranial capacity of 854 cubic centimetres would have weighed 230 kilogrammes, while a man with so small a brain would have weighed only nineteen kilogrammes. Both propositions failed the test of logic in Dubois's view and he concluded his Cambridge address: 'From all these considerations it follows that *Pithecanthropus erectus* undoubtedly is an intermediate form between man and the apes . . . a most venerable ape-man, representing a stage in our phylogeny' (Dubois 1898: 79–96).

Approaching the problem of interpretation from another direction, it could have been shown that a modern man with a thighbone the size of the Java specimen would have weighed about seventy kilogrammes and, with a cranial capacity of 855 cubic centimetres, would have made a perfect candidate for man's immediate ancestor. In other words, neither an ape nor an ape-man but a slightly less brainy man. And there the arguments might have ended, but Dubois was absolutely committed to his belief. He is not known to have made any converts at the Cambridge congress, though he may have earned an apologist or two; none the less, his conclusions invited comment and scientists travelled to Holland to examine the fossils and discuss their interpretation. But Dubois found these visits increasingly tiresome, especially as so few of the visitors shared his views. Science had honoured him with gold medals, diplomas and honorary degrees in recognition of his work, but it would not give him what he most wanted – general agreement with his belief that *Pithecanthropus erectus* was neither ape nor man but a link between the two. Finally, Dubois retaliated by severely restricting access to the fossils.

By thus alienating the sympathizers as well as his critics, and by withdrawing himself, as well as the fossils, from the international scientific community, Dubois harmed himself more than he affected scientific opinion. If he had been able to change his mind instead of closing it with the fossils, the remaining forty years of his life might have been less difficult.

In the event, scientists everywhere rejected his views on fossil man and at home in Holland his work was even less appreciated. The Church reviled him from the pulpit and the academic establishment showed him very little respect. In 1898 he was appointed Assistant Professor of Crystallography, Mineralogy, Geology and Palaeontology at the University of Amsterdam, but it was not a prestigious post. The salary was less than he had earned as a lecturer in anatomy little more than a decade before.

During the years of seclusion Dubois described the Wadjak skulls found in 1889 and 1890 as representing the recent ancestors of Australia's aboriginal population (Dubois 1920: 1013–51) and published a number of papers on the geology and hydrology of Holland. He also refined his Law of Phylogenetic Cephalization, postulating a 'co-efficient of cephalization' and publishing a series of papers which culminated in a formula whereby all mammals could be placed in an evolutionary sequence in respect of brain size and body weight. The sequence was a geometric progression, with one convenient gap. 'Putting the cephalization of Man equal to 1,' wrote Dubois (Dubois 1935: 578–85), 'we find exactly 1/4 for the *Anthropomorphae* inclusive Gibbons; about 1/8 for the majority of our large Mammals: Ruminants, Cats, Dogs etc.; about 1/16 for Kanchils, Civet-Cats, Hares, Large Bats (*Megachiroptera*) etc.; about 1/32 for Mice, Moles, Leaf-nosed Bats (*Phyllostomidae*) etc.; about 1/64 for Shrews, common Small Bats (*Microchiroptera*) etc.

'The only real void space in the series,' Dubois observed, 'is between Man and the anthropomorphous Apes (incl. Gibbons). This void marks the place of *Pithecanthropus*,' the fossil having twice the cephalization of the apes and half that of man, he computed.

For a time it was rumoured that Dubois had abandoned his belief in evolution and returned to the Catholic faith, destroying the fossils in expiation of his sins and in remorse for the pain he had caused his sister, who was a nun. But it was only a rumour.

The fossils appeared again in 1923, when discreet but persistent representations finally found favour with Dubois and some scientists were invited to examine them. Ales Hrdlicka of the Smithsonian Institution and H. H. McGregor of Columbia University were among the first. They were given every facility and courtesy, but their conclusions still differed from Dubois's. The Java fossils had belonged to an early form of man, they said, not an ape or an ape-man. By now it must have been abundantly clear to everyone except Dubois that the amount of controversy surrounding his fossils reflected a severe lack of definitive evidence. He had spent the greater part of his life trying to wring from those few scraps of bone the proof they could never provide, not simply because their evidence was too fragmentary for unequivocal interpretation but also because the judgement Dubois wished to impose upon them was wrong. It is a sad tale: if the fossils had been more complete Dubois could not have avoided the truth; less complete and he could not have built any serious claims upon them.

The argument lingered on while others searched for the more complete fossils that would either corroborate or confound the theories and beliefs of their protagonists. Eventually, new evidence was found, the first in 1929, when Dubois was over seventy years old. It was a skull from Peking, with undeniable similarities to the Java specimen, but Dubois dismissed its significance out of hand, simply because it contradicted his own views on human evolution. The Peking skull was just another example of the Neanderthal race, he said (Dubois 1933: 415–23).

Then came a stream of discoveries from Java: a skull from the banks of the Solo river at Ngandong, not far from Trinil, and others from Sangiran, about seventy-five kilometres away. In all, a dozen fine Java specimens were recovered, most of them under the direction of the German palaeontologist Ralph von Koenigswald, who called the Sangiran specimens *Pithecanthropus*.

As the evidence of affinity between Dubois's fossils and the new specimens became increasingly difficult to resist, so Dubois's efforts became more desperate. In 1935 he attempted to show that von Koenigswald's *Pithecanthropus* was in fact a very large ape of gibbon-like appearance, weighing about 104 kilogrammes (Dubois 1935). In 1940 he claimed the new skulls variously resembled the Neanderthals of Europe and the Proto-Australians he had discovered from Wadjak (Dubois 1940). But by then events had overtaken Dubois and his interpretation.

In 1938 von Koenigswald described a superb skull from Sangiran as *Pithecanthropus* (Koenigswald 1938), and in 1939 he collaborated with Franz Weidenreich, then working in Peking, to define the precise relationship between the Java and the Peking fossils (Koenigswald and Weidenreich 1939: 926–9). The similarities far exceeded the differences that Dubois would have stressed. The new specimens matched what there was of Dubois's fossils and supplied enough of what was missing to satisfy everyone that the Java and Peking fossils all represented an early form of man, with almost nothing of the ape about him. *Pithecanthropus erectus* was not an ape-man. Subsequently, in fact, the name was changed to *Homo erectus* (Mayr 1951: 109–18). Needless to say, these conclusions did not satisfy Dubois. In his eighty-third year he embarked on a tedious attempt to challenge the evidence von Koenigswald and Weidenreich had presented. These papers were the last he published, and they reflect the acrimony of a weary old man. There is a touch of irony too in his very last paragraph:

It is most regrettable, that for the interpretation of the important discoveries of human fossils in China and Java, Weidenreich, von Koenigswald and Weinert were thus guided by preconceived opinions, and consequently did not contribute to, on the contrary they impeded, the advance of knowledge of man's place in nature ... Real advance appears to depend on' obtaining material data in an unbiassed way, such as the *Pithecanthropus* fossil remains ... (Dubois 1940: 1275).

Eugene Dubois suffered a heart attack and died sixteen days after delivering those words. In an obituary, Arthur Keith wrote: 'He was an idealist, his ideas being so firmly held that his mind tended to bend facts rather than alter his ideas to fit them' (Keith 1942).

When Eugene Dubois died, in 1940, the study of fossil man was facing a crisis of classification. During the eighty years that had passed since William King attached the name *Homo neanderthalensis* to the fossils recovered from the cave in the Neander Valley (see p. 11) and thus initiated the practice of applying formal zoological distinction to the evidence of human ancestry, no fewer than twenty-nine genera and 100 species of early man had been created around the various hominid fossils recovered in different parts of the world (Campbell 1965). Like Dubois's *Pithecanthropus erectus*, many of the descriptions were primarily a means of accommodating new (or reconsidered) discoveries within a favoured scheme of human evolution. The literature was filled with 'Missing Links', their putative ancestral status and relationships so confused that it was virtually impossible to reconstruct a plausible scheme of human evolution from the fossil evidence as then presented (Mayr 1976: 530).

This confusion appalled many observers, but appealed to the biologist Ernst Mayr as an opportunity to test the systematic approach then gaining favour in studies of evolutionary biology. The systematic approach classifies organisms strictly according to the features they have in common; could this method clarify the classification of hominid fossils? Adopting a dictum of fourteenth-century philosophy known as Occam's Razor – 'it is vain to do with more what can be done with fewer' – Mayr looked for the simplest arrangement of hominid taxa that could be reconciled with the plethora of names and produced a startling result: one genus and only three species (Mayr 1944, 1951).

Subsequent developments have rendered the scheme something of an oversimplification, as Mayr notes in a 1976 comment on the original paper, but it established a sound basis of classification for the study of early man.

In the new classification, Mayr described mankind's upright posture as the generic characteristic of hominids and grouped all known fossils in a single genus: *Homo*. Species within the genus could be most readily distinguished by characteristics derived from their upright posture, he said, such as the freeing of the hands for new functions and the evolution of the brain. Mayr defined three species of *Homo* on these grounds and distributed the fossils among them accordingly. The most ancient, *Homo africanus*, included the small-brained australopithecines (see Chapters 5, 7); the most recent grouped the Neanderthals and Cro-Magnon together as *Homo sapiens*, immediately antecedent to modern man; and between the most ancient and most recent he put the Java and Peking hominids, calling them *Homo erectus*.

Mayr's classification made *Homo erectus* an archetypal 'Missing Link': poised between ancestral and descendent groups, affined to both but separated from each by an expanse of time broad enough to accommodate the notion that one had gradually evolved into the other. The simple logic and intellectual authority of this unilineal scheme was persuasive. Some years later it was conflated into the single species hypothesis (Brace 1964; Wolpoff 1971), a view of human evolution which looked upon the development of the brain as the primary hominid adaptation and the evolving culture it inspired as a process which could not have tolerated the existence of more than one hominid species at any one time. In this scheme of things, human evolution was a gradual ascent to modern man, and while the fossil record remained sparse enough to define only a few well-marked stages along the route, it seemed a reasonable hypothesis. Since then, however, fossil discoveries have complicated the issue at every stage, and *Homo erectus* has been no exception.

By the mid-1980s, *Homo erectus* was the earliest widely known hominid species. Its existence in Indonesia and China was confirmed; fossils from North Africa, Chad, Kenya and Tanzania established the species's presence in Africa; more controversially, some specimens from sites in Europe had been attributed to the species. And *Homo erectus*, as represented by these specimens, spans an immense breadth of time: more than 1 million years. The oldest, from the shores of Lake Turkana in northern Kenya, dates from 1·6 million years ago; the youngest, from Dali in central China, is about 200,000 years old. This wealth of material, said to represent the existence of a single hominid species through expanses of time and space, has become the nub of a very intriguing question: was human evolution a process of gradual transformation from one species to another through time, or did it proceed by leaps and bounds, with species remaining essentially the same (in stasis) for an extended period of time, then evolving rapidly during a relatively short period? Gradual evolution or stasis punctuated by rapid change? The options are mutually exclusive; both cannot be right. But both have their adherents, who call upon the same collection of *Homo erectus* fossils to promote their views. This surely throws the validity of either the evidence or the argument into question. First, the evidence.

Most of the *Homo erectus* fossils are skulls and teeth; fossils representing other parts of the *erectus* skeleton were virtually unknown until 1984, when a team excavating on the west shore of Lake Turkana experienced what Richard Leakey and Alan Walker have described as 'the exquisite pleasure of unearthing almost an entire *Homo erectus* skeleton, the first discovered of such antiquity – 1·6 million years old – and the earliest set of one individual's bones found *in situ*'. The shape of the pelvis indicated that the individual was male, and analysis of tooth and bone development suggested that he had been no more than twelve years old when he died and had been very well built. The boy's height was about 1·6 m (5 ft 5 in), tall for a twelve-year-old, and if the growth pattern of *Homo erectus* matched that of modern humans he would have stood 1·8 m (6 ft) high as an adult. Furthermore, although the Turkana boy's skull was distinctive, his skeleton was essentially human in its form and proportions. 'Suitably clothed and with a cap to obscure his low forehead and beetle brow, he would probably go unnoticed in a crowd today,' concluded Leakey and Walker (1985: 629), echoing the comment on Neanderthal Man made thirty years before (see p. 15).

The 'strapping youth' from West Turkana demonstrates the extent to which a single piece of evidence can simultaneously broaden an interpretation in palaeoanthropology and leave its central argument unaffected. The post-cranial skeleton confirms the view that the human form has remained essentially unchanged for 1·6 million years, and therefore it has not been subject to a process of gradual evolution during that time. But what about the skull? It seems to have changed a great deal. Was the change gradual, or did it occur abruptly after a long period of stasis? Thus the argument continues to revolve around the evidence of Homo erectus skulls.

The idea of stasis in Homo erectus is said to have originated (Bilsborough and Wood 1986: 307) in a comparison made in 1976 between a 1·5-million-year-old Homo erectus skull then just discovered on the east shore of Lake Turkana and the Homo erectus skulls from Peking, which are at least 1 million years more recent (Leakey and Walker 1976: 572–4). Since then, the idea has been pursued most actively by Philip Rightmire of the State University of New York. Among several features of cranial anatomy he has analysed, Rightmire considers the brain size of Homo erectus particularly important, believing that a gradual increase in brain size through time would be a strong indication of gradual evolution (if it had occurred), while the absence of any increase would indicate stasis. Rightmire found no significant evidence of increasing brain size and concluded that Homo erectus had been a morphologically stable species (Rightmire 1985).

And while Rightmire has concluded that the Homo erectus fossils offer evidence of stasis in the species (and therefore in human evolution), those same fossils have supplied other experts with evidence of the opposing view – gradual evolution. Milford Wolpoff of the University of Michigan, for instance, has compared thirteen anatomical features of Homo erectus skulls grouped in three time ranges and concluded that the species was evolving gradually through time (Wolpoff 1985). When two experts draw such diametrically opposed conclusions from the same evidence, the validity of the science comes into question. Other palaeoanthropologists have described Wolpoff's study as superficially persuasive but unconvincing (Delson 1985), and have accused Rightmire of deriving sweeping conclusions from a limited number of features (Bilsborough and Wood 1986: 308).

The problem is that palaeoanthropology lacks a recognized and universally applied method of analysis. Different experts use different methods on the same fossils and, not surprisingly, come up with different results. Lately, however, analysis has been identified as a central problem and there are signs of progress towards a solution.

During a discussion of *Homo erectus* held in New York in 1984, an 'old hand' spoke of how the preliminary analysis of any fossil evidence should be conducted: 'You've got to have "green fingers" for them,' he said. 'I only need to look at a skull, and hold it, to know if it's *Homo erectus* or not . . .' It was a polarizing moment, one participant has observed. Though the speaker carried on, unaware of the effect of his words on his audience, the meeting paused intellectually, alerted to the intuitive method of analysis which has been responsible for many problems of interpretation in palaeoanthropology. Glances were exchanged among the listeners, and then the meeting relaxed again, confident that most palaeoanthropologists employ more rigorous methods of analysis these days.

During the late 1970s a new approach to the analysis and classification of fossil hominids began to challenge the method of evolutionary systematics that Mayr had tidied up and made respectable. The new approach is called cladistics. It was devised in the 1950s by the German entomologist Willi Hennig (1913–76) as a means of classifying living species according to their evolutionary relationships (Hennig 1966). By the mid-1980s the cladistic approach was firmly established as an unequivocal means of establishing, and defining, the presence or absence of evolutionary relationships among fossil hominids.

In brief, cladistic classification groups specimens on the basis of features they share and others do not. Some of the shared features may be unique to the group, others may be derived from an earlier form, and the evolutionary relationship between groups can be defined on the basis of their unique and/or derived features. The procedure is reminiscent of that employed by Richard Owen in 1855 when he cited the absence of eyebrow ridges in man as proof that man and the apes did not share a common ancestor (see p. 6). The capacity of cladistics to impose a new perspective on evolutionary classification is demonstrated very clearly by an exchange of views on the topic reported in the pages of *Nature* (Halstead 1978; Patterson *et al.* 1979). At a meeting held at Reading University, one exasperated advocate of evolutionary systematics had exclaimed that he supposed cladists would say a lungfish was more closely related to a cow than to a salmon. 'Yes,' a cladist replied, 'I cannot see what is wrong in that.'

The exasperated evolutionary systematists subsequently accused the cladists of 'religious fervour'; to which the cladists replied with charges of 'McCarthyism and a witch-hunt', but the difference of opinion seems to have centred around the meaning of the term 'relationship' in evolutionary classification. As the cladists pointed out, it was Ernst Mayr, the architect of modern systematic classification, who summarized Hennig's definition of relationship in evolution as 'the relative recency of common ancestry'. In terms of this unequivocal definition, the genetic and behavioural similarities of the modern forms are irrelevant; the lungfish and the cow share derived characteristics not found in salmon, and therefore must share a more recent common ancestor than that shared by the lungfish and the salmon.

The case of the salmon, the lungfish and the cow is likely to become a classic example of cladistic analysis and the reaction it sometimes provokes. It is, of course, an extreme example that makes both the method and the conclusions of cladistics very clear, but not all applications produce such startling and conclusive results. Applied to the study of *Homo erectus*, for instance, cladistic analysis has not solved the problem of whether the species represents gradual evolution or stasis, but it has made it clear that the present evidence cannot provide a solution.

'The power of cladistic analysis lies in its clarity,' says Bernard Wood (1984: 109), a leading proponent of the method in palaeoanthropology. It is not the only way of analysing the affinities of fossil hominids, as Wood points out, but it does apply an impressive degree of logic and rigour to the problem of hominid classification. Unlike the intuitive method, cladistics oblige a scientist to justify each stage by which an interpretation is reached. It is not enough to say 'I have green fingers and know this to be true'; assumptions unsupported by demonstrable facts must be explicitly stated and their consequences examined. The aim of the cladistic method is to produce unequivocal conclusions. Often, its conclusions are themselves inconclusive, but an identified lack of knowledge is now welcomed in preference to the ill-defined and subjective claims made by 'old hands' who employed the intuitive method.

4
PILTDOWN MAN
(1912)

Arthur Keith (1866–1955), anatomist, was one of a British scientific triumvirate whose beliefs and work profoundly affected investigations into the evolution of man for nearly fifty years. His associates were Arthur Smith Woodward (1864–1944), palaeontologist and Keeper of Geology at the British Museum of Natural History, and Grafton Elliot Smith (1871–1937), an anatomist whose speciality was the study of the brain. All three gentlemen were knighted for their contributions to science, and their talents were memorably displayed in discussions concerned with the significance of alleged fossil human remains found at Piltdown, Sussex, between 1908 and 1915.

In an autobiography written late in life, Keith remarked that 'the ideas which a man devotes his life to exploring are, for the greater part, those which come to him in the first tide of his inquiries' (Keith 1950: 122). The observation is certainly sustained by the facts of his own career. In the first year of his medical studies Keith was awarded a copy of *The Origin of Species* for his distinctive work in the anatomy class. While working as medical officer to a mining company in Siam immediately after he qualified, Keith dissected monkeys in the hope of determining whether or not the animals shared the affliction of malaria that plagued the human population and he discovered an absorbing interest in comparative anatomy as the means of elucidating the evolutionary development of mankind. Within a year he dissected thirty-two assorted primates, and on returning to England in 1892 arranged to receive and dissect primate carcasses from the London Zoo. He dissected human foetuses as well, and the comparative anatomy of the ligamentous structure of the feet and hands of monkeys and human babies became both the subject of his doctoral dissertation and the basis of his views on the evolution of man's erect posture (Keith 1894: 149–335). At home in Scotland Keith performed cerebral dissections on farmyard cats of all ages to clarify his understanding of the development of the individual brain, and in London he studied primate skulls at the Royal College of Surgeons and at the British Museum of Natural History. He carefully noted about 150 observations on each of over 200 skulls and it was here, in the winter of 1894, Keith later wrote (1950: 170) that he learned 'the alphabet by which we spell out the long-past history of man and ape' from the evidence of fragmentary fossils.

In 1895 Keith met Dubois. He made a reconstruction of the Java skull and wrote an article on the specimen for a popular journal (concluding that the specimen was essentially human, but of a lowly kind). Thereafter he wrote frequently on the subject of human ancestry and, on his appointment as Hunterian Professor of Anatomy at the Royal College of Surgeons in 1908, vowed to uncover and write 'the anthropological history of the British' (Keith 1950: 317).

In *The Descent of Man*, Charles Darwin had implied that the early forerunners of man probably retained some characteristics of the ancestor they shared with the apes. Males were probably furnished with great canine teeth at one time, he said, but as they acquired the habit of using stones, clubs and other weapons for fighting they would have used their jaws less and less, with a consequent decrease in the size of the canines and some restructuring of the jaw (Darwin 1871: 80). Scientists of the day drew several important conclusions from Darwin's observation. Reshaping the jaw would have provided the space essential for the movement of the tongue in articulate speech; the ability to handle stones and clubs presumed an erect posture; both speech and erect posture require a considerable development of the mental abilities. Thus the crucial developments of mankind's evolutionary path were clearly defined. But which came first? Development of the brain? The erect posture? Or the ability to speak? Darwin hardly commented upon the question but, as the slowly accumulating fossil remains inspired competing interpretations of their imprecise evidence, it was clear that some idea of the manner in which human evolution had proceeded would help by suggesting the features that fossils ought to possess. If man had walked before he could talk, then fossils could be expected to demonstrate the fact.

As a result of his work on the feet and hands of apes and human babies, Arthur Keith believed erect posture was an ancient attribute and the large brain mankind's most recent acquisition (Keith 1912a: 78). An opposing view was ardently championed by Grafton Elliot

Smith, whose important and pioneering work on the function and evolution of the vertebrate brain had convinced him that 'the brain led the way.' At its most primitive, the brain had discerned little more than the sensation of smell, he said. Later, vision had been acquired and then 'an arboreal mode of life started man's ancestors on the way to pre-eminence', for, while they avoided the fierce competition for size and supremacy waged among carnivores and ungulates on the earth below, 'the specialization of the higher parts of the brain gave them [the primates] the seeing eye, and in the course of time also the understanding ear; ... all the rest followed in the train of this high development of vision working on a brain which controlled ever-increasingly agile limbs.' Thus 'the Primates found in the branches the asylum and protection necessary for the cultivation of brain and limbs,' he said, and the erect posture developed when they had become 'powerful enough to hold their own and wax great'. It was 'not the real cause of man's emergence from the Simian stage, but ... one of the factors made use of by the expanding brain as a prop still further to extend its growing dominion' (Smith 1912: 575–98).

Arthur Smith Woodward appears to have contributed little to the early stages of the debate. In 1885 he remarked upon the preponderance of 'Missing Links' in the fossil record (Woodward 1885) and subsequently he stated that 'we have looked for a creature with an overgrown brain and ape-like face' (1913: 783), missing from the chain connecting man and his primate ancestors, but by far the greater part of his career was devoted to the study of fossil fish rather than fossil man. In all, Smith Woodward published more than 600 papers on fossil fish and related palaeontological subjects – more than 300 before he became Keeper of Geology at the British Museum in 1901 – and only thirty or so on fossil man. (These figures, of course, also reflect the relative abundance of the fossils in question.)

By 1908 the fossil evidence of early man was still very slight. Specimens from France and Belgium had confirmed the existence of a Neanderthal race; there were the enigmatic Java discoveries, and a lower jaw found in a sandpit near Heidelberg in 1907 suggested that mankind's late Pleistocene ancestors had been able to talk and bore a receding chin as evidence of their simian associations. These specimens added a measure of information to the story of mankind's evolution in general, but of the British anthropological history that Arthur Keith had vowed to write there was no indisputable evidence whatsoever. Fossils had been sought in the caves and gravels of England, Ireland, Scotland and Wales; some remains had been found, but their antiquity was questionable and their aspect distinctly modern. For the most part, therefore, the remains of fossil man in Britain were granted little credence. It was held to be more likely that each was a case of recent remains interred in old deposits rather than a genuine example of early man in Britain.

The Galley Hill skeleton was a case in point. The bones were found to the east of London, in gravels deposited by the River Thames when it flowed 100 feet above its present level. The deposits were considered to be of early Pleistocene age; crude stone tools found near the skeleton were similar to others found elsewhere in associaton with extinct fauna of the same period, so the related geological and archaeological evidence seemed to suggest that Galley Hill Man was very old indeed. The anatomical evidence, however, clearly showed that the specimen represented *Homo sapiens*. The cranial capacity (about 1,400 cubic centimetres) was well within the modern range, the chin did not recede, the jaw structure was compatible with the faculty of speech and the thighbone indicated an habitual erect posture. Furthermore, the skeleton was unusually complete and had been found with its parts in close proximity. All these factors combined to convince most authorities that the Galley Hill remains were of recent origin and had been entombed by the hand of man not nature (Keith 1925a: 258).

The Galley Hill skeleton was discovered in 1888 and consigned soon after to the obscurity of a private collection in East London, where it remained until 1910, when Arthur Keith decided that the evidence merited reappraisal. Over a period of months he confirmed the skeleton's affinities to *Homo sapiens* and agreed that the remains had been buried in the ancient deposits, but, whereas these factors had caused earlier investigators to reject the claims of great antiquity, Keith deduced from them that Galley Hill Man was as ancient as the deposits in which he had been buried, and that the burial was not recent but ancient. 'We hardly do justice to the men who shaped the [artefacts],' he wrote, 'if we hold them incapable of showing respect for their dead' (Keith 1925a: 258). The implications of these deductions were considerable: if large-brained, talking, walking *Homo sapiens* had existed at the beginning of the Pleistocene, as Keith claimed, then all the crucial evolutionary development of man must have taken place long before; true men had remained unchanged for a very long time, and the Neanderthal and Java fossils represented not the ancestors of man but a 'degenerate cousin'.

Geologists, in particular, did not agree that true man could be so ancient. But Keith claimed this was because they had grown up with a belief in the recent origin of man and therefore expected to see a sequence of anatomical change marking the evolution of man (Keith 1925: 265). In fact, the geologists' views simply conformed with the rationale of their palaeontological training, which taught that the long and absolute lack of evolutionary change Keith proposed would be unique among the higher vertebrates, and therefore unlikely. But Keith, the anatomist, was untroubled by these niceties of palae-ontology and quite prepared to believe mankind is unique. After this his claims for true man's exceptional antiquity became a point of faith. He called upon it to explain the anomaly of apparently modern human remains found beneath ancient deposits at Ipswich (Moir 1912; Anon. 1912; Keith 1915). And, at a meeting of the British Association for the Advancement of Science held in Dundee in 1912, he offered perhaps the first full and authoritative exposition of the claim that mankind acquired both large brain and erect stature a very long time ago and has remained relatively unchanged ever since.

Remarking upon the Neanderthal and Java fossils, Keith told his distinguished audience: 'thus we have a knowledge – a very imperfect knowledge – of only two human individuals near the beginning of the Pleistocene period. The one was brutal in aspect, the other certainly low in intellect.' If these are the ancestors of modern man, he said, then we have to accept 'that in the early part of the Pleistocene, within a comparatively short space of time, the human brain developed at an astounding and almost incredible rate'. To Keith it seemed more reasonable to reject Neanderthal and Java from man's ancestry and assume they were simply contemporaries and cousins of true man's large-brained ancestor, whose evolutionary development had occurred long before. 'Is it then possible,' he asked, 'that a human being, shaped and endowed as we are, may have existed so early as the Pliocene?' Briefly reviewing the evidence he had presented, Keith concluded that it was. 'The picture I wish to leave in your minds,' he said, 'is that in the distant past there was not one kind but a number of very different kinds of men in existence, all of which have become extinct except that branch which has given origin to modern man. On the imperfect knowledge at present at our disposal it seems highly probable that man as we know him now took on his human characters near the beginning of the Pliocene period' (Keith 1912b: 758). At the same meeting, Grafton Elliot Smith confidently extended the pedigree of man's ancestors back to the Eocene, explaining how the 'steady and uniform development of the brain along a well-defined course throughout the Primates right up to Man . . . gives us the fundamental reason for "Man's emergence and ascent"' (Smith 1912: 577).

Thus the leading anatomists of the day expounded the theories of human evolution that they hoped palaeontologists might one day substantiate with the evidence of human fossil remains. Just a few months later, in December 1912, Arthur Smith Woodward, perhaps the leading palaeontologist of the day, unveiled Piltdown Man and thus presented the anatomists with a conundrum in which the expectation of theory and the logic of observed fact were wonderfully counterpoised.

Though he was responsible for the reconstruction and presentation of Piltdown Man, Smith Woodward had not discovered the remains. The first pieces of fossil skullbones were brought to him by Charles Dawson, an amateur geologist who had already contributed important palaeontological specimens to the British Museum collections. Dawson (1864–1916) was a solicitor practising at Uckfield in Sussex, a position which left time for a wide range of other activities (in 1909 he published *A History of Hastings Castle* in two volumes and at the onset of his terminal illness was investigating a case of incipient horns on the head of a carthorse), but geology and palaeontology were the interests he pursued most energetically. In 1885, at the age of twenty-one, Dawson was elected a Fellow of the Geological Society for his contributions to the science, though little appeared in the literature under his own name. 'He preferred to hand over his specimens to experts who have made a special study of the groups to which they belonged,' an obituary recounts (Woodward 1916: 477–9), rather than describe them himself, and Smith Woodward was surely rewarding this respectful deference to greater knowledge when he named Piltdown Man *Eoanthropus dawsoni* ('Dawson's Dawn Man') and made Dawson principal author of their joint paper (Dawson and

Woodward 1913: 117–44). Dawson presented the geological and archae-ological evidence of the discovery to a crowded meeting of the Geo-logical Society on 18 December 1912, while Smith Woodward, the palaeontologist, first described the anatomy of the specimen, drawing attention to features which appeared to support his claims concerning the evolution of man, and only then discussed the palaeontology of the site, a subject to which his qualifications might have been more justifiably applied.

The details of Dawson's initial discovery are imprecise; not even the exact year is known. Dawson told the meeting how he had been attracted to the site 'several years' before when he traced some unusual brown flints found on a farm near Fletching to a small gravel pit on a farm adjacent to Piltdown Common, Sussex. He asked the labourers who occasionally worked there to keep any fossils they might en-counter, and on a subsequent visit they presented him with a small, concave, tabular object. It was part of a coconut shell, the men said, which they had found and broken in the course of their digging. They had kept one piece for Dawson and discarded the rest. Dawson, however, realized that the object was part of a fossil human skull. Thereafter he visited the site frequently and 'some years later – in the autumn of 1911', he found another fragment of the same skull among the spoil heaps. Believing the pieces might match the proportions of the Heidelberg jaw, in May 1912 Dawson took his finds to the British Museum for more accurate assessment. Smith Woodward was im-pressed with the importance of the discovery and joined Dawson in the search for more remains that summer, though only as a private, weekend holiday affair and without the involvement of any British Museum resources. Apparently they wished to keep the discovery wholly to themselves. At first, just one labourer was employed to do the heavy digging in the small pit, but later they were joined by Father Teilhard de Chardin and another French priest who was also then studying at the Jesuit College near Hastings. Teilhard de Chardin shared Dawson's amateur interest in fossils and geology (they had met by chance on their rambles about the Sussex countryside) and in later years Chardin was to become a recognized authority on the fossil evidence of early man.

During the summer of 1912 solicitor, palaeontologist and priests scrutinized every spadeful dug from the pit and sifted through all the spoil heaps of previous years. In one heap they found three pieces of the right parietal bone from the skull – one piece on each of three successive days – and later Smith Woodward found another fragment which fitted the broken edge of the occipital bone and connected with the left parietal bone found by Dawson. 'Finally, on a warm summer evening after an afternoon's vain search,' Smith Woodward recounts (Woodward 1948: 11), 'Mr Dawson was exploring some untouched remnants of the original gravel at the bottom of the pit, when we both saw half of the human lower jaw fly out in front of the pick-shaped end of the hammer he was using. Thus was recovered the most remarkable portion of the fossil which we were collecting.' In addition, the pit supplied three flint artefacts, fragments of an elephant tooth, some beaver teeth and one much-rolled fragment of a mastodon tooth, while on the surface of an adjacent field the party found a piece of red deer antler and a horse's tooth, both fossilized and both presumed to have been thrown over the hedge by the workmen. In all, this was a remarkably comprehensive haul.

According to Dawson's determination, the Piltdown gravel bed lay about eighty feet above the level of the River Ouse, deposited there before the river began excising the valley through which it presently flows. The gravel bed could be divided into four distinct strata, he said, and the fossils had come from the third, which lay about three and a half feet below the land surface and was distinguished by a dark ferruginous appearance and the presence of ironstone. The fossil fauna from the pit were of early Pleistocene, or even Pliocene, age, and the flint artefacts appeared to be similarly ancient. All of this strongly implied that the human remains found in the same deposit represented the earliest known example of true man.

Arthur Smith Woodward completed an anatomical reconstruction of the remains some time during the autumn of 1912. He worked alone, apparently without the advice, assistance or even knowledge of his colleagues at the British Museum (Weiner 1955: 120). He made a cast of the interior of the reconstructed skull and invited Grafton Elliot Smith to comment upon the brain of Piltdown Man when the specimen was unveiled at the Geological Society in December, but Elliot Smith has made it clear that he did not help with the reconstruction of the skull (Smith 1913a: 145–7).

The audience that packed the Geological Society's lecture room on

18 December 1912 was larger than any before, and the Piltdown skull they had come to see perfectly fulfilled the expectations of many who attended. Smith Woodward's reconstruction had produced a creature with the jaw of an ape, the skull of a man and a cranial capacity (1,070 cubic centimetres) appropriate to an intermediate stage between man and ape. A small minority thought the combination of ape and human characteristics was just a little too good to be true, and Smith Woodward himself accurately defined the point when he told the meeting: 'while the skull, indeed, is essentially human, only approaching a lower grade in certain characters of the brain [as described in Elliot Smith's contribution to the same meeting] ... the mandible appears to be almost precisely that of the ape' (Dawson and Woodward 1913: 134–5). Elliot Smith, however, did not find the combination beyond the bounds of reason. The Piltdown brain was the most primitive and the most simian so far recorded, he said, and its association with an ape-like jaw was not surprising to anyone familiar with recent research into the process by which the human brain had evolved from the brain of the ape (Smith 1913: 147).

Arthur Keith, on the other hand, was among those who had misgivings. He was jealous that the remains had been given to a palaeontologist at the British Museum and not to him, an anatomist known to be specially interested in the anthropological history of the British. But then, he knew that Smith Woodward regarded his belief in the antiquity of *Homo sapiens* as 'an amusing evolutionary heresy' (Keith 1950: 324). At the Geological Society meeting, Keith hailed Piltdown as perhaps the most important discovery of fossil human remains ever made but took exception to some aspects of the reconstruction. The chin region and the form of the front teeth were too much like the chimpanzee, he said (Keith 1913a: 148).

The arguments concerning the association of jaw and skull, and the form of the reconstruction, would never have arisen if the remains had been more complete. But the problem was, of course, that the anatomical features capable of proving or confounding the association of jaw and skull were exactly those missing from the original specimens: the chin region of the jaw, which would have clearly demonstrated the form of the canines; and the knob on the end of the jawbone, which would have shown the form of the joint in which the jaw articulated with the skull.

In June 1913 Arthur Keith acquired casts of the remains and made his own reconstruction of the Piltdown skull, one which assembled the available parts in accordance with anatomical principles and supplied the missing parts in accordance with his belief in the antiquity of *Homo sapiens*. The chin and front teeth were entirely human and the cranial capacity was 1,500 cubic centimetres, greater than the average for modern man. A few weeks later the conflicting interpretations of anatomist and palaeontologist were reviewed by the participants at an International Congress of Medicine held in London during August. At the British Museum, experts from the world of medical science viewed Smith Woodward's anatomical reconstruction of the original remains, and at the Royal College of Surgeons Arthur Keith showed them where the palaeontologist had gone wrong.

Because of a misconceived notion of the nature of the jaws and teeth on fossil man, Smith Woodward had fitted a chimpanzee palate and jaw on a skull that could not possibly carry them, Keith said, with the result that the upper joints of the backbone were so close to the palate that there was no room for windpipe or gullet and Piltdown Man would have been unable to either eat or breathe. The Smith Woodward reconstruction was anatomically impossible, he said (Keith 1913b). If skull and jaw truly belonged together, then the skull must be large enough to accommodate the massive jaw and the front teeth must be human enough to match the articular capacity.

In the course of the ensuing discussions Grafton Elliot Smith lent his support to the palaeontologist's reconstruction, but Smith Woodward did not respond publicly to Keith's challenge until 16 September 1913, when he told a meeting of the British Association for the Advancement of Science assembled in Birmingham of further discoveries at Piltdown.

Fortunately, Mr Dawson has continued his diggings during the past summer, and, on August 30, Father P. Teilhard, who was working with him, picked up the canine tooth which obviously belongs to the half of the mandible originally discovered. In shape it corresponds exactly with that of an ape, and its worn face shows that it worked upon the upper canine in the true ape-fashion. It only differs from the canine of my published restoration in being slightly smaller, more pointed, and a little more upright in the mouth. Hence, we have now definite proof that the front teeth of *Eoanthropus* resembled those of an ape, and my original determination is justified (Woodward 1913: 786).

The Piltdown canine settled the argument about the chin so conclusively in Smith Woodward's favour that Arthur Keith was forced to concede an important point of his belief in the antiquity of *Homo sapiens*. Despite the evidence of Galley Hill and Ipswich, it seemed that some of man's ancestors in the early Pleistocene had displayed distinctly ape-like characteristics after all. But the argument about the size of the Piltdown brain-case was still unresolved. Smith Woodward believed it must have been relatively small because, in his view, the association of the primitive jaw with a *large* brain-case would be a most improbable combination of primitive and modern features. Keith, on the other hand, insisted that the brain must have been large because the association of a large jaw with a *small* brain-case was anatomically impossible. The 300 cubic centimetres separating the estimates of anatomist and palaeontologist soon became a subject of heated debate in the pages of *Nature* and elsewhere. But Smith Woodward was only slightly involved; in his stead, Grafton Elliot Smith promoted the smaller estimate and thus the palaeontologist was able to remain a passive observer while the merits of his Piltdown reconstruction were argued by two anatomists. In Keith's view the anatomical errors responsible for the small brain-case were manifest and glaringly obvious; he was surprised and irritated by Elliot Smith's refusal to acknowledge them. Acrimony developed between the two men and, although Keith eventually came to terms with most of the colleagues with whom he argued during his career, he and Elliot Smith were never friends again.

The difference in the estimates of the Piltdown brain size resulted solely from the manner in which the existing fragments were assembled and their curves projected to delineate the parts missing in between. A large area of the forehead and the roof of the skull were among the important missing pieces, as Keith pointed out in a letter to *Nature* (Keith 1913c: 197), but he believed it was possible to reconstruct a complete skull from what remained of it by applying the principle of symmetry. 'The right and left halves of the mammalian head and skull are approximately alike,' he continued, but Smith Woodward's reconstruction showed a 'great discrepancy between the right and left halves', the extent of which was largely responsible for his low estimate of brain size; if the symmetry of the palaeontologist's reconstruction was restored by adding to the right side of the skull, then the cranial capacity was substantially increased.

In reply, Elliot Smith stressed the position of the middle line of the skull as the most important factor in reconstructing a skull, and attributed Keith's alleged misplacement of this feature to his having worked from casts of the Piltdown fragments without reference to the original specimens (Smith 1913b: 267). He made little mention of the asymmetry of the skull, though it is interesting to note that such a feature was fundamental to his subsequent theory that the left- or right-handedness of a person is shown in the relative sizes of certain parts of the left and right hemispheres of the brain (Smith 1927: 184). A few weeks later Keith pointed out that Elliot Smith's remarks did less than justice to F. O. Barlow, who had made the casts, and even reflected badly upon the conduct of Smith Woodward, who, he wrote, had permitted 'the freest access to the specimens', even to those who, like himself, 'regarded the original reconstruction of the skull and brain cast as fundamentally erroneous' (Keith 1913c).

Keith championed his views in *The Times* and challenged Grafton Elliot Smith's conclusion at a memorable meeting of the Royal Society where he claims to have earned the reputation of a brawler; but behind the public controversy he was, by his own admission (Keith 1950: 327), beginning to have private doubts about the validity of the argument. The problem as he saw it was quite simple: can a skull *ever* be reconstructed accurately from just a few fragments of the original? Such skills were obviously essential to anyone aspiring to study the progress of human evolution, because most of the evidence was contained in fragmentary fossil remains. Several authorities claimed to possess the skills needed to reassemble such fragments, but in the case of Piltdown Man, their differing results begged the question: is there, or is there not, a *science* of fossil reconstruction?

To test his own skills scientifically, Keith arranged that some colleagues should cut fragments exactly duplicating the Piltdown remains from a modern skull in their possession, which he would then reconstruct according to his anatomical principles and afterwards compare with a cast of the original. The results were close enough to restore Keith's confidence in his skills and reconfirm his belief that Piltdown Man had possessed a large brain; the experiment was described at a meeting of the Royal Anthropological Institute and published in a scientific manner (Keith 1914, 1915: 537–78). But nevertheless, the reconstruction of the modern skull was wrong in one important respect: Keith failed to reproduce the proper form of the forehead, of which there was almost no evidence at all among the Piltdown remains.

While the deliberations concerning the form and size of the Piltdown skull were exercising the skills of the experts in London, Charles Dawson continued the search for more remains. The gravel pit seemed to have been worked out and in wandering further afield, he examined newly ploughed land and the heaps of stones raked from the fields. His endeavours were attended by extraordinary good fortune. Sometime before 20 January 1915, in a field about two miles from the site of the original discovery, Dawson found a fragment of fossil bone which, he was certain, had belonged to a second Piltdown Man. The fragment was a piece of the forehead, retaining a portion of the eyebrow ridge and the root of the nose. In July 1915 he found a molar tooth at the same site and on another occasion a piece of the back of the skull.

Unhappily, Dawson became seriously ill with anaemia in the autumn of 1915. The condition worsened and turned to septicaemia, of which he died in August 1916. His last discoveries were presented before the Geological Society by Arthur Smith Woodward in February 1917, where it was concluded that the new evidence must support the contention that *Eoanthropus dawsoni* was a definite and distinct form of early man, as originally supposed, for, as Smith Woodward pointed out, the occurrence of the same type of bone with the same type of molars in two separate localities must add to the probability that they belonged to one and the same species (Woodward 1917). The frontal bone revealed the form of only a small area of the interior surface, and one devoid of obtrusive features, but none the less Grafton Elliot Smith found that its evidence corroborated his opinion that the Piltdown skull presented features 'more distinctly primitive and apelike than those of any other member of the human family at present available for examination' (Smith 1917: 8). Arthur Keith attended the meeting too, and in the ensuing discussion effectively abandoned his opposition to the specimen. He never accepted the small brain Smith Woodward postulated, but he succumbed to the persuasive logic of the amazing discoveries and their presentation. The new Piltdown finds 'established beyond any doubt that *Eoanthropus* was a very clearly differentiated type of being', Keith said, adding that the frontal bone was particularly valuable because it cleared up any doubt as to the contour of the forehead (Keith 1917: 10).

The triumvirate of British palaeoanthropological science was now united in believing that the Piltdown remains represented the earliest known ancestor of *Homo sapiens*, a unique link between mankind and the ape-like creatures from which he had evolved. And perhaps their knighthoods (Sir Arthur Keith, 1921; Sir Arthur Smith Woodward, 1924; Sir Grafton Elliot Smith, 1934) reflected a shade of patriotic pride colouring this conviction that the ancestor of man was an Englishman.

But while the three experts were gathering around Piltdown Man, the creature was still under attack from other quarters. And the attacks were concerned not simply with the size of the skull, but with the more fundamental question of whether or not the jaw and skull belonged together. Arthur Smith Woodward, it will be remembered, had drawn attention to this problem when the remains were first presented to science; at that same meeting, David Waterston, Professor of Anatomy at King's College, had remarked that it was very difficult to believe that the two specimens could have come from the same individual (Waterston 1913a: 150). Later Waterston strengthened his opinion; in a letter to *Nature* he wrote: 'it seems to me to be as inconsequent to refer the mandible and the cranium to the same individual as it would be to articulate a chimpanzee foot with the bones of an essentially human thigh and leg' (Waterston 1913b).

Similar views were voiced elsewhere. In America Gerrit Miller compared casts of the Piltdown fossils (he never saw the originals) with the corresponding parts of twenty-two chimpanzees, twenty-three gorillas, seventy-five orang-utans and a series of human skulls, concluding that 'a single individual cannot be supposed to have carried this jaw and skull' without assuming 'the existence of a primate combining brain-case and nasal bones possessing the exact characters of a genus belonging to one family, with a mandible, two lower molars and an upper canine possessing the exact characters of another' without any blending of their distinctive characteristics. Miller concluded that the remains must represent two individuals despite the amazing coincidence of their discovery in such close proximity, and created a completely new species of chimpanzee (*Pan vetus*) to accommodate the peculiarities of the Piltdown jaw (Miller 1915).

In 1921 the French authority on fossil man, Marcellin Boule, approached 'the paradoxical association of an essentially human skull with an essentially simian jaw' with the question: 'Is *Eoanthropus* an Artificial and Composite Creature?' Boule considered the evidence and concluded that Piltdown Man was at least composite (if not artificial). The jaw had come from a chimpanzee, he said, and the skull was human but had belonged to a race of men quite distinct from the Neanderthals and closely related to the ancestry of modern man (Boule 1923: 171, 471).

Many authorities in America and France supported the views put forward by Miller and Boule; objections to the paradoxical association of ape jaw and human skull were also raised in Italy and Germany. All in all, the anatomical evidence was hard to deny; indeed, if the jaw and skull had been discovered in separate excavations no expert would have dreamt of suggesting they belonged to the same species, but at Piltdown the scientific evidence of anatomy collapsed against the circumstantial evidence of palaeontology. The first remains had lain within feet of each other on the same geological level (or so it was said) and therefore *must* belong together; and the discovery of matching remains some distance away supported the conclusion. As Grafton Elliot Smith remarked: there was no reason to assume 'that Nature had played the amazing trick of depositing in the same bed of gravel the brain-case (*without* the jaw) of a hitherto unknown type of early Pleistocene Man displaying unique, simian traits, alongside the jaw (*without* the brain-case) of an equally unknown Pleistocene Ape displaying human traits unknown in any Ape' (Smith 1927: 73). Rational minds found it much more likely that jaw and skull belonged together, especially since the creature thus formed so closely resembled the form of man many authorities believed had existed at that stage of human evolution.

In 1922 Elliot Smith, in conjunction with a colleague, made another reconstruction of the skull, supplementing those by Keith and Smith Woodward. The cranial capacity was 1,200 cubic centimetres, its form was more in keeping with the structure of the jaw and Marcellin Boule, for example, found Elliot Smith's contribution persuasive. The new facts should eliminate or at least lessen the 'anatomical paradox', he wrote, expressing the view that the balance of the argument now inclined more towards Smith Woodward's theory. Boule was glad of this, he said, for he esteemed 'both the knowledge and the personal attributes of this scientist' (Boule 1923: 472).

There can be no doubt that the prestige and status of Arthur Smith Woodward were very largely responsible for the degree of acceptance that Piltdown Man achieved. His pronouncements on the fossils constituted a very small part of his work, as we have seen, but they carried the ring of conviction. Arthur Keith has remarked that Smith Woodward liked to set a puzzling specimen on a table where the light from a window caught it at all hours of the day, so that as he passed and repassed it in the course of his work, a chance glance might reveal aspects he had not seen before and the significance of the fossil would gradually become clear. The Piltdown specimens were afforded this treatment (Keith 1948a), so we must assume that the palaeontologist was satisfied with what he saw.

In the early stages of the debate Elliot Smith had said examination of the originals was essential to correct interpretation. Indeed, opposition stemmed mainly from those who had dealt with casts only and several sceptics who subsequently handled the originals are known to have changed their minds. The American-based anthropologist Ales Hrdlicka was one of these. Having examined the originals extensively he remarked on the great difference that exists between the study of a cast and its original. 'It is very probable,' he reported, 'that ... some of the conclusions arrived at by some authors would not have been made had they been able to study the jaw itself.' Hrdlicka accepted Smith Woodward's designation of the remains as 'a being from the dawn of the human period' (Hrdlicka 1930: 65–90).

One Sunday morning in July 1921 another sceptic, Henry Fairfield Osborn, President of the American Museum of Natural History, spent two hours after church examining the Piltdown remains. He concluded that 'paradoxical as it had appeared to the sceptical comparative anatomists, the chinless Piltdown jaw, shaped exactly like that of a chimpanzee ... does belong with the Piltdown skull, with its relatively high, well-formed forehead and relatively capacious brain case' (Osborn 1927: 53).

But behind the controversy, it must be noted, there was unanimous agreement among the experts on a point which had a most pervasive effect, particularly in respect of the beliefs and predispositions that were presented to the anthropology students of the day. The experts may have disputed the association of the Piltdown jaw and skull, they may have argued about the absolute size of the brain, but of one thing they were all certain: the Piltdown remains proved beyond doubt that mankind had already developed a remarkably large brain by the beginning of the Pleistocene. And the implications of this were very important: firstly, a brain so large at that time must have begun its development long before, which implied that true man was very ancient indeed; and second, since the Piltdown remains of this 'true man' were older (as it was believed) than the Java and Neanderthal fossils, they firmly dismissed those 'brutish' creatures from the line to the status of 'aberrant offshoots', evolutionary experiments that led to extinction – cousins of mankind perhaps, but not ancestors.

Thus Piltdown Man contributed to a consensus view in the 1920s and 1930s which led to the neglect of some significant discoveries because they did not conform with accepted beliefs, while others, less accurately founded, were welcomed because they conformed only too well. Regardless of the continuing controversy over their details, the Piltdown remains became a standard requiring mention in related literature and a measure against which subsequent discoveries had to be compared. This Piltdown effect, as it might be called, is well demonstrated in the work of Louis Leakey (1903–1972), who studied anthropology at Cambridge during the 1920s and was an admiring disciple of Arthur Keith.

In 1934 Leakey published a popular book on fossil man called *Adam's Ancestors*. In it he supported Keith's appraisal of the Galley Hill remains and described Piltdown Man as a good candidate for the ancestry of man. 'The Piltdown skull is probably very much more nearly related to *Homo sapiens* than to any other yet known type,' Leakey wrote, and would have granted the specimen full ancestral status if it had been 'vastly more ancient' than the Kanam mandible he had recently found in East Africa and which, he believed, must represent the oldest ancestor of true man (Leakey, L. S. B., 1934: 221) (see p. 139).

We have concentrated so far on the anatomists' and palae-ontologists' view of Piltdown Man, but a third approach, geology, was available to science, and it was from this direction that the riddle was eventually solved. Charles Dawson had said that the remains were found in a gravel bed lying about eighty feet above the level of the River Ouse. This implied an antiquity not much less than that of other river terraces in Britain and Europe, and, indeed, on the evidence of the extinct fauna they were said to contain, the Piltdown gravels could hardly have been younger. Thereafter, Dawson's estimate was repeated as fact by other authorities and, in particular, gained considerable respect from the support of W. J. Sollas, Professor of Geology at Oxford, who even improved upon the Dawson estimate.

In his book *Ancient Hunters* (Sollas 1924: 192), Sollas converted eighty feet to twenty-five metres, bracketed twenty-five with thirty and thus correlated the Piltdown gravels with those lying on terraces thirty metres above other rivers (the Thames, for instance), concluding that the Piltdown remains must, therefore, date from the early Pleistocene. Thereafter, Sollas's assessment became the most authoritative reference on the geology and age of the Piltdown deposits. 'Thirty metres' was frequently converted to '100 feet' and in turn offered to support a contention that the fossils might be even older than originally thought, perhaps even of Pliocene age, though the only Pliocene deposits known from that part of England were of marine origin and above the 500-foot contour. All of which undoubtedly helped to obscure the fact that Dawson's original estimate was based on an erroneous assumption.

Dawson had claimed the Piltdown gravels were part of a plateau lying above the 100-foot contour line, and he had calculated their height in relation to these features. But the gravels are actually part of a larger, well-defined terrace which maintains a constant height of fifty feet above the River Ouse throughout its extent. The portion in which the fossils were found is no exception, as was clearly revealed on the six inch to one mile Ordnance Survey map of the district published in 1911. If this had been noted in 1913, and the stratigraphy of the area accurately ascertained, it may have seemed more correct to correlate the Piltdown gravels with the fifty-foot terraces of the River Thames rather than with anything older, in which case the Piltdown fossils could only have been of late, not early Pleistocene. Had this been pointed out, interest in the remains would probably have evaporated very quickly: the fossils might have seemed odd and anomalous, but no one could have claimed any great antiquity for them, especially since Smith Woodward had always said that the skull was the same age as the deposit in which it had been found.

But the error was not noted in 1913; and it drew no comment in 1926 when a map giving the correct elevation appeared in a Geological Survey publication with text repeating Dawson's estimate (White 1926). In fact, the error and its significance were first mentioned only in 1935, when the attributes of the Piltdown skull seemed difficult to reconcile with those of another skull found at Swanscombe. The Swanscombe specimen came from gravels of the 100-foot terrace of the River Thames itself, and when the problem of its correlation with the Piltdown remains arose at a meeting of the British Association at Norwich, Kenneth Oakley, a geologist at the British Museum, challenged Sollas's assertion that the Piltdown gravels were part of the thirty-metre terrace. He drew attention to the 1926 map of the area and its author's observation that the deposits more satisfactorily corresponded with those of the fifty-foot terrace.

The Swanscombe remains were found by Alvan T. Marston, a dentist with an interest in fossils, in a gravel pit not far from the site of the Galley Hill discovery. They comprise the rear half of a skull; there is no clue whatsoever to the form of the face, the jaw or the forehead. The cranial capacity was estimated to be 1,325 cubic centimetres and comparative anatomists could find little to distinguish the specimen from *Homo sapiens*. Yet the Swanscombe skull had come from deposits no younger than those at Piltdown, and the Piltdown skull was held to be so old and so distinct from *Homo sapiens* as to merit the creation of a new genus, *Eoanthropus*. Clearly something was amiss. The geology at Swanscombe was well documented and the Swanscombe skull's affinities were well defined, so Marston concluded that the fault must lie with the Piltdown specimen. The jaw must have belonged to an ape, he said, and the skull must have belonged to a man more recent than even the Swanscombe remains, whatever the circumstances of the discovery. Marston summarized the problem in 1937:

that the Swanscombe skull had to be considered in its relations to the Piltdown was inevitable, and once this was embarked upon the gross inconsistencies of the large-brained, Pliocene, ape-jawed, eolithic medley became apparent. The relegation of the Piltdown skull to a later date will remove the disharmony which has occasioned so much difficulty for those who have tried to describe it as an early Pleistocene type (Marston 1937: 394).

By the 1930s, fossil evidence accumulating from other parts of the world seemed to suggest that the brain had not led the way in the evolution of mankind. Fossils of no less antiquity than that proposed for Piltdown Man revealed distinctly man-like jaws and teeth, while the brain remained relatively small, so that it became increasingly difficult to reconcile the large brain and ape-like jaw of Piltdown Man with a reasonable interpretation of mankind's evolution as suggested by the new evidence. Scientific papers repeatedly drew attention to the differences rather than the similarities between Piltdown and the new fossils. The triumvirate of British anthropology (they became two with the death of Elliot Smith in 1937) remained convinced of the specimen's validity and regarded the new evidence as proof of the theory that two lines (at least) of hominid evolution had once co-existed, the surviving line represented by modern man, Piltdown and little else, while all the new discoveries represented lines that had led to extinction. To other authorities, however, Piltdown simply did not fit; the specimen was a chimaera, a once-intriguing riddle about which there seemed little more to be said.

But the truth, if discernible at all, must be contained in the evidence. The question was: could it ever be extracted? Oakley had actually begun to answer this question in 1935 when he had referred to the observation that Dawson had estimated the height of the Piltdown gravels incorrectly. The implications of Dawson's error were clear: the age of Piltdown Man was derived solely from its association with extinct fauna of the early Pleistocene found in the same pit; but if the deposits were younger than had been claimed, then the older fossils must have come from somewhere else and there could be no compelling reason to believe that *all* the Piltdown fossils were of equal antiquity. The extinct fauna was indisputably older than the deposit, but Piltdown Man could be the same age or even younger. The next question was: is there some way of determining whether or not bones found close together in a single deposit are actually the same age? This question became a subject of Kenneth Oakley's research programme after the war, and although the solution of the Piltdown riddle was not his specific interest, it was an important result of his endeavours.

Fossils absorb fluorine from the soil in which they are buried. and Oakley's research explored the observation that the amount of fluorine in a fossil steadily increases with time and therefore might give some indication of its geological age. The phenomenon had been noted by J. Middleton in 1844, who remarked that the 'accumulation of fluorine seems to involve the element of time, so interesting to geological investigations' (Middleton 1844: 431–3) and attempted to establish a timescale based on fluorine content by which the absolute age of fossils could be determined. Taking the quantity of fluorine in a bone of an ancient Greek known to be 2,000 years old as his standard, Middleton dated fossils from the Siwaliks at 7,700 years and an extinct pachyderm at 24,200 years, age estimates which even then must have seemed a trifle ungenerous. Furthermore, Middleton had overlooked that fact that, because the soil's fluorine content varies considerably from place to place, fossils found in different deposits are likely to have absorbed quite different amounts and therefore cannot be dated one against the other reliably on this basis.

Middleton's observations were not pursued and the significance of fluorine in fossil bones slipped into obscurity until it was discovered anew by Adolf Carnot, a French mineralogist. In 1892 Carnot published tables showing the increasing amounts of fluorine in fossil bones from progressively more ancient deposits; the following year he reported on the fluorine contents of a fossil mammoth bone and a human bone from the same deposit; they were different, he said, and therefore the bones must be of different ages (Carnot 1893). This observation was fundamental to the potential of fluorine content as a means of dating fossil bones. It could never provide an absolute timescale, such as Middleton had sought, but it could provide a useful relative scale and, furthermore, a means of assessing whether or not bones found together in a deposit had all been there for the same length of time. But even Carnot's work passed unnoticed; the principle of fluorine dating again slipped into obscurity, and there it remained for fifty years until it was rediscovered by Kenneth Oakley.

In 1943, while Oakley was assessing Britain's phosphate resources, a colleague showed him Carnot's 1892 tables giving the fluorine content of fossil bones. Oakley realized that Carnot's work suggested a means of comparing the age of fossils within a single deposit, and for several years thereafter believed this primary observation on fluorine dating was his alone. Only after he had refined and tested his methods did he learn of Carnot's 1893 paper, and later still of Middleton's work.

The quantity of fluorine absorbed by a fossil is never large, even in the oldest bone, and measurement involves complicated chemical analysis. At the instigation of Oakley and the British Museum, preliminary trials were conducted by the Government Chemist during 1948 to establish the most satisfactory procedure, and the perfected fluorine dating method was used to assess the relative age of a fossil assemblage that same year. For this first ever test, Oakley and his colleague M. F. A. Montagu selected the Galley Hill skeleton (Oakley and Montagu 1949). The results profoundly contradicted Arthur Keith's belief in the great antiquity of the specimen.

Briefly, Oakley and Montagu showed that the fossil fauna from the Middle Pleistocene gravels contained about 2 per cent fluorine, those from Upper Pleistocene deposits in the same sequence about 1 per cent and the post-Pleistocene bones not more than 0·3 per cent. The Galley Hill skeleton, which, it will be recalled, had been found in the oldest gravels, contained only about 0·3 per cent fluorine. Therefore it matched the post-Pleistocene bones and could not have been older; the skeleton must have been of recent origin, entombed in the ancient deposits by man, not nature, despite Keith's assertions to the contrary. The antiquity of the Swanscombe skull, on the other hand, was confirmed by the fluorine test; the bones contained 2 per cent fluorine, perfectly matching the Middle Pleistocene fauna with which it was associated.

So the antiquity of Galley Hill Man was dismissed and of Swanscombe Man confirmed. Where did that leave Piltdown Man, with his combination of 'ancient' ape-like jaw and 'recent' large brain? In October 1948 Kenneth Oakley was authorized to apply his fluorine dating method to the Piltdown material, the Keeper of Geology at the British Museum having deemed it likely that the results might help resolve the riddle of its age and association. Every available bone and tooth from the assemblage was analysed, thirty-six specimens in all, including ten pieces of the *Eoanthropus* material and six of the extinct fauna from which the Lower Pleistocene age of *Eoanthropus* had been derived. The fluorine content of the entire assemblage ranged from a minimum of less than 0·1 per cent to a maximum of 3·1 per cent. The higher levels all were found in the extinct fauna, confirming their antiquity; the remains of Piltdown Man contained an average of only 0·2 per cent, clearly showing that he was not as old as the Lower Pleistocene fauna with which he was supposed to have been associated. *Eoanthropus dawsoni*, Dawson's Dawn Man, was probably no older than *Homo sapiens* from Galley Hill, it seemed.

Oakley's results were published in March 1950 (Oakley and Hoskins 1950). 'That the figures scarcely provide any differentiation between *Eoanthropus* and the recent bones requires some explanation,' he remarked, but the deeper implication of his observation was not fully realized until three years later.

Meanwhile, Oakley had simply added another twist to the riddle. The combination of jaw and skull was puzzling enough when both were believed to be of great antiquity, as we have seen, but if both stemmed from the recent past further problems arose. The skull was reasonable enough, but what about the jaw? No man could have possessed such an ape-like form at so late a stage in human evolution. This may seem to have vindicated the contention that jaw and skull represented different individuals, but this in itself presented another problem: if the jaw did not belong to the skull, obviously it came from somewhere else. But where? The great apes are totally absent from the fossil record of Britain and Europe and are highly unlikely to have inhabited the region during the upheavals of the Ice Age. So Oakley provided no comfort for either side of the Piltdown controversy.

With the ageing and passing of its protagonists, the controversy had lost much of its impetus by 1950. Although Piltdown Man so completely contradicted the evidence of the small-brained hominid fossils with man-like jaws subsequently found in Africa and the Far East, most anthropologists were content to consign the riddle to a 'suspense account' and await clarification rather than actively search for it.

But one evening towards the end of July 1953 a chance remark by Kenneth Oakley promoted Joseph Weiner, an anatomist working with Wilfred le Gros Clark at Oxford, to ponder the problem again as he drove home. In the early hours of the morning he found the key to the riddle. If Piltdown Man was not as old as had been claimed, if the strange jaw with man-like features matched no apes living or extinct, if it belonged neither to the skull nor to the deposit in which the specimens were found, then all 'natural' explanations of the Piltdown phenomenon were eliminated. Which left only an 'unnatural' alternative, reasoned Weiner (1955: 26–35). Could it be that the man-like features of the jaw were artificial and that the whole assemblage had been deposited in the Piltdown gravels with the express intention of suggesting to its discoverers that man in the early Pleistocene had possessed an ape-like jaw and a large brain?

The proposition seemed outrageous, but as Weiner weighed the evidence, the case for a deliberate hoax gained strength on several counts. The discovery of the second Piltdown remains so precisely echoing the first some years before considerably lessened the likelihood of either or both being an accident. The fact that the chin region and the articular knob were missing strongly suggested that these critical diagnostic features had been deliberately removed. The pieces of the puzzle began to fall into place.

Next day, Weiner examined the casts of the Piltdown remains in the collection of the Department of Anatomy at Oxford and discussed his theory with le Gros Clark. Even on the casts, the wear of the molar teeth seemed more compatible with artificial than natural abrasion; and similarly on the canine, where artificial abrasion would also explain the apparent paradox, first noted by a dentist in 1916 (Lyne 1916), of such excessive wear on such an immature tooth.

Weiner and le Gros Clark took their case to the British Museum and during the autumn of 1953 the riddle of Piltdown Man was finally resolved, forty-one years after it had first arisen. The teeth confirmed Weiner and le Gros Clark's preliminary observations. Further fluorine testing revealed that the jaw was not just recent but not long dead; the skull was slightly more ancient. The remains were all stained to match the Piltdown deposit; so too were the mammalian fossils with which they were associated. The hoax had been ingeniously planned, carefully carried out and totally unsuspected.

When the news was released in November 1953 it excited comment from many quarters. In the House of Commons a motion was put forward proposing a lack of confidence in the trustees of the British Muesum, 'because of the tardiness of their discovery that the skull of the Piltdown Man is partially a fake'. The proposers were angry at the 'sycophantic servility' of the museum tradition, which had itself been playing a hoax on the public with this 'so-called Missing Link', they said, but the motion aroused more laughter than serious debate: Speaker – 'not sure how serious the motion is (laughter), but sure [we] have many other things to do besides examining the authenticity of a lot of old bones' (loud laughter). Lord Privy Seal – 'the government had found so many skeletons to examine when they came into office that there had not yet been time to extend the researches into skulls' (laughter) (Anon. 1953).

A letter to *The Times* asked: 'Sir, May we now regard the Piltdown Man as the first human being to have false teeth?' (Kramer 1953).

Humour may cover embarrassment satisfactorily, but it could never dispel the question: Who dunnit? Dawson, Smith Woodward, Elliot Smith and de Chardin have all been accused by some and excused by others. Several books and articles (Costello 1985–6; Blinderman 1986; Pryce 1986; Spencer, in prep.) have been published on the subject and from time to time 'new' evidence is produced to throw new light, but so far there is no definite, incontrovertible answer. The evidence simply is not conclusive enough. A case could be made against each of the characters involved (including some not mentioned in this chapter), but none would stand serious cross-examination and judgement would depend heavily upon the predispositions of the judge.

The inconclusive nature of the Piltdown affair reflects a fundamental problem of the science as a whole, for the fossil evidence of human evolution rarely offers just one clear interpretation. At the same time, however, the Piltdown affair makes two pertinent points: first, accurate geological and stratigraphical determinations are essential; and second, when preconception is so clearly defined, so easily reproduced, so enthusiastically welcomed and so long accommodated, as in the case of Piltdown Man, science reveals a disturbing predisposition towards belief before investigation, as perhaps the hoaxer was anxious to demonstrate.

5

Australopithecus africanus

(1925)

Grafton Elliot Smith's contribution to the Piltdown affair was largely inspired by his belief that the imprint of the brain's fissures and convolutions on the interior of a fossil skull permitted some comparative assessment of the owner's intellectual development. His researches had suggested to him that the significant differences in the brain development of apes and man could be recognized on casts taken from the interior of their skulls; so if the form of the ape's 'primitive' brain and of man's 'evolved' brain was known, Elliot Smith reasoned that it should be possible to define and recognize the intermediate stages on casts taken from the fossil skulls of early man.

The idea was not universally accepted by any means, but among those with whom it found favour was Raymond Dart, a fellow Australian and Senior Demonstrator in Anatomy at University College, London, who was working under Elliot Smith from 1919 to 1922, while the latter was still busy with the problems of the Piltdown reconstruction. The evolution of the brain and the nervous system was Dart's own special interest, which Elliot Smith helped to supplement with an interest in the evolution of man, so Dart was especially well equipped to recognize the significance of certain hominid fossils that came his way a few years later.

Raymond Dart was born in a suburb of Brisbane on 4 February 1893, one of nine children. He graduated from medical school in 1917, served with the Medical Corps in France and, after a spell in London, was appointed Professor of Anatomy at the Witwatersrand University, Johannesburg, in 1922, at the instigation of Elliot Smith and Arthur Keith.

Many might have found it flattering to be appointed a full professor at twenty-nine but, all in all, the Witwatersrand Medical School in 1922 was not the most attractive proposition for a young anatomist with interest in neurological research and the evolution of man. Johannesburg was still a pioneer town of tin-roofed houses and impermanent appearance. Barely fifty years old, founded on a gold-rush by the kind of people such events attract, the city was struggling to establish identity and respectability. The University had received its charter just three years before and the Chair of Anatomy was vacant only because its incumbent had been forced to resign in disgrace following his divorce. Dart was hardly a welcome replacement. He was an Australian, and the University Board did not approve of Australians any more than it approved of divorce. The Principal himself wrote expressing regret that an Australian had been appointed, but presumably the choice was limited.

The medical school awaiting the new professor was an un-prepossessing place: a double-storeyed building standing among weeds behind an old garrison wall. The anatomy department comprised just three or four small rooms and a dissecting hall whose walls bore signs of its occasional use for football and tennis practice. The department was devoid of electricity, water or gas and, apart from a few scraps of cadavers remaining from the previous course, almost entirely lacking in essential facilities. No library, no museum, no specimens, an abysmal lack of equipment. 'There wasn't a bloody thing,' says Dart, 'except what I happened to carry out with me from England' (Dart 1978). He had left England feeling more like an exile than a man elevated to a professorship (Dart 1959: 26) and for the greater part of the first two years in Johannesburg he was a very unhappy man.

The events which changed Dart's life irrevocably and introduced an important new dimension to the study of fossil man began in the early part of 1924 when Dart's sole female student, Josephine Salmons, noticed a fossil baboon skull gracing the mantelpiece of a friend's living-room. She told the professor of it and he, then unaware of any fossil primates from anywhere south of the Fayoum deposits in Egypt, asked her to borrow the specimen if she could and bring it to him for examination. The skull was indeed that of a baboon, Dart confirmed the next day, possibly of a new and primitive species. It had been found in the course of lime-quarrying operations near a place called Taung, one among many such items discovered there; in fact, unbeknown to Dart, a new species of fossil baboon had already been reported from the deposit by a government geologist (Haughton 1920). Dart wanted more specimens if they were available and immediately sought the advice of R. B. Young, a colleague in the university's geology department. Young knew the Taung quarry and, as it happened, was due to visit the area. He agreed to look for primate fossils while he was there and to ask the quarry managers to preserve any they might discover.

The Taung fossils had been preserved in cave deposits that typically occur along valleys cut through the dolomitic rock of South Africa's inland plateau. But how were such cave deposits formed and how did fossils accumulate in them? Dolomite is a limestone; caverns were initially formed in it when the water table of the region was so high that it covered the rock entirely. The water percolated through cracks and areas of weakness in the rock, leaching away the soluble calcium salts and thus carving out caves and tunnels. As the rivers cut valleys through the dolomite, the water table dropped with the level of the surface water. At last the caves and tunnels were left high and dry. Rain continued to percolate through rock fissures, of course, and this water leached out the soluble calcium salts as before. But instead of being washed away, these substances now accumulated within the cave system, in the form of stalagmites and stalactites.

Eventually this slow but inexorable process of deposition might fill entire caves, but frequently a rockfall or erosion would open them to the surface first. In that case external debris would fall in and mingle with the purer chemical deposition; animals could enter or perhaps fall in and die there, leaving their bones to fossilize among the accumulating debris in perfect alkaline conditions as the caves gradually filled. It was a continuous process of erosion and deposition that over millions of years has left the dolomite plateau of South Africa dotted with caves and cave deposits containing fossils (Partridge 1973; Brain 1975).

Stalagmites and stalactites and such primary cave deposits consist of pure lime. Lime is an important constituent of cement, and, as the South African building boom gathered momentum after the First World War, every workable deposit in the country became a valuable resource. The purer the better, of course, but even those where the pure lime was surrounded and interfingered by a secondary deposit were worth exploiting. The secondary deposits comprised the earth and debris that had fallen in once the cave had been opened to the surface; they were mixed with varying proportions of lime and compacted to rock hardness. The fossils lay within this rock and were revealed as the lime-workers blasted and quarried the deposits. The Taung quarry was an extensive operation and it is certain that large quantities of fossil bone were shovelled into the lime-kilns before Dart's pronouncements on a fossil found there in 1924 brought worldwide attention to the significance of the deposits.

In a 1974 publication commemorating the fiftieth anniversary of the discovery (Terry 1974), it is said that Young first saw the fossil in question on the desk of the quarry manager, where it served as a paperweight, having been brought into the office some time before by a workman convinced he had found the fossilized remains of a bushman. In a newspaper report of the day, however, Young himself tells how he arrived at the Taung quarry just after blasting operations had taken place. 'One large piece of rock had apparently been split in two,' he says; 'embedded in the one fragment was the "Missing Link" fossil, the face itself hidden in the rock. The brain portion was found quite loose, but it fitted exactly into position in the skull, each fracture corresponding. Dr Young carefully packed the find and after returning to Johannesburg, handed it to Professor Dart' (*Star* 1925).

In his popular book *Adventures with the Missing Link*, Dart gave yet another version of the fossil's discovery. Two large boxes of rocks, mailed to him from the Taung lime-works on Young's instructions, arrived while he was donning white tie and tails for a wedding to be held at his house. With collar unfixed, the guests arriving and the groom waiting, he hurriedly wrenched open the boxes. The contents of the first were disappointing, but in the second he immediately recognized a fossil brain-cast with distinctly hominid features and, after further ransacking the boxes, also found the back of the forehead and face into which the cast fitted. 'I stood in the shade holding the brain as greedily as any miser hugs his gold,' he writes; 'here, I was certain, was one of the most significant finds ever made in the history of anthropology ... These pleasant daydreams were interrupted by the bridegroom himself tugging at my sleeve. "My God, Ray," he said, striving to keep the nervous urgency out of his voice. "You've got to finish dressing immediately – or I'll have to find another best man. The bridal car should be here any moment."' (Dart 1959: 6).

A fossil brain-cast, or more correctly, an endocranial cast, is formed when the skull cavity of the dead creature, lying undisturbed in a cave, fills with debris – for instance, bat droppings, sand, lime –

which subsequently fossilizes along with the bone. In the case of the Taung specimen, only a little more than half the skull cavity was filled, giving a cast of the right side only and a flat surface on the left covered with glistening white crystals. Endocranial casts are extremely rare. Five are known from South Africa; the Taung specimen was the first ever to be recognized. That it was formed in the first place is remarkable enough; that it was recovered in the course of a mining operation, which, by its very nature, is destructive, is even more remarkable; but, following such a fortuitous chain of circumstances, that it should have found its way into the hands of one of the three or four men in the entire world capable of recognizing its significance is most remarkable of all.

In the course of his pioneering work on the brain and endocranial casts, Dart's professor at University College, Grafton Elliot Smith, had identified the lunate sulcus, which is a fissure between two convolutions towards the rear of the brain, and suggested that the gap between the lunate and the parallel sulcus (another fissure close by) is an important indication of evolutionary development. In apes the sulci are close together; in man they are farther apart. Dart, of course, was familiar with this work, and the first glance at the Taung endocranial cast told him that the gap between its lunate and parallel sulci was about three times greater than that in living apes. In terms of cranial capacity, the cast was large for an ape, but still far, far smaller than anyone thought possible for the ancestor of man. Even so, Dart felt that 'by the sheerest good luck', the fossil had brought him 'the opportunity to provide what would probably be the ultimate answer in the . . . study of the evolution of man' (Dart 1959: 16).

Seventy-three days later (during which time Dart had worked in his spare time with a variety of tools, including his wife's knitting needles, sharpened for the fine work), the matrix was removed from the rock into which the cast fitted and the face of the Taung specimen was exposed. There were no great eyebrow ridges, nor did the jaw jut forward, as in the apes. The large brain had not belonged to a large adult ape, it was revealed, but to an infant with rounded forehead, a full set of milk teeth and the first molars just emerging.

The Taung fossil had reached Dart in mid-October; by Christmas he had uncovered most of its detail; by mid-January he had written a preliminary paper on the discovery and posted it, with photographs, to *Nature* in London. During this period Dart's resources were limited. He had worked on the fossil entirely alone, without colleagues for discussion, a library for reference or museum specimens for comparison. His most useful aid had been a book that he had brought from England which included some drawings of infant chimpanzee and gorilla skulls. In comparing these drawings with the Taung specimen, Dart saw enough to convince him that the fossil differed from both the chimpanzee and the gorilla as much as they differed from each other. And in the presentation of his findings (Dart 1925) Dart drew bold conclusions from his unavoidably limited observations.

The Taung specimen represented a creature that was advanced beyond the apes in two distinctly human characteristics, he said: its teeth and the 'improved quality' of its brain. The creature could appreciate colour, weight and form, he claimed; it knew the significance of sounds and had already passed important milestones along the road towards the acquisition of articulate speech. Furthermore, the forward position of the foramen magnum (the hole in the base of the skull through which the spinal cord passes) suggested to Dart that the Taung skull must have balanced on the top of the vertebral column in a manner approximating that of modern man. Therefore, the creature had walked upright, he concluded, with hands free to become manipulative organs and available for offence and defence, a proposal rendered all the more probable, Dart reasoned, by the absence of 'massive canines and hideous features'.

As regards the evolutionary pressures that may have given rise to this 'Missing Link', Dart pointed out that the creature had lived on the fringe of the Kalahari Desert, 2,000 miles from the easy picking of the tropical forests, at a time when, geologists claimed, the climate was no less harsh than in modern times. Compared with the luxuriant forests of the tropical belts, where 'nature was supplying with profligate and lavish hand an easy and sluggish solution, by adaptive specialization, of the problem of existence', Dart suggested that the relative scarcity of water and 'fierce and bitter mammalian competition' for food and with predators, made southern Africa the perfect laboratory for sharpening the wits and quickening the intellect during the 'penultimate phase of human evolution'. Of the other candidates then proposed for the ancestry of man, Dart alluded to the chimpanzee-like features of the Piltdown jaw and referred to Dubois's Java

Man as 'a caricature of precocious hominid failure', an ape-like man destined for extinction, while the Taung specimen represented 'our troglodytic forefathers', intermediate between the apes and man. He proposed a new zoological family to accommodate the phenomenon, the *Homo simiadae*, and named the Taung child *Australopithecus africanus* as the first known genus and species of the group.

Dart has said that he prepared his preliminary report 'proudly' and with 'a sense of history'. When he sent it off to *Nature*, he fully expected some scepticism from the British scientific community but hoped that he would be taken seriously at least. Considering the woefully inadequate facilities in Johannesburg, Dart had assembled a paper of commendable perspicacity. In some respects it tended more towards inspirational interpretation than cool scientific appraisal, and occasionally Dart lapsed into a florid style not normally encountered in *Nature*. None the less, the editors deemed the report important enough to merit immediate attention (no mean compliment in itself) and pre-publication review by four of Britain's most distinguished anthropologists – Arthur Keith, Arthur Smith Woodward, Grafton Elliot Smith and W. L. H. Duckworth, the triumvirate of the Piltdown affair (see Chapter 4) and one other. These gentlemen received proofs of the report on 3 February 1925, but they hardly had time to collect their thoughts before Fleet Street descended upon them for comment on that morning's cables from Johannesburg announcing that the 'Missing Link' had been found there by Professor Dart. The next day, and indeed for several days thereafter, the news occupied much space in the papers. Sir Arthur Keith endeavoured to instil a note of scientific calm with the comment that 'we have a rumour of this kind three or four times a year', but his efforts had little effect. 'Missing Link 5,000,000 years old', 'Ape-Man of Africa had commonsense', 'Missing Link that could speak', 'Birth of Mankind', 'Missing Link 500,000 [*sic*] years old', etc., ran headlines around the world above stories in which Dart expounded variously and at length upon the aspect and talents of the ancestor he believed was represented by the fossil from Taung.

In the first days of his thirty-third year, Raymond Dart became a celebrity. Press inquiries and congratulatory cables inundated him, publishers offered book contracts and General Smuts and the University Principal who disliked Australians both congratulated him. Then, on 14 February, the first serious scientific comment appeared, when *Nature* published the reports of the four experts they had asked to review the paper (Keith *et al.* 1925). Although all four saw more immediate affinities to the apes than to man, the reports were sympathetic. They all emphasized the difficulty of assessing a fossil, especially a juvenile fossil, from a preliminary report and a few photographs. To judge the claims Dart had made, they needed more material and looked forward to receiving full-size photographs, casts of the fossils and the monograph Dart had promised. Of the four, Sir Arthur Smith Woodward was the least complimentary. He concluded his report with an expression of regret that Dart had chosen such a 'barbarous' combination of Latin and Greek in naming the specimen *Australopithecus africanus*.

Australopithecus africanus was intended to be descriptive. It means 'the southern ape of Africa' and its form follows the precedent set in 1922 by *Hesperopithecus*, the 'western ape' (see p. 102). Of course, *Australopithecus* is also akin to the name of Dart's homeland; but he always expressed the utmost surprise if it was ever suggested that he chose the name to reflect his own origins.

Names apart, the most important requirement during the months following the announcement of the discovery was that Dart should publish a thorough description of the remains and make casts available to his senior colleagues with the same dispatch as he had preliminarily described it. The scientific establishment was not impressed with his extravagant speculations in the popular press, nor by the popular acclaim he had achieved. Dart may have been disappointed that reaction was 'criticism rather than adoration of their potential ancestry', as he has written (Dart 1959: 40), but criticism is after all part of the process by which interpretative science proceeds and a scientist with new evidence has some obligation to present it in the fullest possible scientific manner. Dart continued to promote his interpretations of the discovery in the popular press. Meanwhile, expert opinion was steadily hardening towards the conclusion that *Australopithecus* was a form of chimpanzee, its man-like attributes due to the phenomenon of parallel evolution.

It is generally supposed that Dart and the Taung specimen were unfairly attacked by the scientific establishment of the day. In the publication commemorating the fiftieth anniversary of the discovery, it is told how the fossil caused 'sensation and argument' wherever it was mentioned and brought 'an avalanche of scorn' upon Dart. But was the scientific reaction really unfair, given the time and the circumstances?

In the first place, Dart's reputation did not inspire confidence. According to Wilfred le Gros Clark (1967b: 26), the memory of an unorthodox theory Dart had once proposed about the evolution of the nervous system still lingered in some minds, suggesting a readiness to draw far-reaching conclusions from limited evidence. Also, significant portions of the Taung report depended upon the interpretation of an endocranial cast, at a time when such interpretations in general were still regarded with some scepticism. And then there was 'the extraordinary repetitious coincidence between Dart's discovery and that of Dubois in Java', as le Gros Clark puts it. Both Dart and Dubois were anatomists with an interest in the evolution of mankind. Both went to outlandish places and both found a 'Missing Link' within a few years of arrival. The coincidence of Dubois's discovery was remarkable enough. That Dart should now come along with an almost identical second coincidence 'seemed almost too much of a good thing,' writes le Gros Clark. 'At any rate,' he continues, 'combined with the few awkward features of Dart's preliminary article . . . it seems to have alerted the minds of anthropologists generally to the possibility that in his too enthusiastic zeal Dart had claimed far more for his *Australopithecus* skull than was warranted by the evidence.'

Eventually some casts of *Australopithecus* were made and Dart produced a head-and-shoulders representation of the creature, but the manner of their subsequent display in London did little to improve his standing. The casts, in fact, were not intended for appraisal by his senior colleagues; on the contrary, they were intended to edify the general public – from a showcase in the South African pavilion at the British Empire Exhibition which opened at Wembley in the summer of 1925. When Arthur Keith wished to inspect the cast he had to peer at it through a glass case, jostled by other visitors, standing beneath a banner proclaiming 'Africa: The Cradle of Humanity', set before a chart alleging that all mankind had evolved from the ancestor represented by the Taung child.

Once again Dart had flouted convention, and Arthur Keith, for one, was not amused. He wrote to *Nature* (Keith 1925b: 11), complaining that students of fossil man had not been given an opportunity of purchasing casts of *Australopithecus* but must visit the Wembley exhibition if they wished to make further study of the specimen. But despite the limited facilities for calm scientific appraisal at Wembley, Keith was able to conclude that the Taung skull had belonged to a young anthropoid ape 'showing so many points of affinity with . . . the gorilla and the chimpanzee that there cannot be a moment's hesitation in placing the fossil in this living group'. Any claim of 'Missing Link' status was preposterous, he said, and as for its being the ancestor of mankind, well, that was like claiming 'a modern Sussex peasant as the ancestor of William the Conqueror'. The last remark referred to Dart's apparent inability to provide data contradicting suggestions that the skull was younger than he claimed, younger even than Piltdown or Heidelberg, to which he said it was ancestral.

Dart attempted to make light of these remarks, but he had nothing substantial to add and fared badly, the more so when his letter appeared in *Nature* together with another cold rejoinder from Keith on the same page (Dart and Keith 1925: 462).

Thereafter, Dart and the Taung child were hardly more than a music-hall joke, while in the study of fossil man Dubois's release of the Java material and the discovery of hominid fossils in China diverted attention. In South Africa, Dart concentrated on building up the Witwatersrand Medical School. He did not instigate any exploration of cave deposits around the country, or actively seek more remains of *Australopithecus*, but he did complete the monograph on the Taung specimen.

In 1930 he sent the manuscript to Elliot Smith for consideration by the Royal Society, and he himself followed a year later, hoping to convince everyone that *Australopithecus* really was all he claimed for it. He arrived in London with the fossil six years to the day after the initial *Nature* announcement. Finally, Dart had bowed to convention, but he was too late to be persuasive.

Elliot Smith, Smith Woodward and Keith welcomed him warmly enough, but they were all much more interested in telling him about the skull recently discovered in China than in hearing the Taung tale all over again. Elliot Smith had just returned from Peking and was to address the Zoological Society on his visit; he invited Dart to accompany him to the meeting, suggesting that he might like to tell the audience of the Taung child. Dart readily agreed, for it seemed a splendid opportunity to present his case properly; but the result was otherwise. As he later wrote:

This was no setting in which to vindicate claims once daring but now trite . . . I stood in that austere and chilly room, my heart bounding with the hope that the expressions of polite attention on the four score faces before me might change to vivid interest as I spoke. I realized that my offering was an anti-climax but with undiminished optimism launched into my story . . . What a pitiful difference between this fumbling account and Elliot Smith's skilful demonstration: I had no plaster casts to pass round, no lantern slides to throw on the screen to emphasize my points. I could only stand there with the tiny skull in my hand, telling the audience what I saw as I looked at it – all of which had been previously published, with illustrations . . . My address became increasingly diffident as I realized the inadequacy of my material and took in the unchanging expressions of my audience . . . (Dart 1959: 62).

Dart found little joy in London that year, and just before returning to South Africa he was told that the Royal Society would publish only the section of his monograph concerned with the teeth of *Australopithecus*. Why the rest of it was rejected is not known, although le Gros Clark has suggested that it may have been written in an unsuitable style. He also wondered 'why some of the senior anatomists in London at the time did not advise and help him redraft his monograph in a form acceptable for publication' (Clark 1967b: 26).

Meanwhile, Keith had acquired a cast of the specimen and was preparing to publish nearly 100 pages on the Taung skull in the revised edition of his textbook *New Discoveries Relating to the Antiquity of Man* (Keith 1931); and the Austrian anatomist Wolfgang Abel published another 100 pages on the fossil in a European journal (Abel 1931). Both these authors opposed Dart's interpretation of the fossil. Keith aligned it with the chimpanzee, while Abel chose the gorilla. A third author, Louis Leakey, similarly cast doubt upon the validity of Dart's claims by omitting all mention of *Australopithecus* from his book *Adam's Ancestors*, published in 1934.

The trouble was that although Dart had drawn the right conclusions from the Taung skull, it was more by inspired speculation than anything else, for there was very little evidence to substantiate his conclusions. The fossil could be ancestral to man, but it had many ape-like characteristics too. Moreover, the fact that it was a juvenile specimen made final diagnosis almost impossible because juveniles and adults differ greatly in all primate species and juveniles of different species resemble each other more than adults do. More than anything else, Dart needed more evidence, fossil evidence, to support his contentions, and it surely existed in the South African cave deposits; but he chose not to look for it.

In 1925 Dart refused the Witwatersrand Education Department's offer of money and time to travel abroad and write his monograph with access to comparative collections and good libraries. Recalling this decision later, he wrote that he did not want to leave his anatomy department and his home for so long, and was unwilling to be bound by the condition that he should donate the Taung fossil to the University (1959: 56). Later still he was to regret his decision; today the fossil is part of the University's permanent collection and Dart wonders if it might have been wiser to have toured the world in search of support for his *Australopithecus*. 'It's no good being in front if you're going to be lonely,' he says (Dart 1978). And equally regrettable is the fact that while Dart was lonely, for ten years and more untold numbers of *Australopithecus* remains were probably burned in the lime-kilns. At the time, the world of palaeoanthropology was much more interested in the discovery of Peking Man.

6

PEKING MAN

(1926)

The story of Peking Man is an intriguing tale with an unhappy ending, but like a good fairy story it begins with dragons. Not the malignant, fire-breathing dragons of Western mythology whose purpose is best fulfilled on the end of Saint George's lance; no, in Chinese mythology dragons are benign creatures, all-powerful perhaps, but kindly disposed towards mankind. They rule the seas, the rivers and the rain; when dragons quarrel above the clouds, thunder and rain result; when dragons are thirsty they suck the land dry before retiring to palaces beneath the sea. Thus dragons were believed to control the seasons and dragon worship therefore pervaded the life of the rural Chinese. Emperors were born of dragons who attended their mothers on stormy nights; beautiful azure dragons descended from the skies to be present at the birth of wise men like Confucius; rubies were petrified drops of dragons' blood; perfume was dragons' saliva; and, more down to earth, dragon bones and teeth, pulverized and mixed in strange potions, could cure a multitude of ills. This particular belief still persists: ethnic Chinese drugstores (in London and San Francisco as well as Shanghai and Hong Kong) still dispense Lung Ku – dragons' bones – and Lung Ya – dragons' teeth. These dragon relics are, in fact, fossil bones and teeth, found in the ancient sedimentary deposits of China and purchased from peasants who 'mine' them during the dry season, when the dragons are in their watery palaces and there is little profit in agriculture.

'Dragon bones' were first brought to the attention of palae-ontologists and anthropology by K. A. Haberer, a German naturalist who travelled to China in 1899, hoping to explore the hinterland. Unhappily, the disturbances of the Boxer Rebellion restricted his movements severely. He was confined to the ports, so he explored the drugstores instead of the hinterland and returned to Europe with a collection of 'dragon' bones representing no fewer than ninety species, with not a single reptile among them, dragon or otherwise. Haberer's collection was described by Max Schlosser in a monograph on the fossil mammals of China (Schlosser 1903). Schlosser gave details of fossil elephants and camels, bears, hyenas, rhinoceroses, giraffes, horses – and a solitary primate, represented by an upper molar tooth that he felt could be either human or ape. The tooth's affinities were no more certain than that, he said, while adding the tantalizing observation that China might be a good place to search for the early ancestors of mankind. Nowadays that particular tooth is regarded as representing an ape, but in the first decades of the century Schlosser's observations accorded well with a growing conviction that mammalian life had originated in Asia and from there had dispersed to populate the world; and any tooth of the higher primates was enough to suggest the birthplace of man. Schlosser's monograph aroused a good deal of interest among palaeontologists and anthropologists.

These specialists were not the first Westerners to find China interesting. Following the footsteps of Marco Polo, enterprising 'foreign devils' travelled extensively through the country during the late nineteenth and early twentieth centuries. Some were naturalists, others were adventurers, but none travelled without an eye for some kind of foreign profit and exploitation. By the time of the First World War, however, the Chinese authorities believed they were directing foreign exploration towards the greater benefit of Chinese interests. Thus it was that Johan Gunnar Andersson, a Swedish mining expert appointed as adviser to the Chinese government, discovered large deposits of iron ore that were exploited by Chinese entrepreneurs most profitably while war raged in Europe. Demand fell with the advent of peace, however; so did the incentive to pay his salary as regularly as Andersson expected, and he therefore sought an income elsewhere.

Andersson's hobby was collecting fossils. Perhaps prodded by Professor Wiman of Uppsala University, who was certainly aware of China's potential as a repository of palaeontological treasures, and no doubt using the salary default to full advantage, Andersson negotiated an arrangement with the National Geological Survey of China whereby he would collect Chinese fossils for Swedish institutions. Expenses (including Andersson's salary) would be met by the Swedish China Research Committee, established expressly for that purpose, and its Chairman, His Royal Highness the Crown Prince of Sweden, personally attended to the diplomatic aspects of the negotiations. In return for the collecting privileges, the Chinese would receive a duplicate set of fossils. As Andersson later wrote (1934: xx), it was an arrangement 'both beneficial to Chinese science and generous to Swedish museums'. It was also a coup that gave Sweden considerable control over palaeontological investigations in China for a decade and restricted American expeditions to the further reaches of the Gobi Desert when they searched for early man in Asia during the 1920s.

One might imagine that after centuries of medicinal exploitation 'dragon bones' would have been scarce in China. But not so: Andersson's endeavours met with immediate and considerable success. Soon he was excavating several sites at once and, when his first collections were lost in a steamer sunk by a typhoon, he was able to replace them all during the following year. It is difficult to assess exactly how much material Andersson collected, but it is hardly an exaggeration to say that Professor Wiman built Uppsala's Palaeontological Institute around the fossils he sent to Sweden; even today, the material is still not fully described.

By 1921 Wiman had gathered a select band of scientists and students to assist with the preparation and description of the Chinese material, but he was becoming concerned about the manner in which the fossils were collected. Andersson was not a palaeontologist; furthermore, he left the excavating to his Chinese labourers, who were not as careful as was desirable. Wiman felt there should be an expert in charge and persuaded Otto Zdansky, a young Austrian palaeontologist, to spend three years in China ensuring that the excavations were handled 'in a more businesslike way' (Zdansky 1978). Zdansky had recently completed a doctoral thesis on fossil turtles and was willing to go to China, but, because Wiman offered no remuneration beyond travel and living expenses, only on condition that he was given the right to describe his finds himself. 'After all,' Zdansky explains, 'the publications would be all I got out of my stay in China.' Wiman accepted the condition and so, with Schlosser's monograph prominent among his baggage, Zdansky set off for China in the summer of 1921.

Zdansky quarrelled with Andersson very soon after arrival. He threatened to return to Europe immediately; Andersson placated him, but thereafter the relationship between the two men was decidedly cool. Zdansky went to the regions Andersson suggested, but once he was there, the excavations were entirely Zdansky's affair. To familiarize himself with Chinese conditions before venturing into the more remote regions, Zdansky first investigated a disused lime-quarry about fifty kilometres from Peking known to contain large quantities of recent fossils. He established his headquarters in the neighbouring village called Chou K'ou Tien and began work on a column of secondary infill which the lime-workers had left standing in the quarry. The column was packed with fossils; there were some rodents and small predators among them, but most seemed to be of common and possibly still-surviving forms.

Not long after Zdansky had begun exploring the deposits, Andersson paid a visit, bringing with him Walter Granger, Chief Palaeontologist on the American Museum of Natural History expedition in search of early man, which was just then getting under way; and that day a local resident advised the three men of another deposit with bigger and better 'dragon bones' in a quarry about 150 metres from the Chou K'ou Tien railway station. In a matter of hours the new site provided fossils of rhinoceros, hyena and bovids (ruminants of or related to the ox family) and that evening a 'happy trio' raised their glasses to the prospect of further discoveries. Zdansky agreed to spend two or three weeks exploring the site.

Andersson had noticed fragments of quartz dotted through the deposit; he became convinced they were primitive tools of early man and on a subsequent visit said to Zdansky: 'I have a feeling that there lie here the remains of one of our ancestors and it is only a question of your finding him. Take your time and stick to it until the cave is emptied, if need be' (Andersson 1934: 101). Zdansky, however, did not agree that the quartz fragments might be tools. He felt they were just splinters fallen from the veins of quartz that traversed the limestone.

Even so, he did find evidence of early man at Chou K'ou Tien during the late summer of 1921: a single molar tooth that was unmistakably human. 'I recognized it at once,' Zdansky recalled later, 'but I said nothing. You see, hominid material is always in the limelight and I was afraid that if it came out there would be such a stir, and I would be forced to hand over material I had a promise to publish. So I said nothing about it' (Zdansky 1978). The fossil tooth Zdansky had found was, in fact, the first evidence of Peking Man.

Andersson's interest in finding early man may have been awakened by Schlosser's monograph, but it was surely encouraged by Walter Granger, and was undoubtedly confirmed by the arrival in Peking of all the experts and equipment that were to explore Mongolia and China under the auspices of the American Museum of Natural History. The expeditions conducted from 1921 to 1928 were inspired by the 'brilliant prediction' of Fairfield Osborn, then President of the Museum, that 'Asia would prove to have been a great dispersal center for northern terrestrial mammalian life' (Andrews 1932: Intro.). But whatever the inspiration, the avowed intention of the expeditions was 'to seek and discover the ancestry of man'. Popularly known as 'The Missing Link Expeditions', the scale on which they were organized and the flamboyance with which they were conducted might have seemed to guarantee success, but they were restricted by one important consideration: namely, a 'gentleman's agreement' with Andersson and a formal undertaking with the Chinese National Geological Survey that 'the expeditions would not enter upon geological, palae-ontological or archaeological explorations in Northern China' (Andrews 1932: 572). This effectively confined the Americans to the wastes of Mongolia, an area of deposits so ancient they could never contain the remains of man. As cynics suggested, they might as well have looked for fossils in the Pacific Ocean.

None the less, the Americans were provided with ample resources: $600,000 to be precise, with undertakings of more to follow. Their leader, Roy Chapman Andrews, a colourful zoologist and explorer, envisaged ten years of exploration in China. The problems he faced were enormous, but Andrews found a solution for many of them in motorized transport. Cars and trucks could travel 100 miles a day, ten times faster than a camel, and thus should enable the Americans 'to do approximately ten years' work in one season', Andrews reasoned; and he claims to have achieved that ratio. But for all their benefits, motor vehicles brought problems peculiar to themselves. Accidents were frequent, with 'many people killed and injured', and fuel was a constant headache. The fleet of five cars and two trucks required 4,000 gallons each season; this weighed twelve tons and would have left little space for the expedition's personnel, equipment and discoveries if carried in the vehicles themselves. So Andrews resorted to camels, employing several score as a fuel train. Forty-four-gallon drums proved difficult to pack on a camel's back, and they had to be returned after use, so disposable five-gallon cans were used instead. Each camel carried twelve of these, weighing 400 pounds – perhaps an excessive load, but one that quickly lessened as the cans expanded, rubbed and leaked when subjected to a camel's rolling gait under a desert sun. A full 50 per cent of the fuel was lost in this way the first year, but Andrews reported that better packing reduced leakage to 25 per cent in 1925.

Logistics notwithstanding, the American expeditions achieved remarkable results. They found a fossilized redwood forest and the grave of a shovel-tusked mastodon with jaws five feet long; they sent over 26,000 specimens back to America and described more than 1,000 fossil and living forms new to science. In all they collected enough data for hundreds of scientific articles and for twelve volumes of final reports. But in respect of fossil man, the expeditions were a failure. As Andrews wrote in a paragraph of his report headed 'The Unfinished Task': 'we have not been successful in one subject of our search – the "Dawn Man". It is a scientific tragedy that Chinese opposition to foreign investigations should end our work when that goal might be attained. Still, we have shown the way, broken trail as it were. Later, others will reap a rich harvest. We are more than ever convinced that Central Asia was a palaeontological Garden of Eden' (Andrews 1932: 453).

The 'Chinese opposition' that Andrews mentioned in his report led ultimately to the expulsion of the American Museum team from their new-found 'Garden of Eden' and stemmed principally from Chinese objections to the manner in which the Americans had disposed of some fossilized dinosaur eggs found in 1923.

The expedition found twenty-five dinosaur eggs in all, the first known to science (Andrews 1932: 208), and the discovery aroused widespread excitement. When Andrews returned to America, newspapers clamoured for exclusive rights to the story, some offering thousands of dollars. But Andrews refused all in favour of *Asia* magazine, to whom he was contracted for popular articles. Eventually the story and pictures were made available to the press free of charge, but Andrews and his colleagues at the American Museum determined to cash in on the enormous interest aroused by auctioning one egg to the highest bidder. Not only would the sale contribute directly towards expedition expenses the following year, they reasoned, but it would also publicize the shortage of funds and perhaps encourage private donations. The egg went to Colonel Austin Colgate for $5,000 and Andrews raised $284,000 that winter, but he soon had reason to wish the publicity campaign had not been quite so successful. The Chinese, Mongolian and Russian authorities assumed that every egg obtained was worth $5,000 and, not surprisingly, drew the conclusion that the fossil collection Andrews and his team had removed from Central Asia was of enormous commercial value. They never could be persuaded otherwise, and, with a change of government and civil strife not helping, cooperation gradually turned to direct opposition and the American Museum had to withdraw, pending 'the dawn of a more tolerant era of sympathy and co-operation with foreign scientific endeavor', as Andrews wrote in the preface to his report, *The New Conquest of China* (Andrews 1932: ix).

While the Americans were having difficulties with the Chinese during this period, Sven Hedin, a Swede who adopted a more individualistic mode of exploration, was enjoying considerably more success, though he had not the slightest interest in the search for early man. Born in 1865, educated with royalty and the last man in Sweden to be knighted, Hedin was a romantic figure who spent the greater part of his life in the Far East. He wrote several books on his travels and achieved popular fame with one in which he claimed to have rediscovered Marco Polo's Silk Road, which even the Chinese had been unable to find. Hedin was an adventurer more than a scientist or a businessman. He managed to allay Chinese suspicions that he was removing valuable treasures from the country, but his expeditions often had a commercial application: in 1925, for instance, his travels through Tibet, Mongolia and China were financed by Lufthansa, the airline then seeking topographical details for their proposed air route to Peking.

The strength of Hedin's position in China at that time was that he knew how to manipulate the Chinese authorities to his own ends, and he knew how to raise money in Sweden and elsewhere. As such he was a threat to both the American and the Swedish explorers; even though he declared no interest in the search for early man, his presence in the country compounded the uncertainties of an already complicated situation.

Meanwhile, Andersson's expeditions were achieving a commendable degree of success. Apart from the fact that Zdansky had actually discovered some evidence of early man within weeks of arriving in China (the fossil tooth he had decided to keep to himself), he and Andersson had also uncovered the beginnings of deciduous vegetation among the fossils of southern Manchuria; in central China they found a rich field of fossil plants including many new to science. Fossil fish, turtles, cockroaches and dragonflies came from eastern China; from there too came some strange dinosaurs. One of them was fully ten metres long; Zdansky and his men cut out the near complete skeleton in great blocks of sandstone and, in Sweden, four men spent a year preparing and reassembling the bones. From the structure of the bone and the form of the skeleton, Wiman deduced that the creature had lived in the water rather like a very large, long-necked hippopotamus. He called it *Helopus zdanskyi*, which means marsh-footed and acknowledges its discoverer. Wiman regarded *Helopus* as a most important discovery.

But despite the success of the expedition's palaeontological endeavours, it was a recurrent disappointment to Andersson that all the sites they investigated were far too old to contain the remains of man. In fact, the only site they had encountered with fauna recent enough to have been contemporary with man was the very first they had visited, Chou K'ou Tien. And there, of course, he had seen the quartz fragments. 'I could never forget the thought of hominid remains in this cave,' he wrote later; and in 1923 he persuaded Zdansky to return to the site. Of course, Zdansky already had in his pocket, so to speak, the very thing Andersson most wanted: the hominid tooth found two years earlier. He was aware of the worldwide interest in the search for early man. But still he said nothing of the tooth to Andersson. The fact that he disliked the man eased any qualms and, in any case: 'I wasn't interested in what Andersson wanted,' Zdansky recalls; 'I wanted only the fauna of the cave' (Zdansky 1978).

Zdansky returned to Sweden in 1923 to study and describe his discoveries and later that year published a preliminary paper on the Chou K'ou Tien deposits, with Andersson as co-author (Zdansky 1923). The hominid tooth was not mentioned and, indeed, its existence might have remained a secret until Zdansky finally published his monograph (Zdansky 1928) if the Crown Prince of Sweden had not

made a visit to Peking in 1926. It will be recalled that the Crown
Prince was Chairman of the Swedish China Research Committee
which had funded Andersson's work. To mark the Prince's visit to
Peking in the course of a world tour, Andersson arranged a scientific
meeting and wrote to Professor Wiman, asking for details of any
important discoveries that could be announced to coincide with the
Prince's visit. Wiman responded with a description of the magnificent
Helopus zdanskyi and asked Zdansky if he had anything to contribute
that might 'give an additional spice to the meeting'. 'Yes, I have,'
replied Zdansky, and promptly dispatched a description of two
hominid teeth from Chou K'ou Tien (he had found a second while
sorting the material), together with photographs and lantern slides.

Andersson's first response to this sudden revelation that Zdansky
had found the ultimate prize and never disclosed it while in China is
not recorded. Later he wrote that Zdansky had thought the first tooth
was an ape's when he found it, but in October 1926 he kept his
counsel and saved the 'spice' for the very end of the meeting. As
Zdansky had expected, the news caused a sensation: his discovery was
immediately labelled 'Peking Man' and reported as 'The oldest human
type whose remains have been found in the strata of the earth' (Anon.
1926).

As a palaeontologist of uncompromising determination, Zdansky
had resolutely avoided the glamour of the search for early man; he
sought the broad picture of ancient life, in which man was an insig-
nificant detail. But in the audience at the Peking meeting sat an anatomist with an interest in fossils for whom fossil man filled the entire
canvas. His name was Davidson Black, a Canadian who was Professor
of Anatomy at the Peking Union Medical College, an establishment
generously endowed by the Rockefeller Foundation of New York.

Black was inspired by the Chou K'ou Tien teeth. With only the
photographs and a written description to hand (reports that Black
worked from the originals are erroneous, according to Zdansky),
Black compiled a report on the discovery which he submitted to
Nature and *Science* (Black 1926a, 1926b). The teeth are 'two specimens
of extraordinary interest,' he wrote, 'which cannot otherwise be
named than *Homo ?sp*. [an unidentified species of the genus *Homo*]
... the actual presence of early man in Eastern Asia is no longer a
matter of conjecture,' he said, and, recalling Schlosser's prediction,

concluded that 'the Chou K'ou Tien discovery . . . furnishes one more link in the already strong chain of evidence supporting the hypothesis of the central Asiatic origin of the Hominidae.' Thus wrote the anatomist.

A few months later Zdansky published a preliminary paper (Zdansky 1927) presenting the more cautious view of the palaeontologist. Noting that the discovery was 'decidedly interesting but not of epoch-making importance', he wrote:

I am very sceptical towards a great deal of prehistoric–anthropological literature, and convinced that the existing material provides a wholly inadequate foundation for many of the various theories based upon it. As every fresh discovery of what may be human remains is of such great interest not only to the scientist but also to the layman, it follows only too naturally that it becomes at once the object of the most detailed – and, in my opinion, too detailed – investigation. I decline absolutely to venture any far-reaching conclusions regarding the extremely meagre material described here, and which cannot be more closely identified than as ?*Homo sp.* [*sic*].

With this honest and accurate assessment of the evidence and ideas then prevailing in the search for early man, Otto Zdansky retired from the story of Peking Man. He completed his monographs in 1928 and thereafter was appointed Professor at Cairo University. And with his retirement, the Swedish option on early man in China effectively lapsed. The two teeth Zdansky dug from the Chou K'ou Tien deposit (and another found later in among the collection) still reside in the Palaeontological Institute at Uppsala, but the subsequent discoveries they inspired were destined for a much less satisfactory resting-place.

Within days of the sensational announcement of the fossil teeth at the Peking meeting, Black convened a smaller, more select gathering in his office. With the Crown Prince in the chair, representatives of the Geological Survey of China and of the Rockefeller Foundation in attendance, Black and Andersson gained unanimous approval for a joint Chinese/Swedish/American expedition to Chinese Turkestan two years hence. But while he was negotiating this cooperative endeavour (which in fact never came to fruition), Black was also applying to the Rockefeller Foundation for money to conduct a systematic two-year research project on the Chou K'ou Tien deposits. The Foundation responded generously. Black arranged that the project would be conducted in conjunction with the Geological Survey and undertook to study any hominid fossils recovered in his laboratory in Peking.

The second round of excavations at Chou K'ou Tien began on Good Friday, 1927. Otto Zdansky had been invited to take charge but declined in favour of the Cairo appointment. In his stead Professor Wiman sent another of his graduate students, Birger Bohlin, who had recently completed his doctorate on the fossil giraffes Andersson had sent from China. Like Zdansky, Bohlin was primarily interested in the broadest aspects of palaeontology but, unlike Zdansky, his work in China was narrowly circumscribed from the start. 'I went to China chiefly because I wanted to go somewhere,' says Bohlin, 'but I was ordered to find man. You could see from a distance that Davidson Black wanted fossil man. The rest was just by-product. He gave me some directions of how to work at Chou K'ou Tien: he said I should remove the whole deposit in six weeks and take it back to Peking. In the first few days I saw that this was impossible' (Bohlin 1978).

With 5,000 dollars' worth of explosives, a small army of Chinese labourers and the able assistance of C. Li, a Chinese geologist, Bohlin managed to blast and examine 3,000 cubic metres of deposits in six months. He uncovered the plan of the cave, revealing a deposit about 800 metres square and between eleven and seventeen metres thick. But for all that, evidence of early man eluded them until three days before work was to finish for the year. Then, on 16 October, Bohlin found a single hominid tooth poking from a corner of the cave. 'Here you are,' he told Li triumphantly. 'We can go home now.'

'Do you think one is enough?' replied Li.

Not long after Bohlin's return to Peking, Davidson Black identified the single tooth to his satisfaction as a child's, matching the second tooth that Zdansky had discovered in Uppsala. On reflection, he decided that both must come from the same jaw and both must have been related to the adult represented by the third tooth – remarkably fortuitous discoveries among such a vast quantity of excavated deposit. Then, comparing the Bohlin tooth with corresponding teeth from a chimpanzee and a ten-year-old child, Black concluded that 'the newly discovered specimen displays in the details of its morphology a number of interesting and unique characters, sufficient it is believed, to justify the proposal of a new hominid genus' (Black 1927). He called the creature *Sinanthropus pekinensis* (Black and Zdansky), and so, despite his caution, Zdansky found his own 'extremely meagre material' used in a manner he could never approve, with his own name appended in honour of the first discovery.

In the light of subsequent finds at Chou K'ou Tien, Davidson Black's creation of a new genus on the basis of one tooth is often viewed as a bold and inspired move. At the beginning, though, many authorities considered the announcement irresponsible. The first announcement produced no correspondence in the journals and little comment in the newspapers, though the indifference which greeted *Sinanthropus* was probably not unrelated to almost simultaneous dethroning of *Hesperopithecus haroldcooki*, another solitary molar hailed as a human ancestor and, in view of its relation to the story of Peking Man, worthy of a brief digression.

Hesperopithecus had been presented to the world in April 1922 by Henry Fairfield Osborn (the palaeontologist who inspired the American Museum of Natural History expeditions to China). The specimen comprised a small water-worn tooth found in the Snake Creek fossil beds of Nebraska by Harold J. Cook, a geologist. Cook sent the tooth to Osborn, who, on receipt, replied: 'The instant your package arrived I sat down with the tooth, in my window, and I said to myself: "It looks one hundred per cent anthropoid . . . we may cool down tomorrow, but it looks to me as if the first anthropoid ape of America had been found"' (Osborn 1922). This was an event that American anthropologists had been 'eagerly anticipating' for some time. *Hesperopithecus* means 'ape of the land where the sun sets', but in the London *Times* on 20 May 1922 Grafton Elliot Smith extended the description somewhat and welcomed the tiny tooth as 'the earliest and most primitive member of the human family yet discovered . . . one would regard so momentous a conclusion with suspicion,' he continued, 'if it were not for the fact that the American savants' authority in such matters is unquestionable.' The shape and structure is like a palimpsest to the anatomist, he said, revealing the ancestry of the creature that once owned it. The palaeontologist Arthur Smith Woodward took a rather less favourable view of *Hesperopithecus*: if the tooth were set differently in its hypothetical jaw, he remarked, its owner could just as well have been an extinct form of bear as an early kind of man (Woodward 1922).

The arguments surrounding *Hesperopithecus* were as much concerned with detail absent from the tooth as with detail present on it; by 1925 they were still unresolved, inspiring Osborn to write: 'In the whole history of anthropology no tooth has ever been subjected to such severe cross-examination as this now world famous tooth of *Hesperopithecus*. Every suggestion made by scientific sceptics was weighed and found wanting' (Osborn 1925). Subsequently, however, a Mr Thompson of the American Museum of Natural History searched for more specimens of *Hesperopithecus* in the Snake Creek deposits. He found several teeth, some quite unworn, among which there was sufficient resemblance to the original tooth to establish their overall affinity beyond doubt, and sufficient detail on the unworn specimens to show quite clearly that all the teeth had come from the jaw of an extinct wild pig.

'An ancient and honourable pig no doubt, a pig with a distinguished Greek name,' commented a *Times* leader when the news was released, 'but indubitably porcine'. *The Times* wondered whether the worshippers who had so eagerly proclaimed themselves made in the image of *Hesperopithecus* were now left desolate; and concluded: 'If there is a place where the spirits of forsaken gods congregate . . . to condole with one another on ruined temples and smokeless altars, there also, aloft in the branches of a monkey puzzle tree overlooking the asphodel meadow . . . conscious of his own distinction as one who has received the offering of unsuperstitious science, should sit the spirit of the Evening Ape' (Anon. 1928). Palaeontologists had been badly bitten by the Nebraska tooth, Elliot Smith remarked later (Smith 1929).

As this salutary lesson on the dangers of applying bold and inspired interpretations to limited evidence was rumbling to its climax, in Peking Birger Bohlin had painted a charming portrait of Peking Man among the flowers of Chou K'ou Tien (which he photographed and made tinted copies of throughout his life), and Davidson Black set off for America and Europe with the tooth of *Sinanthropus pekinensis* in a specially made brass capsule that was variously suspended from his watch-chain or about his neck. Ostensibly he was on holiday, but he also toured the world of anthropology to present *Sinanthropus*. The trip was not marked with much success. Some colleagues were critical, some indifferent and others plainly rude. But Black was unmoved; according to Elliot Smith, rejection had no effect on Black 'beyond awakening his sympathies for anthropologists who are unfairly criticized and to make him redouble his efforts to establish the proof of his claim' (Hood 1964: 93).

A little more of that proof awaited Black on his return to Peking in December 1928: half a lower jaw with three teeth in place. Again, Bohlin had found the fossil, and again it was found a few days before excavations ceased: the only hominid specimen among over 400 large boxfuls of fossils recovered that year. The teeth matched *Sinanthropus*, and the shape of the jaw seemed to show ape-like characteristics, so Black felt his earlier claims were vindicated, but even so, the evidence of early man recovered from Chou K'ou Tien during his years of expert, expensive and extensive excavations was not impressive: four teeth and a fragment of jaw.

The Rockefeller Foundation grant had been for two years' work; now that the money was spent, could these meagre hominid finds possibly convince the trustees in New York that further investment was justified? On the face of it, probably not, and it is therefore quite likely that but for the collapse of his plans to explore Chinese Turkestan with Andersson for two or three years beginning in 1929, Black would not even have asked. It was at this point that the devious dealings of Sven Hedin worked to the benefit of those seeking the fossil evidence of early man. Naïvely perhaps, Black and Andersson had sought the advice of Hedin while planning their joint Chinese/Swedish/American expedition two years before. They had confided its destination, objectives and intent; and when Hedin subsequently returned to Sweden, he organized an expedition of his own to achieve these ends, thereby absorbing all the Swedish money available for such an undertaking. The Swedes would not support a second expedition; the Americans (that is, the Rockefeller Foundation) would not foot the entire bill to duplicate what was, in effect, Sweden's unilateral action, and the Chinese had no money at all, so the Black and Andersson enterprise was abandoned.

The expedition had long been Black's cherished dream; he had already arranged a three-year release from his duties at the Medical College and was sorely disappointed that his plans could not proceed. But he quickly saw that the collapse of one project could be turned to the advantage of another. He knew that the Rockefeller trustees were sympathetic to his plight, and as money had already been budgeted for the expedition (Black had requested $20,000 per year), perhaps it

could be used to extend the search for early man. Black applied to the
Foundation accordingly. But the proposal that reached the New York
offices in January 1929 was not simply for funds to continue excavations at Chou K'ou Tien; it was much more ambitious. Black proposed
the creation of a laboratory to investigate cenozoic geology and
palaeontology throughout China (cenozoic means 'recent life' and is
the name of the geological era extending from the present to about 65
million years ago). The Cenozoic Research Laboratory should be a
special department of the Geological Survey of China (then in dire
financial straits and kept afloat by private mining interests), Black
proposed, though it would be housed in the Anatomy Department of
the Rockefeller-funded Medical College in Peking. Eventually the
laboratory would deal with all aspects of geology and palaeontology
throughout China, including prehistoric archaeology, but Chou K'ou
Tien would be of particular concern from the start. An important
condition was that all fossils and artefacts must remain in China:
research material would never again be sent abroad for study and
preparation. Black presented an impressively bold and inspired plan,
and the Rockefeller Foundation responded with a grant of $80,000 to
cover its initial establishment. Black's mood changed from depression
to jubilation: 'things have turned out very differently than I . . .
supposed possible,' he wrote to Sir Arthur Keith; 'it's better to be
born lucky than rich' (Black 1929).

At the conclusion of the first Chou K'ou Tien excavations Birger
Bohlin had joined Sven Hedin's expedition (where an early task was
to purchase the equipment left by the American Museum of Natural
History expedition on their expulsion from China), but Black did not
look again to Sweden or to America for a replacement. Instead he
relied on Chinese geologists and palaeontologists to manage the excavations under his own direction, with the further help of occasional
visitors like Teilhard de Chardin, the Jesuit priest and expert on
fossil man who subsequently contributed extensively to the study of
the geology and the fossil fauna of the Chou K'ou Tien deposits.

By 1929 a total of 8,800 cubic metres of fossil-bearing deposit had
been removed from the site and 1,485 cases of fossils packed off to
Peking. There were a few more hominid teeth among them, but substantial remains to underpin the shaky foundations of *Sinanthropus
pekinensis* still eluded Black. He may have been confident all along,

but not until December 1929 — once again at the very end of the season — did the combination of Rockefeller dollars and Black's conviction finally pay the dividend his critics demanded: a relatively complete skull.

The skull was discovered by one of the Chinese scientists, W. C. Pei, just when work had been halted forty-two metres below the highest point of the deposit by rock that could be breached only by extensive quarrying. Pei was curious to know what lay beyond and found two caves opening away from the southern extremity of a fissure low in the deposit. He was lowered into one of them on a rope and explored it 'with great difficulty', finding only a few hyena vertebrae.

The other cave was less deep, and since it opened horizontally, on 29 November Pei was able to crawl in and explore the interior. The weather was bitterly cold. On 1 December he began removing the uppermost part of the material filling the cave. At four o'clock the next afternoon he found an almost complete hominid skull, which he was able to remove from the deposit with relative ease. On 6 December Pei left Chou K'ou Tien in the early morning and delivered the specimen to the Cenozoic Laboratory in Peking by noon the same day (Pei 1929).

The skull Pei had found represented the culmination of Davidson Black's work in China, substantiating his claim that fossil evidence of early man would be found in Peking, and presenting scientists with the first hint in many years of evidence that was both new and credible. The specimen served to divert attention from the Piltdown riddle and helped to eclipse the significance of Raymond Dart's *Australopithecus*. Once all the matrix had been removed from the skull, however, it became clear that *Sinanthropus pekinensis* was not unique after all. Despite the slight dental distinctions Black had emphasized when proposing the new genus and species on the basis of teeth alone, the new specimen was very similar to the *Pithecanthropus erectus* fossils that Eugene Dubois had found in Java (Koenigswald and Weidenreich 1939). Subsequent discoveries at both sites confirmed the association, and the Java and Peking fossils were grouped together as *Homo erectus*. But Davidson Black did not live to see this. He died suddenly, aged forty-nine, of a heart complaint while working at his bench in the Cenozoic Research Laboratory during the night of 15 March 1934.

After Black's death, Teilhard de Chardin took charge of the Chou K'ou Tien excavations, and a year later Franz Weidenreich arrived in Peking to take over as head of the Cenozoic Research Laboratory. Within two years, excavations at Chou K'ou Tien were abandoned in the face of guerrilla fighting in the surrounding hills and the growing menace of Japanese occupation of the whole of north-eastern China. But by that time a large section of the hillside had been removed. In all, fourteen skulls in varying degrees of completeness were found, together with eleven mandibles, 147 teeth, portions of seven thigh-bones, two upper armbones, one collarbone (of doubtful attribution) and one wristbone (Day 1986: 371). During a total of 1,873 days worked on the site, the excavators had blasted and sifted through the equivalent of a solid rock 'haystack' about twenty-three metres long, fifteen metres broad and forty-six metres high. Of course, such effort pales into insignificance against the tons of rock that are mined from holes kilometres deep to produce every ounce of gold, but the remains of Peking Man were no less a treasure for all that.

When the Japanese military threat finally halted excavations in 1937, Weidenreich retired to the laboratory, where he devoted himself to the detailed study of the fossils' anatomical structure. Careful casts and drawings were made, photographs were taken and Weidenreich issued a stream of authoritative monographs on the mandibles, the teeth, the brain-casts, the long bones and, finally, a truly monumental work on the skull. No fossils had ever been so assiduously documented (Weidenreich 1936, 1937, 1941, 1943).

Because of its American connections, the Cenozoic Research Laboratory was regarded as a pocket of foreign interest during the early stages of the Japanese incursion and was not molested. But with the beginning of the Second World War in September 1939, the growing danger of conflict between Japan and America posed a serious threat to the laboratory and the fossils it housed. The official under-standing, of course, was precisely as Davidson Black had stipulated: the Chou K'ou Tien fossils must remain in China. But the Chinese seem to have overlooked their responsibilities in this respect when the government moved from Peking. In January 1941, the director of the Geological Survey, Dr Wong, suggested from his refuge in south-west China that Weidenreich should take the fossils with him on his return to America. Weidenreich declined. He feared the fossils would be confiscated if customs officials found them among his personal baggage and, in any case, considered them much too valuable to expose to an unprotected voyage at so dangerous a time. The diplomatic pouch was the obvious alternative and apparently Weidenreich suggested to the American Ambassador that the fossils should be sent to the United States in official baggage not subject to customs examination. But his suggestion was rejected and so, while Weidenreich travelled safely to America in April 1941 with a complete set of casts, photographs, drawings and data, the original fossils remained in the safe at the Cenozoic Research Laboratory (Shapiro 1974).

At this late stage, the wisest course would probably have been to hide the fossils somewhere in China, but in July they were packed in two large boxes, taken to the United States Embassy for safe keeping and, in August, Dr Wong himself asked the US Ambassador to arrange their shipment to America. The Ambassador could hardly refuse such a direct request but, for some unexplained reason, three months passed before his instructions reached the appropriate authorities. By then it was mid-November 1941; the Japanese attack on the American naval base at Pearl Harbor was barely three weeks away.

Now the story becomes confused, but it seems certain that the fossils left Peking early in December in the care of a US Marine contingent who were to sail for America in the SS *President Harrison*. War was declared between Japan and America while the marines were on their way to the port. The *President Harrison* ran aground trying to evade a Japanese warship and never docked. The marines were held by Japanese troops and the fossils in their care have never been seen again. The casts and Weidenreich's work on the originals are all that remain.

Since the war, work on the Chinese fossils that Roy Chapman Andrews collected in such vast numbers has continued in America. In Sweden, Bohlin continued his work on the fossils Andersson had sent back, and on those he had collected himself on the Hedin expedition. The teeth Zdansky found are still at Uppsala too, the only surviving original remains of Peking Man. It is ironic to reflect that had Otto Zdansky been a less determined scientist, and more concerned with the romance of early man, if he had told Andersson of that first tooth and spent the next two years in the Chou K'ou Tien cave, he might have found the fossils that Black's endeavours subsequently discovered. Then, too, Peking Man would be safe in Sweden instead of wherever he now resides.

In 1949 Chinese researchers resumed excavations at Zhoukoudian (as Chou K'ou Tien has become under the *Pinyin zimu* system of transliteration approved by the Chinese government in 1958). Five hominid teeth were found in 1949, two limb fragments in 1951, a female mandible in 1958 and, in 1966, two skull fragments which fitted the casts of others found in 1934 to form a complete skull (Wu and Olsen 1985: 6). Excavation and research has also been conducted at other sites in China. A skull fragment of anatomically modern man of ancient but ill-defined date was found at Maba in 1958 (Woo and Peng 1959; Wu and Olsen 1985). A skull and mandible, dating from over 500,000 years ago and assigned to *Homo erectus*, were recovered from two separate excavations at Lantian in 1963–64 (Woo 1966). Other *Homo erectus* skulls, dating from about 250,000 years ago, were found at Dali in 1978 (Wang *et al.* 1979) and at Hexian in 1980 (Wu 1982). Fossil apes and hominoids have also been recovered from sites around China, and the abundance of material has given palaeo-anthropology there a distinctly Chinese bias: the study of early man is the study of early China.

Chinese palaeoanthropologists acknowledge that Africa has played a role in the early stages of human evolution, but the wealth of fossil material found within their own national boundaries appears to have convinced them that although the ancestors of the human line may have originated in Africa some 3 million years ago, their descendants spread far and wide soon after and established 'Man's place of origin ... in the southern part of East Asia' – China (Jia Lanpo 1980: 3). Fossil remains described as those of *Ramapithecus* found in Yunnan Province are said to represent the hominid ancestor, and human evolution is believed to have proceeded in a direct line from *Rama-pithecus* to the modern Chinese population. It is claimed 'that tool-using hominids, present in China since at least early Middle Pleistocene times [1 million years ago] and perhaps much earlier, constitute the basal stock from which the various Chinese national minorities ultimately emerged'. Analytical research is said to indicate 'substantial continuity in the development of the mongoloid physical type as well as in the phylogenetic relationships among the various stages of hominid development ... [so that] ... although the modern mongoloid race seems to be a product of only the past few tens of thousands of years of evolution, its origins may be traced into the earlier Pleistocene . . .' (Wu and Lin 1985: 10).

The Institute of Vertebrate Palaeontology and Palaeoanthropology of the Chinese Academy of Sciences instigated a comprehensive five-year study of the Zhoukoudian cave site in 1978, involving 120 Chinese scientists from seventeen Chinese universities and research institutions. This work has convinced its leading participants that evidence from the cave traces 'the development of a single community over a period that spans a significant fraction of the evolution of the genus *Homo*' (Wu and Lin 1983: 78). It is claimed that early man first used the cave shelter about 460,000 years ago, and did not abandon it until about 230,000 years ago. It is said that fossil skulls from the cave indicate an increase in brain size during this period and that 'Peking man became more manlike in anatomy after 200,000 years of cave dwelling' (Wu and Lin 1983: 83). Peking Man used fire throughout his occupation of the cave, the Chinese researchers claim, and they believe the stone tools he left behind reflect increasing technological skill through time. The vertebrate fossil remains recovered from the cave are believed to indicate that deer were Peking Man's commonest prey, which in turn is said to suggest that he was a skilled and efficient hunter. Because successful hunting demands the cooperation of many individuals, Peking Man is presumed to have lived in groups, sharing food and dividing labour between the sexes: male hunters and female child-caring gatherers.

A Sinocentric view of human evolution may be appropriate for a nation that currently constitutes fully one-quarter of the human species, but it does conflict with the majority view among scientists in other parts of the world. Milford Wolpoff supports the Chinese view, but he is arguing primarily for the continuity that his gradualistic scheme of human evolution demands (see p. 50). In 1984 Wolpoff and two others (one Chinese, one Australian) proposed a general theory of hominid evolution which claims that *Homo erectus* in Asia represents one of several ancestral populations of the species from which similar populations of *Homo sapiens* have evolved (Wolpoff *et al*. 1984). The multiple occurrence of complex and identical evolutionary trends that this scheme demands seems highly improbable. Furthermore, claims that the modern Chinese population evolved from distant ancestors in

China are directly contradicted by genetic evidence (see p. 32) suggesting that the entire world, including China, is populated today by the descendants of a small group of modern humans who left Africa no more than 180,000 years ago.

The claims of social and cultural development and continuity at Zhoukoudian also conflict with current views outside China on these aspects of human evolution. Between 1950 and the 1980s, opinions on the role of hunting in human evolution have changed dramatically: gathering and scavenging are now thought likely to have been at least as important. In 1984 archaeologists Lewis Binford and Nancy Stone conducted a reappraisal of the Zhoukoudian evidence in China and concluded that Peking Man was more likely to have been a scavenger than a hunter. Furthermore, he had used fire only during the last stages of his occupation of the cave, claims of earlier usage having been based on a misinterpretation of bones stained by minerals and decomposed plant material, and they found that the evidence of social grouping around a 'home-base' was ambiguous and inconclusive (Binford and Stone 1986: 467–8).

The findings of Binford and Stone attracted oblique accusations of their having been disrespectful to their Chinese hosts (Olsen 1986: 470), but, along with the other contradictions summarized above, they seem unlikely to have much effect upon the study of early man in China. There is an important difference between western and Chinese attitudes towards palaeoanthropology. In the West, scientists treat the Chinese fossil evidence as part of the broad picture of human evolution worldwide; in China, it is part of national history – an ancient and fragmentary part, it is true, but none the less one that is called upon to promote a unifying concept of unique origin and continuity within the Chinese nation.

7

Australopithecus SUBSTANTIATED

(1936)

While the scientific establishment continued to argue over the merits of Piltdown Man and was diverted by the discoveries from Peking, the significance of the South African fossil that Raymond Dart had named *Australopithecus africanus* in 1925 was neglected. After his skirmish with fame and controversy Dart applied his talents to the creation of a creditable anatomy department at the Witwatersrand Medical School. Meanwhile, lime-quarrying kept pace with the country's development and the cave deposits, together with the fossils they undoubtedly contained, were shovelled into the kilns with hardly a thought for anthropological significance. That the potential Dart had identified was left unexploited, even wasted, was the result of circumstance and temperament unhappily combined, as we have seen. That it was exploited twelve years later, and Dart's claims subsequently vindicated, was entirely due to the initiative and effort of one man: Robert Broom.

The biologist J. B. S. Haldane once described Broom as a man of genius, fit to stand beside Shaw, Beethoven and Titian (Haldane 1974), and his biographer, George Findlay, offers the observation that Broom was about as honest as a good poker player (Findlay 1972: 101). On reflection, these compliments may not seem wholly appropriate to a dedicated scientist, but the evidence of Broom's life and work suggests that both are true and neither is a discredit to the man or science.

Robert Broom was born in Scotland on St Andrew's Day, 1866. Poor health and his family's pecuniary problems permitted him only four years of unbroken schooling. None the less, he entered Glasgow University at the age of sixteen and emerged a Bachelor of Medicine and Master of Surgery at twenty-three. At Glasgow he was introduced to the natural sciences while they were still freshly inspired by the work of Darwin, Lyell, Huxley and Haeckel. He was a great believer in 'Missing Links' and searched for them assiduously in later life, but in effect he became a link himself – between the eccentric, idiosyncratic inquiries of Victorian science, among which he was reared, and the mechanistic, statistical investigations of the mid-twentieth century, among which he died in 1951.

Broom held firm beliefs that were often provocatively displayed. He was inclined, for example, to remove all his clothes while hunting fossils in remote hot places (he once misplaced them altogether) in order to enjoy more fully the sunshine he considered so beneficial to health; and so as to demonstrate the benefits of sunshine during sickness, he once left an African 'flu victim inside a hut to die while another sat outside in the sun and was cured (Findlay 1972: 43). To further his anthropological researches he boiled skulls clean on a kitchen stove and buried dead Bushmen in his garden, to be exhumed when decomposition was complete. In another field of scientific endeavour, Robert Broom found and described important fossil evidence of the evolutionary link between the reptiles and the mammals but, although he accepted the theory of evolution, he rejected Darwin's proposal of natural selection as the driving force (Broom 1933, 1950: 91–100). In Broom's view the process was too complicated and the results were much too wonderful to be the product of mere chance. He believed that life on earth was the work and concern of a divine creative force (Broom 1939).

To the casual eye, a predilection for the odd and quirky is immediately evident in the bibliography of 456 papers, books and monographs that Broom published during his lifetime. But a closer look suggests that the explanation of the odd and the quirky was in itself a theme central to the purpose and intent of his scientific inquiries. Robert Broom's first paper, published when he was nineteen, was 'On the volume of mixed liquids' (Broom 1885) and showed that two and two do not add up to four in the case of some chemical solutions: when mixed together the whole becomes less than its parts. His second paper (1888) was on 'a monstrosity of the common earthworm' and described a worm with two tails, each 'furnished with a perfect anus'. In 1895 he described the anatomy of a four-winged chick and the Organ of Jacobson in the duck-billed platypus.

The Organ of Jacobson, a tiny accessory sense organ in the nose of many mammals, was one of Broom's lifelong interests. As a student he collected a specimen from a kitten, and the comparative anatomy of the organ later became the subject of his doctoral thesis (Broom

1895). Subsequently he described its anatomy in anteaters, squirrels, moles, horses, bats, shrews and marsupials, and during the First World War his collection was enhanced by the addition of a rare and fully developed specimen taken from the nose of an unsuspecting woman on whom he was operating for a quite different purpose.

Broom's interest in the Organ of Jacobson developed into a reasoned belief that since the organ was not affected by habit, its varying structure and form should provide clues to the zoological distinction between mammals whose appearance was otherwise very similar. Indeed, he convincingly divided a group of insectivores into three different orders on the basis of such evidence (Broom 1915). And in Australia, where he practised general medicine from 1892 to 1896, Broom found that the Organ of Jacobson in the duck-billed platypus is supported by a structure remarkably similar to that found in snakes and lizards. The platypus is a mammal that lays eggs, and Broom's work on the Organ of Jacobson in its snout provided further detail of the manner by which the mammals had evolved from egg-laying reptiles.

Broom moved to South Africa in 1897 and, turning from living creatures to the evidence of fossil remains, sought clues to the origin of the mammals among the fossil reptiles preserved in the ancient sediments of that country. He identified several important mammalian features in fossil reptilian skeletons and ultimately assembled a series of fossil forms that showed how a group of reptiles had gradually evolved into mammals.

In 1920 Broom was elected a Fellow of the Royal Society; in 1928 he received the Society's Royal Medal for his work on the origin of the mammals. The citation read:

At the time he went to South Africa thirty-five genera and sixty-five species (of fossil reptiles) had been identified. Little was known of their structure and the classification was hopelessly confused. He trebled the number of genera, quadrupled the number of species and worked out the details of the anatomy of most groups and established a classification that is universally accepted (Findlay 1972: 57).

In South Africa, however, Broom's work on the fossil reptiles was not quite so well received. Throughout his life he earned a living from medical practice; but for many years he also ran what amounted to a wholesale fossil business from his consulting rooms, paying collectors to bring him fossils and selling them to museums abroad. In this manner a substantial number of important specimens went to the American Museum of Natural History, who paid rather better than other establishments. Of course, this flow of fossils aided Broom's research as well as his pocket, as the Royal Society Medal amply demonstrated, but the South African museum authorities did not recognize such subtle distinctions. The fossils belonged to South Africa, they said, and Broom had no right to sell them abroad for his personal gain. His behaviour was held to be reprehensible and dishonest. In the early 1920s Broom was forbidden all access to the collections of the South African Museum and his reputation in South Africa sank very low indeed after that, despite much acclaim from abroad. The position eased a little with the death of the Museum Director, and was further improved by the interventions of General Smuts, Raymond Dart and the affairs of *Australopithecus africanus*.

When the first reports of *Australopithecus* were published in February 1925, Broom immediately wrote to Dart, congratulating him on an important discovery and noting that although he (Broom) had achieved so much, he had still not been 'so blessed by fortune' as Dart. 'The missing link is really glorious,' he wrote; 'what a new chapter you will be able to add [to the story of human evolution]. Possibly an adult skull or perhaps a whole skeleton will yet turn up' (Broom 1925a).

Two weeks later Broom visited Dart's laboratory. Unannounced, and ignoring both professor and staff, he strode over to the bench on which the skull reposed and dropped to his knees, 'in adoration of our ancestor,' Dart recalled (Dart 1959: 37). Broom spent a weekend examining the fossil and found nothing to contradict Dart's contentions. Although probably no older than the Pleistocene, the specimen was undoubtedly a 'Missing Link', he reported in April 1925 (Broom 1925b), connecting the higher apes with the lowest human types. *Australopithecus* was surprisingly similar to Java Man, he wrote, and probably the forerunner of Piltdown Man. Broom demonstrated these affinities with a drawing of the adult *Australopithecus* skull he envisaged (and in which jaw and dentition almost precisely duplicated those parts in Piltdown Man), and concluded his report with a reference to the 'considerable probability' that adult specimens would be found.

In common with other authorities, Broom was fully aware that adult specimens were essential if the significance of Dart's interpretation of the juvenile *Australopithecus* from Taung was to be properly evaluated. But adult specimens were not found, nor even sought, in the years immediately following the 1925 announcements; and they were still undiscovered in 1934, when Robert Broom finally gave up medical practice and, at the instigation of General Smuts, accepted the post of palaeontologist at the Transvaal Museum in Pretoria. For nearly two years he worked on the collection of fossil reptiles, writing sixteen papers on twenty-three new genera and forty-four new species, until, in May 1936, he decided to look for 'an adult Taung ape', as he put it (Broom 1950: 39). By then the cave deposits had been neglected for nearly twelve years and Dr Robert Broom was sixty-nine years old. He already considered himself the greatest palaeontologist that had ever lived, Broom later remarked, and saw no reason why he should not become the greatest anthropologist as well (Broom 1946).

It is never unreasonable to suppose that where one of a kind has been found there may be more, but in the case of *Australopithecus* the problem confronting Robert Broom in 1936 was not so much whether the fossils existed as whether there were any left. Dart's Taung fossil owed its initial discovery to the activities of lime-workers, as we have seen; twelve years later, in a country short of lime, there were likely to be more scenes of devastation than discovery. Broom deplored the fact that the deposits had been ignored for so long ('Dart was not much of a fighter,' he said, and had been too easily discouraged by opposition to his pronouncements [in Findlay 1972: 54]). But Broom found some consolation in the thought that even if he did not find the remains of *Australopithecus*, he was certain to find some interesting Pleistocene mammals. He could not afford to travel to Taung, so he began his investigations on some old lime-workings around Pretoria. Within a few weeks he had discovered half a dozen new species of rats and moles, a small sabre-toothed tiger and a giant baboon.

Cave deposits and lime-workings similar to those on which Broom was first engaged are common features of the dolomitic region to the north and west of Pretoria and Johannesburg. There are some near

Krugersdorp, and if circumstances had ever taken Robert Broom to that small market town about sixty kilometres west of Pretoria, he would probably have noted Mr Cooper's general store on the main street, where a sign beside a small display of fossils invited his customers to 'Buy Bat Guano from Sterkfontein and find the Missing Link'. Prodigious quantities of bat guano are frequently deposited in caves; it is a very good fertilizer and, as such, was a profitable adjunct to Mr Cooper's sale of agricultural and building lime from lime-works at Sterkfontein, ten kilometres away. The man in charge of the Sterkfontein quarry was a Mr Barlow, who had been manager at Taung when the first *Australopithecus* was found. No doubt Barlow's interest in fossils had inspired Mr Cooper's window display, but it was one of Dart's graduate students, Trevor Jones, who eventually brought Sterkfontein and its fossils to Broom's attention (Jones 1978). Some of Jones's colleagues regretted Broom's intervention (Wells 1966), feeling perhaps that the subsequent discoveries ought to have been reserved for Dart, but there can be no doubt that Broom had more time and enthusiasm for the quest than Dart had shown. Broom pursued the investigation most energetically and found an adult *Australopithecus* skull at Sterkfontein on 17 August 1936, nine days after his first visit to the site and just three months after he had decided to look for one.

The discovery was almost an exact repetition of events at Taung twelve years before (if R. B. Young's account of those events is accepted; see p. 82). An endocranial cast was found after blasting in the morning and rocks containing associated pieces of skull and face were recovered from the rubble during the afternoon and the next day. The cast was undistorted and lacked only its rear portion, but the face and side of the head were badly crushed and, furthermore, the fossil bone was extremely friable and therefore very difficult to remove from the much harder rock in which it was embedded. Four upper teeth were also preserved, however, and one of these, together with the brain-cast, was in fact the only useful diagnostic feature available in the new specimen. Broom acknowledged the inherent difficulty of comparing such fragmentary evidence of an adult with more complete juvenile remains, but reported to *Nature* (Broom 1936a) that the 'newly found primate probably agrees fairly closely with the Taung ape', despite 'certain distinctive details' in its teeth. Broom was no less confident of the fossil's human affinities and, in the *Illustrated London News*, described his find as 'A New Ancestral Link between Ape and Man' (Broom 1936b).

The skull was first called *Australopithecus transvaalensis*, Broom proposing specific distinction from the Taung specimen on the grounds of his belief that the Sterkfontein deposit was appreciably younger. Subsequently, however, he decided that the differences he had noted in the teeth merited generic distinction and renamed the creature *Plesianthropus transvaalensis*, which means 'near-man' of the Transvaal and defined Robert Broom's opinion of its position in human evolution rather more closely than *Australopithecus*, 'southern ape'.

In November 1936 Robert Broom celebrated his seventieth birthday; in February 1937 he showed casts of the new discovery at a Congress of Early Man held in Philadelphia; in June he received an honorary doctorate from Columbia University; and during a six-month tour abroad he was enthusiastically applauded wherever he lectured. But the acclaim was for Robert Broom more than for the fossil of which he spoke. The Sterkfontein discovery was notable, but hardly conclusive enough to persuade everyone that Raymond Dart had been right after all. Interest in the South African claims had dwindled considerably by 1937; the works of Keith and Abel (see p. 89) were widely regarded as the definitive appraisals of *Australopithecus*, and, although disagreement may have persisted on the question of whether the creature was related to the gorilla or the chimpanzee, there was general agreement with the contention that *Australopithecus* was not an ancestor of mankind. Polite scepticism characterized the majority view that Broom encountered abroad, but his belief in the ancestral status of *Australopithecus* was undiminished and, on returning to South Africa in August 1937, he immediately resumed the search for more substantial evidence.

In fact, Broom's investigations were significantly dependent upon the financial arrangements he made with Barlow, who was encouraged to look out for interesting specimens exposed by the quarrying operations but expected to be paid for fossils of merit. Between August 1937 and May 1938 Broom bought from Barlow a wristbone, a facial fragment, the lower end of a thighbone and a nice piece of upper jaw with four teeth in place. All were undoubtedly remains of *Aus-*

tralopithecus but none matched the significance of the first skull. And then, on 8 June, Barlow produced a palate with one molar still in place that Broom knew to be worth considerably more than the £2 he gave for it. Perhaps Barlow knew too, for he would not reveal precisely where the fossil had come from, and neither would the workmen when Broom returned to question them in Barlow's absence a day or two later.

Broom then tried a more straightforward approach: the specimen was very important, he told Barlow, and had belonged to a large ape-man quite different from those previously found at Sterkfontein. But some teeth had been freshly broken off, he said, and in the interests of science Barlow should assist in the search for the missing teeth and more remains of the creature. Where had the fossil come from?

Relenting, Barlow directed Broom to Gert Terblanche, a young boy whom Broom found at school some five or six kilometres away. In the presence of his headmaster, Gert 'drew from the pocket of his trousers four of the most wonderful teeth ever seen in the world's history,' Broom recounts (Broom 1950: 50). They were the teeth missing from the palate; Broom promptly purchased them, transferred them to his own pocket and, after enthralling pupils and staff with an impromptu lecture on cave formations and fossils, walked with Gert to the hillside where the palate had been found in an outcrop of eroded cave deposit. The place was called Kromdraai; it was but three kilometres from the Sterkfontein site and, as Broom had suspected, the deposit contained more remains belonging with the palate. Within a few days Broom assembled a specimen comprising practically the entire left side of the skull, the palate and a large portion of the right lower jaw.

The face of the Kromdraai skull was flatter, the jaw more powerful and the teeth larger than in the Sterkfontein specimen. The whole aspect of the specimen was larger, more robust and, Broom believed, more man-like than either the Taung or the Sterkfontein skulls, so he afforded the new specimen generic distinction from both of them and called it *Paranthropus robustus*, which means 'robust equal of man'. In *Nature* he described the anatomical features of the new fossil (Broom 1938a) and in the *Illustrated London News* it was heralded as 'The Missing Link No Longer Missing' (Broom 1938b). The scientific establishment responded predictably, chiding Broom for creating new genera on 'extremely slender grounds', advising greater caution and remaining unmoved by the new evidence (Broom 1950: 55). Broom was equally unmoved by the criticism and continued the search for more remains.

Lime-quarrying at Sterkfontein ceased in 1939 and the advent of the Second World War curtailed explorations at Kromdraai, so Broom continued his investigations in the laboratory at the Transvaal Museum, where he worked on the blocks of fossil-bearing rock he had previously removed from the Kromdraai deposit. From the block in which the *Paranthropus* skull had been embedded he recovered much of an elbow joint, an anklebone, some handbones and some fingerbones. Their close proximity to the skull implied that the bones belonged to the same individual and, although they hardly comprised the adult skull and skeleton Broom had hoped Dart would seek and discover, the scant collection did substantially vindicate Dart's claim that a small-brained, bipedal man-like ape with manipulative skills had once inhabited southern Africa. The anklebone Broom had found was quite unlike that of either the gorilla or the chimpanzee, for instance, and more closely resembled the human form, strongly suggesting a habitual upright bipedal gait. The handbones were slender and more suited to manipulative dexterity than to walking on all fours and the elbow joint was similarly man-like. If the bones had been found separately no anatomist would have doubted their human affinities, but at Kromdraai they were associated with a small-brained ape-like skull which many scientists believed to be more closely related to the gorilla or the chimpanzee than to man. Was Broom's new evidence substantial enough to overcome the negative predispositions this association aroused?

Proper presentation of the evidence was important; preliminary reports appeared in *Nature* (Broom 1942a, 1942b) and Broom distributed casts of the Kromdraai remains, but the war undoubtedly diverted attention and judgement was effectively suspended while he gathered together all the evidence of the South African fossil ape-men for publication in a comprehensive monograph (Broom and Schepers 1946). He worked on the volume during much of 1944 and 1945, describing the Taung, Sterkfontein and Kromdraai fossils in turn, attributing them all to one subfamily – the Australopithecinae – while describing the basis for the generic distinctions he made between them. Broom's text filled 133 pages and was illustrated with well over

100 anatomical drawings, all his own work. A further 100 pages of the monograph, reviewing the evidence of the endocranial casts, was the work of the Johannesburg anatomist G. W. H. Schepers. In discussing the affinities of the Australopithecinae Broom concluded that 'these primates agreed closely with man in many characters. They were almost certainly bipedal and they probably used their hands for the manipulation of implements . . . The dentition . . . agrees remarkably closely with the dentition of man.' He added that the brain, though smaller, was of the human type. 'What appears certain,' he went on, 'is that the group, if not quite worthy of being called men, were nearly men, and were certainly closely allied to mankind, and not at all nearly related to the living anthropoids. And we may regard it as almost certain that man arose from a Pliocene member of the australopithecinae probably very near to *Australopithecus* itself' (Broom and Schepers 1946: 142).

The monograph was published in Pretoria on 31 January 1946, a little over two months after Broom's seventy-ninth birthday, and its authoritative and comprehensive presentation was afforded careful appraisal everywhere. The work won a large measure of support for *Australopithecus* and for the first time the scientific establishment began to suspect that Raymond Dart might have been right after all. Sir Arthur Keith acknowledged the man-like attributes of *Australopithecus* but continued to doubt its ancestral status. Wilfred le Gros Clark, the Oxford anatomist, on the other hand, was more wholly impressed by Broom's work. He wrote a favourable review for *Nature* (Clark 1946) and subsequently visited South Africa to examine the original fossils. He found good anatomical reasons to support the contention that *Australopithecus* represented the stock from which mankind had evolved.

Though over eighty, Robert Broom continued to search for more *Australopithecus* remains in 1947; but, while his work and the South African cave deposits were finally achieving recognition, some authorities were becoming concerned about Broom's apparent lack of regard for geological evidence and the recording of stratigraphic detail. Now that Broom had found some important fossils, this information was essential if the relative ages of his discoveries were to be established – especially at Sterkfontein, where the cave entrances had eroded away and lime-workers had removed most of the interior.

Perhaps over hastily, the Historical Monuments Commission issued a ruling which expressly forbade Robert Broom to excavate without the assistance of a 'competent field geologist'. The ruling was presumably intended to do no more than correct a deficiency, but its effect was three-fold. First, it insulted Broom; after all, he had been a medallist in geology at Glasgow University and had held the Chair of Geology at Stellenbosch University for seven years. Second, the ruling inspired Broom to begin excavations at Sterkfontein on 1 April in direct contravention of the Commission, believing, as he wrote later (Broom 1950: 63), 'that a bad law ought to be deliberately broken'. And third, the ruling thus led to the discovery of a superb *Australopithecus* skull on 18 April. The specimen was undistorted and complete but for the teeth and the lower jaw. Broom, with his usual enthusiasm, described it as 'the most important fossil skull ever found in the world's history'; and, indeed, its significance was readily acknowledged by scientists in Europe and America. In South Africa, however, Broom was unanimously condemned at a meeting of the Commission and once more banned from the Sterkfontein site.

The irony of a world-renowned scientist being banned from the site of his investigations immediately following an important discovery did not escape the press and their cartoonists. Public and private pressure mounted and the ban was lifted a few weeks later. Broom triumphantly resumed work at Sterkfontein, with continuing good fortune. At the end of June 1947 he discovered a fine lower jaw which fully confirmed the man-like, rather than ape-like, attributes of the *Australopithecus* dentition; and in August he unearthed the ultimate prize, a nearly complete pelvis and vertebral column with associated legbone fragments, part of a shoulderblade and upper arm. At last, twenty-two years after Raymond Dart announced the new species, Robert Broom had assembled teeth, skulls and skeleton of the adult *Australopithecus*, and the assemblage presented irresistible evidence of the creature's man-like affinities. 'Congratulations on brilliant discoveries. Proof now complete and incontestible,' cabled Wilfred le Gros Clark. 'All my landmarks have gone,' said Sir Arthur Keith; 'you have found what I never thought could be found': a man-like jaw associated with an ape-like skull, the exact reverse of the Piltdown evidence.

Keith's conversion to the belief in the ancestral status of *Aus-*

tralopithecus was absolute. 'Professor Dart was right and I was wrong,' he conceded in a letter to *Nature*. And in *A New Theory of Human Evolution*, written in his eighty-second year and published in 1948, Keith agreed that 'of all the fossil forms known to us, the australopithecinae are the nearest akin to man and the most likely to stand in the direct line of man's ascent' (Keith 1948b: 210). They represented the pre-human stock from which the various divisions of mankind had evolved in the late Pliocene, he said (Keith 1948b: 159), adding the suggestion that for the sake of brevity, if not contrition, they should be renamed 'Dartians' (Keith 1948b: 234).

With *Australopithecus* presenting such convincing evidence that the enlargement of the brain was the final stage of mankind's evolution from an ancestor shared with the apes, Keith now attempted to define the point at which the man-like ape could be said to have become man. In *A New Theory of Human Evolution* he proposed brain size as the measure, suggesting that just as the eruption of the first permanent molar provides a convenient mark for determining the end of infancy and the beginning of childhood in the individual, so the acquisition of a certain brain size could mark the species' evolutionary transition from apehood to manhood. Taking the largest known brain size in the gorilla (650 cubic centimetres) and the smallest known in man (855 cubic centimetres) as the most valid determinants, Keith proposed a cranial volume of 750 cubic centimetres as the 'cerebral Rubicon' to be crossed before the ancestors of mankind may be called truly human. By this measure, Java Man (with an estimated mean cranial capacity of 850 cubic centimetres) and Peking (ranging from 915 to 1,225 cubic centimetres) were justifiably assigned to the genus *Homo*, while *Australopithecus* (435 to about 650 cubic centimetres) had not yet crossed the Rubicon (Keith 1948b: 206).

Of course, Keith's *New Theory of Human Evolution* in part also reaffirmed views he had expressed thirty-six years before when he described the erect posture as mankind's most ancient attribute and the large brain as a relatively recent acquisition (see p. 55). But the evidence of the large-brained, early Pleistocene Piltdown Man he had championed for so long was not so easily accommodated in the new theory. 'If we could get rid of the Piltdown fossil fragments, then we should greatly simplify the problem of human evolution,' wrote Keith (1948b: 229), but 'getting rid of facts which do not fit into a preconceived theory' is not the manner usually pursued by men of science, he continued, and proposed instead that in terms of his new theory, Piltdown Man should be regarded as an 'aberrant' type who first found lonely refuge in England and then extinction there some time after the late Pliocene.

Meanwhile, Broom continued the search for more remains of *Australopithecus*. In September 1948 a site was opened under his direction at Swartkrans, another disused lime-quarry across the valley from Sterkfontein. *Australopithecus* fossils were found within days, and many more have since been found there. In 1950 Broom was the principal author of a monograph on the Sterkfontein hominids (Broom *et al*. 1950) and by then he felt that the impact of his discoveries and publications was such that only two eminent scientists remained unconvinced that the australopithecines represented the ancestors of mankind. The dissidents were W. L. Straus and S. Zuckerman, both of whom still maintained that the fossils were related to the apes, not to man. Zuckerman, a zoologist, bothered Broom most; he had made a pioneering behaviour study of the monkeys in the London Zoo and was a scientist of standing and repute. Zuckerman believed in figures and statistical method and would not accept findings that did not demonstrate some metrical consistency. So, as Broom produced the fossils and his collaborator, le Gros Clark, published reports defining their man-like affinities, Zuckerman (aided by E. H. Ashton) checked their assertions by comparing the dental dimensions of the fossils with the corresponding dimensions of assorted apes. In all, he checked a total of forty-eight overall dimensions in the fossils with those of eighty chimpanzees, ninety gorillas and sixty orang-utans (Ashton and Zuckerman 1950). The results, said Zuckerman, showed that the fossils were more like the apes than like man. Broom had little respect for mathematical method and scoffed at the findings. 'I suppose that because the molar teeth of horse and cow are often identical, Zuckerman would conclude that a horse is a cow,' he said. Le Gros Clark was similarly sceptical, once remarking that measurements of length, breadth and height would proclaim a cube, a sphere and a pointed star identical (quoted in Findlay 1972: 86). None the less, le Gros Clark felt obliged to respond in kind and, using even more diagnostic measurements than Zuckerman, compared the fossils with the adult dentition of 238 gorillas, 276 chimpanzees and thirty-nine orang-utans, as well as with the juvenile dentitions of eighty-nine gorillas, 105 chimpanzees and twenty-nine orang-utans (Clark 1967a, 1967b: 35). The new results directly contradicted Zuckerman's findings. Some lively correspondence ensued, in the course of which a statistician revealed that the Zuckerman team had neglected to divide by the square root of two in some vital computation (Yates and Healy 1951). But 'the mistake was due to a misunderstanding in the interpretation of the analysis of variance,' replied Zuckerman (1966), and made no difference whatsoever to the overall result. Le Gros Clark disagreed, but contrary to some claims (Ardrey 1961: 324), the square root factor did not conclusively settle the argument either way. The argument stands best as a symbol of the gulf separating the idiosyncratic, qualitative approach of an earlier age that Broom employed from the statistical quantitative methods of the mid-twentieth century. Robert Broom died on 6 April 1951 at the age of eighty-four. More than any scientist or discovery before or since, Broom's work on *Australopithecus* fundamentally and irrevocably revised the study of fossil man. At first glance he may seem to have confused the story of mankind's evolution with a profusion of complicated names, new genera and new species, not all of them justified and several introduced as 'Missing Links'. But the significant point is that Broom assigned all except one of the taxa he described to a single zoological subfamily, the Australopithecinae, and he made it quite clear that the habitually erect and bipedal Australopithecinae, with their man-like dentition and relatively small brains, were good candidates for the ancestors of mankind. After Broom, scientists were obliged to fit *Australopithecus* somewhere in their schemes of human evolution. Today, the Australopithecinae comprise one genus and three species: the heavily built *Australopithecus robustus*, known generally as the 'robust' australopithecines and including Broom's *Paranthropus* as well as specimens unearthed in East Africa since the 1960s (see Chapters 8, 11); the lightly built *Australopithecus africanus*, which is often referred to as the 'gracile' *Australopithecus* and includes both the Taung specimen and Broom's *Plesianthropus*; and *Australopithecus afarensis*, represented by fossils from Tanzania and Ethiopia discovered in the 1970s (see Chapter 12). This last species dates from over 3 million years ago and adds further weight to Dart's and Broom's contention that *Australopithecus* stood close to the beginning of the hominid line.

In 1945, while Broom was still busily collecting australopithecines from Sterkfontein and Kromdraai, another rich source of fossil material was located in the Makapansgat Valley, 320 kilometres (200 miles) north of Johannesburg, by a team of students from Witwatersrand University under the leadership of Phillip Tobias, who was studying anatomy under Raymond Dart at the time. Tobias later succeeded to Dart's position at the Medical School, and has become a leading figure in modern palaeoanthropology. His work has broadened the subject in several dimensions (not least on library shelves), and its predispositions may be judged by the effort he has made to establish some personal connection with the original discovery of *Australopithecus*: 'My boy,' he responded when questioned on the point, 'I was conceived on the very day that Dart's announcement of *Australopithecus africanus* was published in *Nature*' (Tobias 1978).

Tobias returned from that first visit to Makapansgat with the skull of a fossil baboon which suggested that the site may be as old as Sterkfontein and therefore a potential source of hominid remains. According to Dart, Tobias reawakened his interest in palaeoanthropology with this evidence (Dart 1959: 100), and thereafter, excavations at Makapansgat provided Dart with the foundations of a theory which has profoundly affected the study of human origins and lingered on in the popular consciousness for decades.

Australopithecine fossils were indeed recovered from the Makapansgat site, but Dart was more particularly impressed by the evidence of their lifestyle that he saw in the cave deposits. He attributed the hominid fossils to a new species, *Australopithecus prometheus* (Dart 1948), on slight evidence that they had used fire (since refuted) and drew far-reaching conclusions from the variety of animal species and body parts found among the fossil remains, and their fractured condition.

A preponderance of certain bones among the remains persuaded Dart that the australopithecines had been using bones as tools and weapons: long bones as clubs and bludgeons, shoulderblades as cleavers, horn-cores and split bones as daggers, mandibles as scrapers and saws. Examination of forty-two baboon skulls (from Taung and Sterkfontein as well as from Makapansgat) convinced him that twenty-seven (64 per cent) of them died from a violent blow to the head. Further investigation along these lines appeared to show that some australopithecines had been killed in a similar fashion, and Dart con-

The remains of Neanderthal Man were discovered in a cave high on
the side of the Neander Valley, near Düsseldorf, in 1857. With the
publication of Darwin's theory of evolution in 1859, Neanderthal
Man became central to arguments provoked by the theory's
implication that man was also a product of evolution. Did the fossils
represent an evolutionary link between modern man and an ape-like
ancestor? the protagonists argued. Was Neanderthal Man a 'Missing
Link' that would substantiate Darwin's theory?

The Neanderthal remains (left) found in a cave near the village of La Chapelle-aux-Saints in France in 1908 are those of an old man with severe osteoarthritis, but the deformed limbs and vertebral column persuaded many experts of the day that the Neanderthals had walked with a slouching gait and had been a degenerate race destined for extinction, and therefore not an ancestor of modern man.

The obvious differences between the Neanderthals and the remains of anatomically modern man of similar antiquity (Cro-Magnon Man, above right, with a Neanderthal from La Ferrassie) strengthened belief that the Neanderthals had become extinct without contributing to the evolution of modern man.

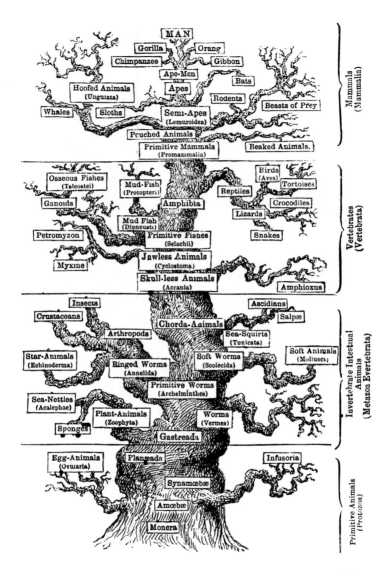

The German zoologist Ernst Haeckel devised an ancestral tree (left, from *The Evolution of Man*, 1879) to illustrate the theory that all forms of life had evolved from single-cell organisms. Man and the living apes were directly descended from a common ancestor, the Ape-Men, he proposed.

Inspired by Haeckel's proposal, the Dutch anatomist Eugene Dubois described fossils he found in Java in 1891–2 as the remains of ape-men. Dubois's full-size reconstruction of this archetypal 'Missing Link' (above) now resides in the basement of the Natural History Museum, Leiden.

4. Feby. 1912
Woodward,
DAWSON & HART,
SOLICITORS.
TELEGRAMS,
"DAWSON, UCKFIELD."
P.O. TELEPHONE No 5.
My dear Woodward,
1908-11
1912
13. Augt
My dear Woodward,
have
together once more.
Keith was most unfair
in the way he tried to
saddle you with dummy
base of the skull after your
explanation
When I saw him in
the morning I pattered

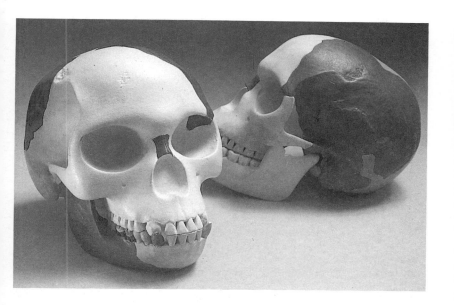

Fragments of skull and jaw bone found near Piltdown, Sussex, in 1912 (left, with correspondence) seemed to combine the large brain of man with the jaw of an ape in one individual (reconstructions above), exactly as some experts had proposed for the intermediate form linking modern man and his distant ancestors.

The implications of the Piltdown discovery misled the study of fossil man for many years, but subsequent discoveries rendered the evidence increasingly contradictory, and in 1953 Piltdown Man was shown to be a fraud. The skull fragments were human and the jaw had belonged to an ape; they were not from the same individual. Piltdown Man was a product of human artifice, not human evolution.

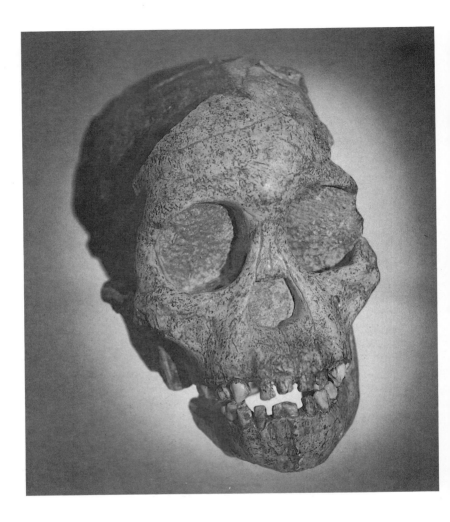

The type specimen of *Australopithecus africanus* (above) was described by Raymond Dart in South Africa in 1925. On the basis of the skull's distinctive features, Dart claimed that *Australopithecus* was an ancestor of man. The claim was scornfully dismissed at the time and for many years after that, but was confirmed by Robert Broom in the 1940s with discoveries (also in South Africa) including a partial skeleton (right) which proved that the australopithecines had walked upright, as Dart had said.

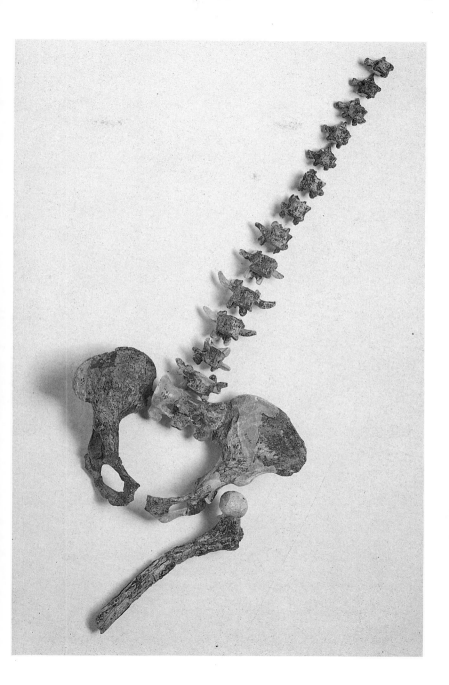

The advent of stone tools was an important landmark in the story of human evolution. Chipped cobbles found at Olduvai Gorge in deposits dating from about 1·9 million years ago are among the oldest known; more sophisticated handaxes and cleavers (above) from Olduvai are about 700,000 years old.

The famous 'Zinj' (right, set against the Olduvai skyline) is a 1·75 million-year-old robust australopithecine found along with stone tools at Olduvai in 1959. The association of tools and skull suggested that Zinj had been a toolmaker, and for a short time he was therefore promoted as the oldest known ancestor of man.

In the late 1950s, development of the potassium–argon dating method at the University of California, Berkeley (left), enabled geologists to determine the absolute age of volcanic rocks. Where applicable, potassium–argon dating gives palaeoanthropologists the precise age of the deposits in which their discoveries were made. Sites at Olduvai Gorge were the first to be dated by the method.

The type specimen of *Homo habilis* (above) from Upper Bed I, described in 1964 as the oldest representative of the genus *Homo*, is 1·7 million years old.

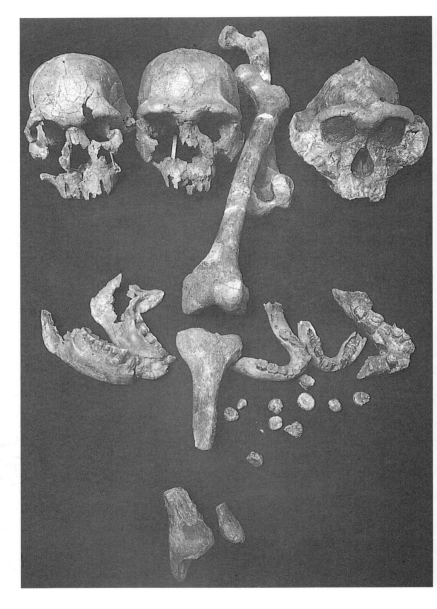

During the 1970s and 1980s, knowledge of early hominid evolution has been vastly extended by discoveries in East Africa.

Fossils recovered by expeditions to Lake Turkana in Kenya include the remains of three hominids species (left) that lived contemporaneously around 1·5 million years ago – evidence showing that hominids have not always been a single-species phenomenon.

'Lucy' (right) is the star of a remarkable collection of hominids found in Ethiopia. Scientifically, she is known as *Australopithecus afarensis*, a new species of hominid described in 1979. *A. afarensis* dates from 3·6 million years and is widely accepted as the earliest known link in the human line.

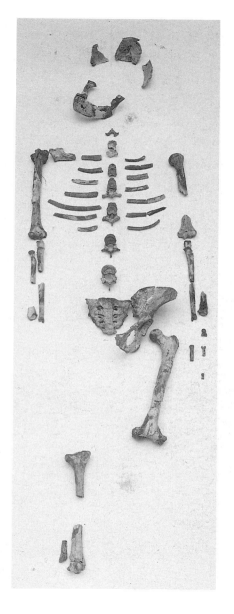

A trail of hominid footprints fossilized in volcanic ash was found at Laetoli, Tanzania, in 1978. The trail dates from 3·6 million years, showing that hominids were fully bipedal and on the road to humanity at that time.

cluded that the australopithecines had been violent carnivores who ate their own kind from time to time.

In 1957 Dart published a monograph entitled 'The osteodontokeratic culture of *Australopithecus prometheus*', detailing the evidence of australopithecine lifestyle he claimed to have discovered among the fossil collections, but the conclusions he drew from that evidence had been published four years earlier, in a paper entitled *The Predatory Transition from Ape to Man* (Dart 1953). Here Dart described the australopithecine ancestors of mankind as essentially 'human in their cave life, in their love of flesh, in hunting wild game to secure meat ... [who] ... seized living quarries by violence, battered them to death, tore apart their broken bodies, dismembered them limb from limb, slaking their ravenous thirst with the hot blood of victims and greedily devouring livid writhing flesh' (Dart 1953: 204, 209). Dart believed that the evidence of ancestral violence he perceived among the fossils explained what he saw as the predominantly aggressive nature of modern man. 'The loathsome cruelty of mankind to man forms one of his inescapable, characteristic and differentiative features; and it is explicable only in terms of his carnivorous, and cannibalistic origin,' he wrote. 'The blood-bespattered, slaughter-gutted archives of history from the earliest Egyptian and Sumerian records to the most recent atrocities of the Second World War ... [proclaim] ... this mark of Cain that separates man dietically from his anthropoidal relatives and allies him rather with the deadliest of Carnivora' (Dart 1953: 207–8).

Though Dart's theory of mankind's bloody ancestry evoked little positive response in academic circles, it found wide popular support – perhaps because its evolutionary perspective was a salving context in which to set painful memories of the recent war. The Hollywood dramatist Robert Ardrey spelled out the Dart version of human evolution in *African Genesis* (1961), a bestseller whose attitude towards man's early ancestors may be summarized by an index entry for 'tools', which instructs the reader to '*see* weapons'. The theme of ancestral violence was pursued in other notable books (for example Lorenz 1966) and found memorable expression in the opening sequence of Stanley Kubrick's film *2001*, wherein the killer man-apes are seen eliminating their less able brethren. Phillip Tobias is understood to have advised Kubrick on the veracity of this sequence.

And as an image of mankind's ancestors as violent (and hairy) little humans was etched in the popular imagination, where it explained the most deplored aspects of modern human behaviour as a legacy of our evolutionary past, scientists were completing the circle with research and interpretations which explained the ancestral status of the australopithecines in terms of their human characteristics and behaviour patterns.

In general, archaeologists, anthropologists and palaeoanthropologists tended to confirm the assumption that early man had been primarily a hunter. Stone tools and postulated living sites dating from 1·9 million years ago were discovered at Olduvai Gorge (see Chapter 8). Studies of the modern day San (Bushmen) of the Kalahari provided a model of a way of life, seemingly based on hunting, that might have characterized that of early man in Africa. Hypotheses concerning the evolution of hunting were proposed (Washburn and Lancaster 1968: 213–29), conclusions about the social structure of early hominids were drawn (Washburn 1963) and the 'home-base' concept was established (Pilbeam 1972: 12; Isaac 1978). Early man went out hunting for food, it was said, while early woman stayed at home and cared for the children, a style of living strikingly similar to that of suburban man in the post-war decades.

More specifically, Phillip Tobias explored the possibility of extracting some indication of how the australopithecines had lived from the evidence of when – that is, at what stage of development – they had died. Tobias sorted fossil teeth from the South African cave sites into five stages of development on the basis of tooth growth, eruption and wear, and assigned them to two broad categories: pre- and post-puberty. He found that a significantly larger number of *A. africanus* individuals had died before puberty than of *A. robustus* individuals, and concluded that further analysis might supply more information on the life and survival patterns of the ancestral hominids (Tobias 1968).

And most specifically of all, in 1975 the palaeontologist Alan Mann published a monograph on early hominid life and survival patterns he had deduced from a study of australopithecine teeth. The monograph, based on Mann's PhD dissertation, was entitled *Paleodemographic Aspects of the South African Australopithecines*, and opened with an admission that 'the fragmentary, incomplete, and scattered condition of these hominid fossils, and the difficulty of relating known samples to a living population, preclude generation of the most elementary demographic statistics' (Mann 1975: 6). But despite use of the suffix 'paleo', careful introductory remarks and disclaimers in the text insisting that his conclusions applied only to the sample he studied and not to the actual australopithecine populations (Mann 1975: 79), Mann's study was widely interpreted as an analysis of australopithecine demography from which valid interpretations of population size, age distribution, social arrangements and the cultural development of mankind's ancestors could be drawn. (A cynic might say that only non-publication could have ensured a different result.)

Since teeth are the hardest part of the body and therefore the most frequently preserved, they are prominent in all fossil collections. Mann analysed over 800 australopithecine specimens from the South African cave sites. He assessed their stage of development with the aid of innovative X-ray techniques, compared his findings with the pattern of dental development in modern chimpanzees and humans, and concluded that australopithecine dental development had followed an essentially human pattern (Mann 1975: 49). With the human characteristics of australopithecine dental development established to his satisfaction, Mann then assessed the age at death of the australopithecines according to the rate of development found in modern humans. His results showed that none had lived beyond the age of forty; 85 per cent died before the age of thirty, their mean lifespan was about twenty years and childhood development was prolonged.

Mann was careful to acknowledge the limitations of his study, but drew some far-reaching conclusions from it none the less. The slow development of the australopithecine teeth could be a result of chronic malnutrition, but it was more likely to indicate a lengthened time of childhood dependency, he suggested, which would be important in the transmission of learned behaviour across generations. Prolonged childhood and learned behaviour implied culture, and thus the study 'furnishes the first direct morphological data for the presence of culture in this hominid group,' Mann concluded (1975: 81–4).

And so a bag of teeth, representing the few individuals whose remains were somehow incorporated in South African cave deposits over a million years or more, helped to strengthen a growing belief that man's earliest ancestors were cultured creatures, living under difficult conditions, lacking the talents that evolution has subsequently

bestowed on their descendants, killing because they had to, but be-
having just as modern human beings would in similar circumstances.
The underlying presumption echoes an old argument: the fossils may
be the remains of human ancestors but they are not apes.

Meanwhile, other studies were encouraging an alternative view of
the apes themselves. For a start, the African apes were found not to be
the innocent vegetarians that Dart had compared with bloodthirsty
human ancestors. At Jane Goodall's Gombe Stream research station
in Tanzania, chimpanzees were observed hunting in organized bands
and eating meat with fair regularity. They killed and ate monkeys,
bushpigs, buck – and occasionally their own kind too (Teleki 1981:
327). Conversely, it was shown that the San people of the Kalahari
depended more upon gathering than upon hunting for their sustenance
(Lee 1968), and a definitive study by C. K. Brain of the Transvaal
Museum in Pretoria directly contradicted the evidence of the australopithecine's bloodthirsty hunting upon which Dart had based his
proposal of a predatory transition from ape to man.

Recording more than a decade of research, Brain's monograph,
published in 1981, shows that the fossil bones found in the South
African cave deposits accumulated naturally over hundreds of thousands of years. The bones either represent the remains of animals who
died in the caves or else they had been carried there by leopards or other
predators – or even by porcupines, whose habit of dragging large bones
back to their dens to gnaw (leaving tell-tale marks on the bones) is well
documented. The bones were broken in rockfalls and under the sheer
weight of the assemblage, not by the action of any human ancestors.
Furthermore, the australopithecines found in the caves, far from being
the bloodthirsty hunters of Dart's interpretation, were most probably
the prey of leopards, Brain concluded. In short, the evidence gave
reason to suppose they were the hunted, not the hunters, as the title of
Brain's monograph suggests: *The Hunters or the Hunted? An Introduction to African Cave Taphonomy* (Brain 1981).

And the australopithecine teeth, from which such far-reaching conclusions have been drawn, have also come under closer scrutiny in
recent years. With the benefit of scanning electron microscopy, two
researchers from University College London, Timothy Bromage and
Christopher Dean, have been able to assess the rate at which australopithecine teeth grew (Bromage and Dean 1985). It has been known

for decades that enamel is laid down in a precise and regular fashion as the tooth grows. Fine incremental lines can be observed on the surface of the tooth, much as growth rings are found in trees and growth ridges on seashells. In the case of primate teeth, however, the growth rate is faster and the process is completed before the tooth erupts. Research has established that the growth lines in teeth actually record a daily deposition of enamel (Beynon and Wood 1987; Dean 1987); applying these data to the incremental lines on a range of unerupted australopithecine teeth, Bromage and Dean discovered that their owners had actually matured at a much faster rate than had been supposed. Even after taking into account several negative factors, they found that the Taung child, for instance, was probably only three years old when it died, not six as had been thought. Similarly, other fossil teeth were also found to be about half the age upon which Mann had based his proposal of prolonged childhood, learned behaviour and culture in australopithecines. In fact, the findings of Bromage and Dean suggest that the growth rate of australopithecine teeth was much more akin to that of the apes than that of modern humans, and further doubt as to the human affinities of the teeth has been raised in a study published by Holly Smith of the University of Michigan (Smith 1986).

Holly Smith assessed a range of fossils according to newly refined standards of tooth development in apes and humans and found some curious anomalies. The least 'human-looking' of the australopithecines, A. robustus, which became extinct 1 million years ago, had a human pattern of tooth development, while the australopithecine candidates for human ancestry were distinctly ape-like.

All this of course suggests that the human line was rather more ape-like and rather less cultured at the australopithecine stage of its evolution than had previously been thought. Alan Mann's response to the development is not sympathetic. The analyses published by Smith, Bromage and Dean are 'absolutely and completely wrong', he has said (Mann 1987). Time will tell.

Meanwhile, the simple dichotomy of 'either human or ape' is fading from palaeoanthropology's view of hominid origins, as the findings of Bromage and Dean, Smith and others point to the conclusion that our earliest ancestor was probably neither ape nor human but a unique combination of both.

8

Zinjanthropus boisei

(1959)

Louis Leakey (1903–72) often expressed affection and admiration for Raymond Dart and Robert Broom, but he never accepted their contention that *Australopithecus* was a direct ancestor of mankind. Leakey believed that human evolution has been a long, slow affair and that man – in common with the rhinoceros and the flamingo, for instance – was shaped millions of years ago and has remained relatively unchanged ever since. The fossil record shows, he said, that most, if not all, vertebrate lineages have their dead branches along which related forms have evolved to extinction, and he saw no reason why the *Homo* lineage should be any different.

In Leakey's view, the hominid line, leading to man, and the pongid line, leading to the apes, branched away from their common ancestral stock about 20 million years ago (Leakey, L. S. B., 1969), and he believed there have been many more branches since then. *Australopithecus*, for instance, left the *Homo* line about 6 or 7 million years ago, he said, and virtually every fossil mentioned in the preceding chapters was no more than an 'aberrant offshoot' from the human stem. Neanderthal, Java, Peking and *Australopithecus* were all, in Leakey's view, evolutionary experiments that ended in extinction. They were 'rather brutish creatures', who may have existed at the same time as the true human ancestor, but played no direct part in the story of human evolution.

These views echo the early pronouncements of Arthur Keith, Leakey's mentor; but whether they were wholly the product of his learning or whether an upbringing as a missionary's son had already predisposed Louis Leakey towards a belief in the antiquity of man's lineage, it is certain that the views were formed early in his career and never changed. Throughout his professional life Leakey expressed the belief that man's ancestry is a long direct line on which the enlargement of the brain was a decisive feature, thin skullbones a distinctive characteristic and the ability to make stone tools a crucial development.

Stone tools are the key to the story of Louis Leakey, his wife, Mary, and their discoveries at Olduvai Gorge. They are also perhaps the most evocative relics of our ancestors. Fossil bones may reveal the physical characteristics of the creatures whose flesh once clothed them – their height, their weight, the relative proportions of the bodies – but the tools they have left behind add an unexpected dimension of understanding. A stone tool may have lain undisturbed for more than a million years, but we can be certain that the hand that made it differs hardly at all from the hand that picks it up today. We heft it, consider using it, perhaps even imagine our lives depending upon it. That we are here to wonder is in itself proof of the evolutionary success of the lifestyle adopted by the early toolmakers. The cutting edge was the beginning of culture and technology. The crude stone tool is a tangible link with those origins.

Louis Leakey perceived the magic of this connection as a boy and undoubtedly it heightened his sensitivity to the subject, predicating his important discoveries and underscoring his success in print and the lecture hall. Uniquely, Louis Leakey was able to envisage and communicate the predicament of early man; and on that plane it is perhaps irrelevant that the bold and inspiring story he told was as much the product of his intellectual and emotional preconceptions as it was a reflection of the evidence and the facts.

Young Louis' earliest ambition was to become a missionary like his father (Leakey, L. S. B., 1937: 55). He was born on 7 August 1903 in a mud-and-wattle house that his parents occupied on the mission station established by the Church Missionary Society among the Kikuyu people at Kabete, fifteen kilometres from Nairobi. When he was twelve years old, Louis received a book on the Stone Age as a Christmas gift from a cousin in England and was immediately inspired to search for flint arrowheads and axeheads in the vicinity of Kabete. He had no clear idea of what he was looking for, or even of what flint was, but this deficiency was probably an advantage, for there is no flint in East Africa and if the young enthusiast had searched assiduously for what was not there he might have overlooked the obsidian flakes that were quite common in the road cuttings and exposed ground of the region. Assuming the shiny black material to be flint (it is actually volcanic glass), Louis collected every scrap he encountered. Subsequently he learned from Arthur Loveridge, the curator of the Nairobi Museum and Leakey's childhood hero, that his collection was obsidian, not flint, but included some pieces that were undoubtedly Stone Age implements. The boy's delight can be imagined. Loveridge encouraged him to make a record of his finds and, at the age of thirteen, Louis Leakey embarked upon a study of the Stone Age in East Africa, determined to continue until he knew all there was to know about it (Leakey, L. S. B., 1937: 56).

Many years later he learned that in 1912 two American archaeologists had visited Kenya in search of early man, intending to initiate extensive investigations if they found any worthwhile evidence. But, trained in the European tradition, they were looking for flint tools and of course found none. Leakey was convinced that had they not searched under this misconception, they would have recognized the obsidian implements, discovered the archaeological potential of East Africa and pre-empted his entire career.

An upbringing among the Kikuyu hardly prepared the sixteen-year-old Leakey for life in the English public school he entered in 1920 in pursuit of formal education and his ultimate ambition – a degree in anthropology from Cambridge. He had gained a fair knowledge of French, Latin and mathematics from his father and the tutors brought to Kabete, but he had no knowledge of the English academic system. He did not know the meaning of the word 'essay', understood nothing of Greek or cricket, made few friends and, by his own account, was very unhappy. But it appears he was an extremely bright pupil in whom pride produced a fierce determination.

He caught up in most things (including cricket) and at Cambridge his upbringing proved to be a distinct advantage, enabling him to gain acceptance for the anthropology course by offering Kikuyu for the Modern Languages Tripos. In his autobiography Leakey says that although the university authorities were perplexed by the proposition, there was no regulation by which Kikuyu could be disallowed; it was spoken by a large living population, the Bible (translated by Leakey's father) was evidence of its written form and Leakey could produce two certificates of competent knowledge, one from a missionary and the other bearing the thumb-print signature of a tribal chief. The only problem was to find an instructor. In the event, Leakey found himself obligated to teach Kikuyu to his supervisor, who subsequently became his examiner as well (Leakey, L. S. B., 1937: 132).

At the beginning of his second year Leakey suffered concussion on the rugby field. Severe headaches ensued whenever he attempted any reading and his doctor recommended a year's absence from all academic work. This was a serious setback to his ambitions, but Leakey solved the pressing problem of financing a year's enforced holiday by joining a British Museum of Natural History expedition to Tanganyika, where its leader, W. E. Cutler, hoped to recover the fossil remains of dinosaurs from some excavations at Tendaguru begun by German archaeologists before the war.

Cutler had collected fossil reptiles in America most successfully but he had never been to Africa. Leakey's knowledge of the continent and its people was undoubtedly useful to Cutler, but Leakey himself appears to have been the major beneficiary of the expedition. He gained invaluable practical experience in excavating and preserving fossils, although the fossils they found were of minor significance. Leakey celebrated his twenty-first birthday at Tendaguru and returned to Cambridge with over 100 ebony walking-sticks, carved by the workmen in their spare time, which he sold on commission through some Cambridge tailors and thus financed a portion of his college bills. W. E. Cutler died of blackwater fever at Tendaguru some months after Leakey had left.

With First Class examination results and sheer enthusiasm to encourage grants, stipends and other financial support, Leakey managed to organize a series of four archaeological expeditions of his own to East Africa between 1926 and 1935. The first two of these explored caves and burial sites in Kenya. An abundance of stone tools and recent skeletal remains was recovered. The latter expeditions continued the investigations in Kenya, but also explored Olduvai Gorge in Tanzania and here set the scene for the culmination of Louis Leakey's career.

Olduvai Gorge is an unavoidable feature of the south-eastern Serengeti Plains. The popular story of its accidental discovery by Professor Kattwinkel in 1911 is hard to credit, though Louis Leakey particularly enjoyed recounting how the German lepidopterist had apparently nearly plunged to his death over the cliffs of the gorge while in absent-minded pursuit of some exotic butterfly. Recoiling from the brink, Kattwinkel descended into the gorge in a more orthodox manner and discovered large quantities of fossil bone lying about the erosion slopes. He made a small collection that aroused excitement in Berlin (Tanganyika was German territory at the time) when it was found to include some bones from a three-toed horse. This extinct creature was well known in Europe from deposits of the early Pliocene period, but the Olduvai deposits seemed much younger that that, implying that the three-toed horse had survived longer in Africa than it had in Europe. This was a startling idea that called for further investigations and so, with the Kaiser's personal blessing, an expedition set off in 1913 to make a thorough study of Olduvai Gorge.

Led by Dr Hans Reck of the University of Berlin, in three months the team completed a geological survey, collected more than 1,700 fossils and confirmed the geological antiquity of the Olduvai deposits, but the significance of this work was quite overwhelmed by the controversy that arose when Reck claimed that a human skull and skeleton found in the lower deposits of the gorge were as old as the extinct animals from the same level. Reck returned to Berlin with the skull wrapped in his personal linen, while the skeleton followed with the other fossils. He announced the discovery in March 1914 and the London *Times* of 19 April that year reported him as saying that the ribs and breast were akin to those of the ape, while the skull was unmistakably human, an observation which he subsequently claimed as proof 'that the human race more or less as it is now is of considerably greater antiquity than has been imagined' (Reck 1914).

The skeleton had lain on its side, knees drawn up in the foetal position. Sceptics suggested that it had belonged to a tribesman of the recent past whose fellows had buried him in the more ancient deposit. But Reck remained firm in his belief that the skeleton was contemporary with the extinct animals among which it was found, even though they were definitely of Lower Pleistocene age, a time when the human ancestor might be expected to look a little less modern than the large-brained Olduvai Man.

To resolve the problem, Reck planned another expedition to Olduvai. Quite independently, but presumably attracted by the controversy, three other German expeditions to the gorge were planned as well; all four were actually on their way when war was declared in August 1914. None reached their destination. Reck stayed in Tanganyika as a government geologist and became a prisoner of war when British forces took the German territory in 1916. After the war, Tanganyika became a British Mandated Territory, no longer so readily available to German science, with the result that the problem of Olduvai Man was still unresolved when the first of Leakey's East Africa archaeology expeditions returned to England, in 1927.

Some fossilized human remains that the expedition had recovered from a burial site near Lake Elmenteita in Kenya resembled Olduvai Man, Leakey thought, but the fossil fauna seemed very different; so he went to Germany to examine the Olduvai collections and discuss the matter with Reck, now returned to the University of Berlin. Reck still believed in the great antiquity of Olduvai Man, but Leakey could not agree; he found the state of preservation very different from that of the extinct animal fossils and this, combined with the faunal disparity between Olduvai and Elmenteita, convinced him that the skeleton was younger than Reck believed, though not as young as the critics had suggested.

In this conclusion Leakey was essentially correct, but he was to change his mind before the problem of Reck's Olduvai Man was finally resolved, and meanwhile his second East Africa archaeological expedition (1928–9) added another twist to the mystery. Skulls were discovered in a cave near Elmenteita which were even more like the Olduvai skull than the specimens found in 1927, yet the associated fauna was very much younger. And then there was the question of tools: why had none been found at Olduvai? At Kariandusi in Kenya, Leakey and his colleagues had collected impressive numbers of handaxes from deposits that Leakey was certain were the same age as Olduvai, yet Reck insisted that despite a most diligent search he had found no stone implements of any kind anywhere in the gorge. But could he have overlooked them? Leakey suspected there was a good chance that he had. Quite apart from the circumstantial evidence, he recalled noticing a rock among Reck's geological specimens in Berlin which strongly resembled the handaxes from Kariandusi (Leakey, M. D., 1979b).

With further investigations patently necessary, Leakey included Olduvai Gorge on the itinerary of his third expedition to East Africa and Hans Reck among its participants. Leakey was so confident that there must be some evidence of Stone Age culture in the Gorge that he bet Reck £10 he would find a stone tool within twenty-four hours of arriving there. Reck was equally confident he would not. The party arrived at Olduvai Gorge just before 10 a.m. on 26 September 1931 and spent the rest of the day establishing their camp and water supply. Reck spent most of the night engaged in the latter endeavour as well. He had difficulty locating the spring he had used eighteen years before and, having awaited the rise of the full moon to light his way back to camp, was frustrated by the occasion of a total lunar eclipse that night. No doubt he had intended to sleep late the next morning, but that plan was frustrated too, by the excited Louis Leakey who had left camp at dawn and found a perfect handaxe very soon thereafter. 'I was nearly mad with delight,' he writes; 'I rushed back with it into camp amd rudely awakened the sleepers so that they should share in my joy' (Leakey, L. S. B., 1937: 252). One of the principal objects of the expedition was thus achieved within twenty-four hours of arrival and Reck lost £10 as well as his night's rest.

Subsequently, thousands of stone tools have been found at Olduvai, and doubtless thousands remain. Why had Reck not seen them on his first visit? It transpired that like the young Leakey at Kabete, Reck had been looking for flint tools but, unlike Leakey, he knew flint very well. Of course, there is no more flint at Olduvai than there is at Kabete; the tools that litter the gorge are made from a variety of volcanic lavas, chert and quartz, and Reck simply did not notice them (though apparently he took at least one back to Berlin as a rock sample). It is a classic example of how training can create pre-conception.

It was at this point, at the age of twenty-eight, with virtually the whole of East African prehistory laid before him, that Leakey's own preconceptions began to colour his interpretations, particularly those concerning the antiquity of large-brained *Homo sapiens*. This tendency was clearly revealed when Leakey and Reck reassessed the contention that Olduvai Man was as old as the Pleistocene fossil fauna found at the same level. Within four days of their arrival at the Gorge, Leakey abandoned the evidence of the physical and faunal inconsistencies he had found so persuasive while examining the fossils in Berlin, and accepted instead his senior colleague's interpretation of the geology, concluding that the large-brained skeleton was as old as Reck had claimed.

Within a week of arrival, the expedition leaders sent a note to

Nature (Leakey, L. S. B., *et al.* 1931) proclaiming that the problem of Olduvai Man was solved. Stone tools reinforced Leakey's conviction. In marked contrast to Reck's previous visit, the 1931 expedition found tools in each of the five geological beds; and among them Leakey claimed to see an evolutionary sequence of manufacturing skills, from the simplest pebble tools of Bed I to the advanced handaxes of Bed IV. Later he claimed these discoveries were important enough 'to startle the scientific world and lead palaeontologists to revise their concepts of the age of *Homo sapiens*'. Reck's Olduvai Man was probably the maker of an intermediate pebble tool culture, he wrote in *The Times* of 3 December 1931, suggesting that '*Homo sapiens* goes back in East Africa to an age in the evolution of modern man far more remote than the evidence found anywhere else in the world suggests' (Leakey, L. S. B., 1931).

A few weeks later, tools and traces of fire attributable to Peking Man were found in the Chou K'ou Tien cave and, in a revealing comment, Leakey told readers of *The Times* that although Peking Man was probably the same age as Olduvai Man, he represented a cousin not an ancestor of *Homo sapiens*. Further excavations at Chou K'ou Tien would probably show that *Homo sapiens* had lived there, Leakey suggested, and was responsible for the tools and the fire, while the remains of Peking Man represented the relics of his meat feasts (Leakey 1932a).

After the Olduvai interlude Reck returned to Europe while Leakey and the rest of the party set off to explore some deposits near a village called Kanjera in the vicinity of Lake Victoria. Fossils had been found there in 1913 and Leakey was anxious to see if the deposits matched the age of those at Olduvai. In a matter of weeks the contemporaneity was confirmed to Leakey's satisfaction, not least by the discovery of two fragmentary skulls as large as those of modern man and his alleged ancestor from Olduvai Gorge, and then by a scrap of hominid mandible from another site (Kanam West) which Leakey claimed also represented *Homo sapiens* and was even older than Olduvai Man. 'The world's earliest *Homo sapiens*,' he called it, 'one step further back than even Olduvai' (Leakey, L. S. B., 1932b).

Neither the Kanjera skulls nor the Kanam mandible were particularly impressive fossils, nor was the evidence for the antiquity of Olduvai Man very convincing; but such was Leakey's reputation in the early 1930s that he persuaded a number of important people to agree with him on all counts. Arthur Keith, for instance, who had rejected Reck's claim in 1914, wrote: 'In the light of the discoveries made by Mr Leakey in the Rift Valley, there can no longer be any doubt as to the antiquity of Oldoway [sic] man ... I have had to reconsider my opinion and acknowledge that Dr Reck was in the right when he claimed Oldoway man as a representative of the Pleistocene inhabitants of East Africa' (Keith 1931: 158).

At Cambridge in March 1933 a conference organized by the Royal Anthropological Institute expressly to examine all aspects of the Kanjera and Kanam finds unanimously agreed with Leakey's interpretations and congratulated him 'on the exceptional significance of his discoveries' (Royal Anthropological Institute 1933). Leakey had achieved considerable success at a relatively young age, but how much of it was due to the fact that his views so closely echoed those of his mentors? Is it simply ironic that Sir Arthur Keith, Professor Elliot Smith, Sir Arthur Smith Woodward and Dr W. L. H. Duckworth (the triumvirate of British anthropology plus one), who all congratulated the thirty-year-old Louis Leakey in 1933, were the very same gentlemen who had cast doubt upon the announcement of *Australopithecus* by the thirty-two-year-old Raymond Dart seven years before? Or does the irony reveal the predispositions of those involved? *Australopithecus* was an ape, the eminent gentlemen had said; but Leakey's fossils differed hardly at all from *Homo sapiens*, despite their apparent antiquity. 'A most startling discovery,' commented Arthur Smith Woodward (1933: 210). However, while Dart's pronouncements were corroborated by later discoveries, Leakey's were soon discounted.

Leakey's moment of unalloyed success was brief. It was first tainted by the findings of independent geologists reconsidering the antiquity of Olduvai Man. They showed that the body had been buried comparatively recently in an ancient Bed II surface exposed by faulting that was subsequently covered again during the deposition of Bed V. Reck and Leakey had to agree (Leakey, L. S. B., *et al.* 1933). Olduvai Man was not the oldest *Homo sapiens*. Reck had been wrong all along and Leakey had only the dubious comfort of learning that his first interpretation of the evidence had been correct. But even that comfort disappeared when a voice of dissension was raised soon after concerning the provenance of the Kanam and Kanjera fossils. It came from

Percy Boswell, the Professor of Geology at Imperial College, London, who suggested that more evidence of the geology and palaeontology ought to be collected before definite conclusions could be drawn.

Boswell was a Senior Fellow of the Royal Society, a most important figure, and it is a measure of Leakey's conviction and straightforwardness that his response to the implied criticism was an invitation for Boswell to join the fourth expedition to East Africa then being planned. If the Royal Society would finance Boswell's trip, Leakey would be happy to accompany him to Kanam and Kanjera so that Boswell might assess the evidence for himself and science. However, commendable though this action was, it did nothing to strengthen Leakey's case; in fact, Boswell's assessment virtually destroyed it.

The first essential was that Leakey should prove to Boswell that the Kanam and Kanjera remains had been found in the deposits precisely as claimed, and not washed or carried there from somewhere else. For some reason Leakey had neglected to make a map recording the position of each discovery in 1932, an omission which became doubly unfortunate when, on returning with Boswell nearly three years later, he found that local tribesmen had removed all the iron pegs he had hammered into the ground to mark the spots. Furthermore, a camera fault had rendered all Leakey's photographs of the sites useless, and those of another expedition member proved to have been incorrectly labelled when he attempted to locate the sites from them. In short, it was impossible to show Boswell the precise location of the finds. This did not entirely disprove Leakey's claims, but Boswell would not accept them on trust. 'It is regrettable that the records are not more precise,' he commented in *Nature*, 'and disappointing, after the failure to establish any considerable geological age for Olduvai Man . . . that uncertain conditions of discovery should also force me to place Kanam and Kanjera man in a "suspense account"' (Boswell 1935).

Louis Leakey's attempts to explain the debacle (Leakey, L. S. B., 1936) were not persuasive and, although his own belief in the conclusions remained unshaken, Boswell's attack dealt a serious blow to Leakey's reputation. After this, controversy (spiced with a measure of good luck), rather than academic approval, distinguished his career.

After the Kanam confrontation, Boswell returned to England while the fourth East Africa archaeological expedition spent several months at Olduvai Gorge, where Leakey's research team comprised himself, a

geologist, a zoologist, a surveyor and a young archaeologist named
Mary Nicol. The expedition concentrated its attention on sections of
the Gorge not thoroughly explored on previous visits, noting geological evidence and collecting palaeontological specimens. Large
numbers of Stone Age implements were recovered too, from horizons
throughout the sequence, which enabled Leakey to substantiate (to his
satisfaction at any rate) the evolution of the stone tool culture at
Olduvai that he had proposed in 1931. He described the simple pebble
tools of Bed I as the Oldowan Culture, and traced the growth of
manufacturing skill from the Oldowan, through eleven stages, to the
relatively sophisticated tools of Bed IV, which he compared to the
Acheulean flint handaxes of Europe (Leakey, L. S. B., 1951).

In all, the vast potential for prehistoric research at Olduvai was
fully confirmed. In 1931 and 1935 Leakey's expeditions explored about
300 kilometres of fossiliferous exposures up and down the Gorge,
ranging in depth from seventeen to 100 metres of cliff and slope face.
They discovered more than thirty promising sites, identifying them
with the initials of expedition members followed by the letter 'K' for
'Korongo', which is the Swahili word for gully.

At FLK Louis Leakey had found the first stone tool in 1931, sig-
nifying the beginning of his work at Olduvai; he named the site for his
wife, Frida Leakey. At MNK, towards the close of the 1935 season,
Mary Nicol found two fragments of a fossilized human skull among
remains of antelopes and pigs and a scattering of stone tools. They
searched for more but found none. The pieces were small and isolated
but undeniably hominid. In effect, they marked the end of the first
stage of Leakey's Olduvai investigations with a hint that Olduvai
possibly held the sort of evidence that no critic could dispute: the
campsites of early man, on which his fossilized bones might be preserved, along with his stone tools and the remains of his meals. And if
the Gorge held the fossils of man in each of its geological levels, then
Leakey would be able to show the process of human evolution from
the Lower Pleistocene to recent times – a prehistorian's dream.

In 1936 Louis Leakey was divorced by his wife and married Mary
Nicol, bringing down upon themselves the opprobrium such behaviour
could attract at that time. Leakey's biographer implies that the divorce
precipitated their move to Kenya, once Leakey realized that, in conjunction with the Kanam affair, the divorce rendered him unsuitable

in some eyes for the academic posts he sought at Cambridge (Cole 1975: 117–25). In any event, it was not until 1951 that stage two of his Olduvai investigations commenced seriously.

For many years academic and government institutions were Leakey's main source of funds, significantly supplemented from his own pocket and by the proceeds of his popular writings. In 1948, however, his financial problems were eased by the generosity of an American-born London businessman with an interest in prehistory, Charles Boise. Early in 1948 *The Times* published a letter from Louis Leakey describing the problems of conducting such research in Kenya. This caught the attention of Boise and inspired him to contribute £1,000 towards the undertaking. Subsequently, Boise visited the Leakeys in Kenya, travelled with them to Olduvai Gorge and became the major contributor to the cost of the excavations that began there in 1951, first in the form of direct financial aid and later through the Boise Fund, which he established at Oxford university expressly for the purpose.

Leakey's early Olduvai investigations had been limited to surface explorations, with very little excavation, mainly because of the expense of the petrol that would have been needed to maintain an adequate water supply for a large workforce. Boise solved the money problem, but now time was the limiting factor. Olduvai Gorge was in Tanganyika; Leakey was a Kenya government employee and could hardly explore the prehistoric site of another country in official time, so work there was restricted to his holidays and unpaid leave.

Accordingly, the Leakeys concentrated attention on the most promising of the sites that the surveys had revealed, in particular BK (Bell's Korongo) and SHK (Sam Howard's Korongo). Both were in Upper Bed II, both were living-floors and both provided large accumulations of stone implements, waste flakes and the fossilized remains of the animals upon which early man had lived. At SHK there were over 2,000 stone implements and evidence of a unique and extensive mammalian fauna. BK proved to be a veritable 'slaughter house', with more than 3,000 stone tools littered among numerous animal bones. Louis Leakey suggested that a group of hominids had driven a herd of massive herbivores into a bog there, dragging out the smaller individuals for slaughter while the largest became inextricably stuck in the mud, where they died. One skeleton was found standing upright (Leakey, M. D., 1971a: 199).

A remarkable feature of the Upper Bed II fauna was the presence of several giant herbivore species. Louis Leakey suggested that optimum feeding conditions were responsible for their development (Leakey, L. S. B., 1965: 76). The giants included a pig the size of a hippo (whose tusk was at first mistaken for that of a primitive elephant); *Pelorovis*, with a horn-span in excess of two metres (first classified as a sheep but later shown to be a relation of the buffalo); and a baboon the size of a gorilla. The size aspect was seized upon in 1954 when the *Illustrated London News* published a review of the latest discoveries from Olduvai Gorge, in which an artist's impression showed the prehistoric creatures looming above their modern counterparts. Olduvai had been the hunting ground of prehistoric man, the headline implied, and at the conclusion of his accompanying article Louis Leakey wrote: 'the remains of the men themselves still elude us, and it is interesting to wonder whether, when found, they will be giants like the animals they hunted, or of normal stature' (Leakey, L. S. B., 1954).

An answer of sorts was provided four years later when Leakey described two hominid teeth found at the BK site in 1955. One was a canine and the other a molar. The canine attracted little attention, but the molar was unusual enough to fall into the category of uncertainty that inevitably attracts controversy, particularly when Louis Leakey suggested that it had come from the lower jaw of a three- to five-year-old human, for the tooth was huge and the child would have been a giant. Leakey's judgement was based upon the cusp pattern of the tooth. In *Nature* he remarked that although the pattern was the most unusual he had ever seen in a deciduous (milk) molar, the tooth none the less had more affinities to fossil and modern man than to the australopithecines. 'We are, therefore, possibly dealing with a very large true hominid which is not of australopithecine type. The teeth, in fact, suggest we are dealing with a human' (Leakey, L. S. B., 1958a). The *Illustrated London News* reported the announcement more colourfully: 'A giant child among the giant animals of Olduvai? . . . a really gigantic human milk tooth has been found at Olduvai Gorge . . . which suggests that [prehistoric] Man in Tanganyika may have been gigantic' (Leakey L. S. B., 1958b).

The tooth was certainly a puzzle, but many found the alternative interpretations proposed by John Robinson a more satisfactory explanation of its size. It was not a milk tooth from the lower jaw of a human child, he said, but a permanent tooth from the upper jaw of an australopithecine adult (Robinson 1959). Robinson had excavated australopithecines with Robert Broom and written a monograph on their dentition, so his word carried weight, but before Louis Leakey's reply pleading uncertainty appeared in print (Leakey, L. S. B., 1959a), events were overwhelmed by an even more contentious discovery.

By the end of the 1958 season, the Leakeys began to feel they had exhausted the immediate potential of Bed II and decided that in 1959 they would first of all look for living sites among the Laetoli deposits south of Olduvai. Three weeks at Laetoli proved totally unrewarding, but soon after their return to Olduvai a hominid tooth was found at MK I, a Bed I site that had yielded many Oldowan tools since its discovery in 1931. The tooth obviously rendered MK I worthy of immediate excavation, but research funds for the year were exhausted.

Leakey returned to Nairobi and managed to arrange an overdraft on his research account sufficient to cover three weeks' excavations at MK I. He also arranged for the operation to be filmed by Des Bartlett for Armand and Michaela Denis's *On Safari* British television series. Bartlett was to arrive on 17 July, bringing with him the Leakey's fourteen-year-old son, Richard. Louis and Mary travelled down a few days in advance. On the morning of the 17th Louis remained in camp, recovering from a slight bout of influenza. Mary took the dogs and walked across to the FLK site, where the first stone tools had been found in 1931 and where she and Louis suspected there might be an Oldowan living-floor.

At about 11 a.m. she noticed a skull just breaking the surface of a slope about seven metres from the top of the bed. At first glance it was not at all like a hominid, for the exposed bone was not solid, as in human skulls, but permeated with air cells like the skulls of very large animals where compensation must be made for excessive weight. She brushed away some of the covering soil and two teeth were revealed, unquestionably hominid but suspiciously australopithecine. 'I was tremendously excited by my discovery and quickly went back to camp to fetch Louis,' writes Mary Leakey (1979a: 75; 1984: 121). But Louis did not share her excitement. 'When he saw the teeth he was disappointed,' she continues, 'since he had hoped the skull would be *Homo* and not *Australopithecus*.'

None the less, FLK proved to be a site of unique significance. It was a living-floor, but an older, less disturbed and more revealing living-floor than any that had been found until then. Many thousands of years before the Leakeys began to uncover its secrets, a group of hominids had camped at FLK. The site was beside a lake whose waters rose and fell periodically; it became littered with the debris of their habitation, then the hominids moved away and shortly thereafter the rising lake waters combined with a fortuitous shower of volcanic ash to preserve some clues of their presence and lifestyle. Organic matter such as skins, wood and the like soon rotted away, but the bones of the animals they had consumed, many of them broken to extract the marrow, were covered over before the weathering effects of sun and rain could fragment them further. Among the bones, the hominids left many stone tools of the Oldowan culture and on the same living-floor, in direct association with the animal remains and the tools, lay the impressively complete skull that Mary Leakey discovered that July morning.

If the skull had been *Homo* it would have been a splendid vindication of Leakey's claims for the Kanam and Kanjera fossils, but the new skull had obvious australopithecine affinities and its implications struck rather deeper than the disappointment of its failure to settle an old argument. They presented Leakey with an awkward dilemma.

At FLK the Leakeys had discovered, for the first time ever, hominid remains of great antiquity indisputably associated with stone tools. By definition a toolmaker *was* man (Oakley 1956), but the skull that lay among the tools was clearly a representative of the australopithecines, the hominids Louis Leakey would not countenance in his story of human evolution and whom most scientists believed incapable of making tools.

By 1959 Louis Leakey may have been the only scientist actively seeking man's origins who still refused to accept Dart's and Broom's assertion that *Australopithecus* was an ancestor of man, but he was one of many still unwilling to accept the contention that the creatures had been capable of making tools. Simple tools of the Oldowan type were known to have been made during australopithecine times, but who made them was another question. The evidence against *Australopithecus* was entirely negative: the brain was not large enough and there was no proof that he had made tools. A few chipped pebbles had been found together with australopithecine fossils in one of the gravel levels of the Makapan caves in South Africa, it was true, and Dart claimed they were tools made by *Australopithecus* (Dart 1955), but other authorities were sceptical. The chipping could have been natural, they said, and the specimens were too heavily weathered to be conclusive.

Then, too, a sizeable collection of more acceptable tools had been recovered from the Sterkfontein caves between 1956 and 1958, though not associated with any fossils. Who had made these? The site had produced large numbers of australopithecine fossils, as we have seen, but John Robinson thought it more likely that the tools had been made by a more advanced hominid from the Swartkrans site, a mile or so away (Robinson and Mason 1957; Robinson 1961). In this conclusion Robinson was congratulated by Louis Leakey for 'proving ... that these "near-men" [australopithecines] were contemporary with a type of early man who made these stone tools and that the australopithecines were probably among the victims which he killed and ate' (Leakey L. S. B., 1958a).

This remark echoed Leakey's comment on the occurrence of tools with the *Sinanthropus* fossils at Peking, made twenty-seven years before (see p. 139); and indeed, it accurately reflected his long-standing and vigorously expounded opinion that the pedigree of Man the Toolmaker was a line of great length and exceptional purity, from which most of the hominid fossils found theretofore were but aberrant offshoots. How extraordinary, then, that it should fall to Leakey to discover the most 'aberrant' of those 'offshoots' lying among some of the earliest known examples of stone tools on the world's oldest and best-preserved living-floor of early man.

Research does on occasion unearth evidence that directly contradicts preconception, but rarely is the confrontation so obvious and unavoidable as that which Louis Leakey found at FLK. The evidence of skull and tools in direct association strongly suggested that a group of australopithecines had made the tools at FLK, where one of their number had died. But if the australopithecines had made the tools, then by definition they qualified as human ancestors, a corollary which seriously conflicted with the Leakey notion of human evolution. So he might have been expected to cling to his preconceptions and suggest that, as at Peking and Sterkfontein, FLK had been the campsite of another hominid, true man, who made tools, ate australopithecines along with all the other animals whose bones littered the living-floor, but was still unknown in the fossil record. In the long term (as discussed in Chapter 10), his preconceptions have proved closer to the truth than the implications of the evidence; but in the short term Leakey took the pragmatic view and resolved the dilemma with a blend of interpretation and preconception that revealed the extent of his faith in both and brought extensive publicity.

Because the skull was virtually intact he concluded that it represented the occupants of the campsite rather than their victims; because of direct association he concluded that the occupants of the site had made the tools with which it was strewn; because the occupants had made the tools he concluded that the skull represented a human ancestor; but because he did not believe the australopithecines had played any part in the evolution of man he concluded that the Olduvai specimen was not an australopithecine, and created a new genus to accommodate the phenomenon: *Zinjanthropus boisei*. *Zinj* is the ancient name for East Africa, *anthropus* means man and *boisei*, of course, honours Leakey's benefactor. *Zinjanthropus boisei*: Boise's East African Man.

Though the recovery of the skull fragments and the subsequent reconstruction of the specimen took some time, Leakey's announcement of the new genus appeared in *Nature* (Leakey, L. S. B., 1959b) less than a month after the discovery. The skull showed no signs of having been broken before fossilization, he said, so there was no good reason to suppose that its owner had been 'the victim of a cannibalistic feast by some hypothetical more advanced type of man'. It was much more likely that the fellow and his kind had themselves made the tools among which he was found. But, whereas for some this might have proved that *Australopithecus* was a toolmaker after all, for Leakey it meant that the Olduvai toolmaker was not an australopithecine. He conceded general affinities but claimed the new skull differed from both *Australopithecus* and *Paranthropus* much more than the two genera differed from each other; he listed twenty points that he felt supported the call for generic distinction and concluded: '. . . the new find represents one of the earliest Hominidae, with the Olduvai skull as the oldest yet discovered maker of stone tools'.

In the *Illustrated London News* he was bolder: '. . . Zinj was a close relative of the "near-men" of South Africa and yet he was a man in the sense that he was a maker of stone tools "to a set and regular pattern" . . . Zinj, moreover, shows a number of morphological characters which are definitely man-like, far more so than any of the South African "near-men" and so he can be regarded almost certainly as being in the direct line of our ancestry' (Leakey, L. S. B., 1960a). And in the *National Geographic* he described 'Finding the World's Earliest Man . . . who lived in East Africa more than 600,000 years ago' (Leakey, L. S. B., 1960b).

It is unlikely that Leakey persuaded anyone but the innocent man in the street with his cry that Zinj was an ancestor of man and the australopithecines were not. John Robinson called the new genus 'unwarranted and biologically unmeaningful', and claimed that the characteristics Leakey saw as distinctive of *Zinjanthropus* were, in his view, either related to the greater size of the specimen or were not real differences at all (Robinson 1960).

But a questionable new genus could not detract from the significance of the specimen itself. The skull was more complete and less distorted than any of the South African forms and its discovery at such an ancient level, along with pebble tools marking the beginnings of human technology, was a major event in the progress of the science. It could hardly have been more appropriate to the centenary of *The Origin of Species* publication.

In the 100 years since Darwin had provided a theoretical basis, zoologists had been striving to establish the path of man's evolution from primal origins. At the same time, archaeologists and prehistorians, encouraged by Joseph Prestwich's confirmation of the geological antiquity of stone tools, also published in 1859, were delving ever deeper for the origins of culture. The two lines of inquiry, both seeking the roots of humanity, appeared to have met when skull and tools were found together on the FLK living-floor in Bed I at Olduvai Gorge. The only problem, from Leakey's point of view, was that the skull at FLK seemed to suggest that Adam's ancestors were not the large-brained man-like creatures he and others had believed in. 'It is now clear that tools ante-date man,' wrote Sherwood Washburn (1960).

The skull's evolutionary significance and the tools' relationship to the origin of man were matters of interpretation, quite distinct from the fact of their indisputable antiquity. Whatever the interpretation of their evidence may be, FLK and Olduvai remained a milestone, a reference point against which earlier and subsequent discoveries could be assessed. The certainty of antiquity stemmed from the geological circumstances of the Gorge which, though not uncomplicated, could be followed more easily than most. The Gorge slices through a 'layer cake' of deposits, revealing a sequence of remarkable clarity. Furthermore, it is packed with fossils, and the advent of new species, combined with the extinction of others through the ascending strata, enables palaeontologists to determine the relative age of Olduvai fossils with unusual accuracy.

Zinj had died among the tools of the FLK living-floor during Lower Pleistocene times. That much was certain, and no one was inclined to dispute Leakey's claim in *The Times* that 'the Olduvai skull represents the *oldest* well-established stone toolmaker ever found anywhere' (Leakey, L. S. B., 1959c). But relative age determinations, even when accurate, are of limited value, particularly in attempts to discern the detail of hominid evolution, all of which is packed within the relatively recent geological past. Something more precise was called for: an absolute timescale that would give ages in years rather than in geological eras.

Estimates of fossils' actual ages frequently appeared in books and articles, it is true, but these were very rough estimates based on guesses of how fast evolution proceeds, or how long sedimentary deposits take to accumulate. These estimates were always known to have little scientific value and they were produced primarily for popular publications (where their inconstancy must surely have confused as many as were enlightened). So the suggestion that Zinj was over 600,000 years old would not have particularly disturbed Leakey's colleagues, even if they were unaware that the suggestion had originally come from G. Mortelmans, a science writer (Leakey, M. D., 1979b). However, not many months later Leakey himself claimed that Zinj was 1·75 million years old; and this claim did startle his colleagues, not only because of the great age but also because Leakey and his co-authors claimed that this was the *absolute* age of the fossils (Leakey, L. S. B., *et al*. 1961). This announcement introduced the potassium/argon dating method to palaeoanthropology, a development that matched the importance of the fossils themselves.

During the 1950s, as the inquiries of palaeontologists and archaeologists approached their rendezvous with Zinj on the FLK living-floor, a select group of geologists and physicists in the laboratories of the University of California at Berkeley were discovering how the age of sedimentary deposits could be determined with far greater precision than the geological timescale allowed. The principle upon which the Berkeley group's work was based is simple enough: certain chemical elements are unstable in that spontaneous disintegration occurs within their atoms; as this disintegration proceeds radio-activity is emitted and different chemical elements are formed successively until a stable state is reached. Uranium, for instance, eventually becomes lead. The rate of disintegration is consistent and can be determined, so that if the relative amounts of unstable and stable elements in a given quantity of material are measured, it is possible to calculate how much time has passed since all the material was in its pristine unstable state, and that of course tells how long ago the element was formed and gives the age of the rocks in which it was found.

The uranium/lead decay was actually used to date rocks as long ago as 1913, but since uranium decays very slowly indeed (a given quantity loses half its radio-activity in 4,500,000,000 years) the amount of decay material in a sample accumulates very slowly too; in fact, it is infinitesimally small and impossible to measure in all but the very oldest rocks. For more recent rocks an element with a faster decay rate was called for, and the Berkeley group turned to potassium. But even here they faced problems of daunting proportions. Many rocks contain potassium, but only about 1 per cent of natural potassium comes in the radio-active form called K_{40}. K_{40} decays into an inert gas called argon (Ar_{40}), losing half its radio-activity in 1,310,000,000 years – which is considerably faster than uranium but still means that in 2 or 3 million years only some 0·1 per cent of the K_{40} will have turned into Ar_{40}.

The quantities were still extremely small, but once the Berkeley group had perfected their extraction methods and succeeded in developing a mass spectrometer capable of measuring billionths of a gram with consistent accuracy, then potassium/argon dating was available to science. Since Zinj it has become an integral part of research into early man. Of course, it is not the fossil itself that is dated but the deposits with which the fossil is associated, which is both a problem and a limitation: a limitation because the required potassium-bearing rocks do not occur at every fossil site and a problem because collecting undisturbed, uncontaminated rock samples of known and indisputable association with the fossils has proved, in some cases, to be hardly less complicated than the laboratory procedures themselves.

The skull that had lain undisturbed beneath the Olduvai sediments for 1·75 million years travelled extensively in the months following its rebirth as *Zinjanthropus boisei*. First he went to Kinshasa, where he was introduced to science by Louis Leakey at the Pan-African Congress on Prehistory which opened there on 22 August, and earned the sobriquet 'Nutcracker Man' in respectful acknowledgement of his enormous teeth. Then he went to London in October and was presented at the British Academy, where he achieved popular fame as the oldest of man's ancestors, though several scientists contested the claim. And in November, Leakey and his charge joined Sir Charles Darwin and Sir Julian Huxley as guests at the University of Chicago's Darwin Centennial (*The Origin of Species* was published on 24 November 1859). Zinj was an unexpected guest; not surprisingly he was welcomed as the archetypal 'Missing Link' – found at last.

While in America, Leakey made an extensive lecture tour. He also told the tale of Olduvai Gorge to the research committee of the National Geographic Society, where, like a magician saving his best trick for the end of the show, he casually drew Zinj from cotton wool wrappings in his briefcase as he concluded a plea for funds to extend the excavations in the Gorge (Payne 1978). The National Geographic Society responded with a grant of over $20,000 and has funded the Leakeys' work with annual grants ever since.

After America, Zinj travelled to Johannesburg, where he resided for several years in Phillip Tobias's anatomy department, and was subjected to exhaustive examination, measurement and comparison. Tobias published the results as Volume II of the Olduvai Gorge series of monographs, according *Zinjanthropus* only sub-generic rank, with the australopithecine affinities firmly asserted by the name

Australopithecus (*Zinjanthropus*) *boisei* (Tobias 1967). In January 1965, Zinj made another journey, this time to Dar es Salaam. He has not moved since, but resides permanently and very securely in a sealed glass case, within a small locked box, inside a locked steel cupboard in the air-conditioned strongroom of the Tanzania National Museum.

During the early 1960s, Louis Leakey was instrumental in enabling an international expedition, combining researchers and resources from France, the United States and Kenya, to explore the fossil beds widely exposed along the Omo river as it drained into the northern end of Lake Turkana (then still known as Lake Rudolf). The region lay just across the Ethiopian border from Kenya and access was best gained from Nairobi.

The Omo Research Expedition was probably the first to be planned as a multi-disciplinary exercise involving geologists, palaeontologists, anatomists and archaeologists whose investigations would ensure that fossil hominid discoveries could be assessed and interpreted in a firm and full scientific context. Initially, it was composed of three groups: a French-funded group under overall direction of Camille Arambourg (1885–1969) with Yves Coppens directing field operations (Coppens assumed overall direction of the French group with the death of Arambourg in 1969); a group funded by the United States National Science Foundation under the direction of F. Clark Howell; and a group supported by the National Geographic Society under the overall direction of Louis Leakey and led by his son Richard (b. 1944).

In 1967, the Kenyan team explored the youngest deposits in the succession and discovered two skulls, an early suggestion that anatomically modern man had lived in Africa as much as 100,000 years ago (Leakey, R. E. F., 1970a: 719; see also p. 28). The French and American teams explored older deposits (dated at between 1 and 3 million years old), where they recovered a total of 231 hominid specimens from ninety-four separate localities. The specimens included 208 teeth, four incomplete skulls, nine mandibles, one complete ulna (lower armbone) and seven other pieces of post-cranial skeleton. Preliminary assessment indicated that they represented four taxa: *Homo erectus* and *H. habilis*; *Australopithecus africanus* and the robust *A. boisei* (Howell and Coppens 1976: 530).

During that first season at the Omo, Richard Leakey chartered a helicopter leased by the American group for a little private exploration along the north-eastern shores of Lake Turkana, in Kenya. He landed close to a promising-looking ridge of sediments and the helicopter's rotor had scarcely stopped before he found a primitive stone tool very similar to the earliest known from Olduvai Gorge (Leakey, R. E. F., 1970a: 719). This development persuaded him to withdraw from the international Omo expedition: 'I already knew how to organize an expedition and find fossils. I wanted to have my own show,' he explained later (1977: 53). With support from the National Geographic Society, he led independent expeditions to East Turkana in 1968 and 1969, establishing a research project which soon eclipsed endeavours at the Omo and has gone on to yield the greatest body of information on early man ever found in one area.

Leakey's first major discovery at East Turkana was a complete hominid skull, a magnificent specimen found in August 1969, unmistakably a robust australopithecine, with distinctive similarities to A. boisei (Zinj) from Olduvai. This find, together with those from the Omo, extended the range of the species from South Africa, where Robert Broom had discovered the first A. robustus specimen, through Tanzania to southern Ethiopia. Many more robust australopithecine specimens have been unearthed subsequently, so that by the early 1980s the species was firmly established as a hominid which had inhabited a wide expanse of southern and eastern Africa from about 2.2 until 1.2 million years ago.

The robust australopithecines were acknowledged to have been an integral part of the African landscape for a million years, but their status in the saga of human evolution was ill defined. They were generally regarded as the inferior relatives of mankind, making their way in the world for a time, but only as a branch-line of hominid evolution and bound for extinction as a consequence of their vegetarian diet, as denoted by heavy and specialized dental equipment. Meat-eating and hunting were still seen as crucial factors in the early evolution of man; 'if you remained a vegetarian, the necessity for culture was not nearly as great,' C. K. Brain explained (1977: 53).

Thus the robust australopithecines were regarded as a kind of evolutionary failure, and because all known specimens were more recent than any gracile australopithecine, scientists concluded that one had evolved from the other, with the oldest A. *africanus* representing the beginning of a line on which the increasingly specialized characteristics of A. *robustus* and A. *boisei* had led to extinction.

In 1979, the description of A. *afarensis* (Johanson and White 1979; see also Chapter 12) added weight to this scheme by providing an ancestor from the temporal distance of between 3 and 4 million years ago from whom the robust australopithecine line could have diverged and evolved to extinction, while the gracile line led on to H. *habilis*, H. *erectus* and modern man. In 1983, the scheme was further strengthened by a study (Rak 1983) which explained the increasing bulkiness of the face in the three species of australopithecine as an evolutionary process of gradual reinforcement and strengthening through time, in response to a diet calling for increased chewing forces which in turn placed increased stress on the facial architecture.

But while science settled comfortably around a majority view regarding the evolutionary trend from gracile to robust which had led to extinction, the fossils had another lesson in store. In 1985, a robust australopithecine skull was found by Leakey's team on the western shore of Lake Turkana which was no less robust than any previously known but was nearly half a million years older than any of them. On the basis of its strong affinities to the Olduvai and East Turkana specimens, the new skull was assigned to the *Australopithecus boisei* taxon (Walker *et al.* 1986). It was found in sediments 2·5 million years old, so its age invalidated the scheme wherein A. *africanus* was said to be the earliest representative of a lineage which led to A. *robustus* and A. *boisei*: A *boisei* could not be the end of the *africanus–robustus–boisei* evolutionary line if it was already present at the beginning.

The immediate response to the new discovery was a flurry of discussion and publications (Delson 1987), during which the majority view of early hominid evolution sprouted an extra branch with notable alacrity. Instead of two branches diverging from A. *afarensis*, three were now postulated: one leading to A. *robustus*, a second to A. *boisei* and a third leading to modern man (Lewin 1986: 721). But the lesson of the robust australopithecines surely concerns the way in which the evidence of chronology and morphology interact in the study of hominid evolution – the long stretches of time that lay between specimens in the fossil record can be bridged with hypothetical schemes of evolutionary development, but in the final analysis it is 'morphology and not time that reveals which taxa (or samples) are most closely related' (Delson 1986).

9

TOOLS

When Mary Nicol joined Louis Leakey's archaeological expedition to Olduvai Gorge in 1935 she was just twenty-two years old and her two most important interests in life were archaeology and Louis Leakey. Convention might have suggested that it was not quite proper for a young lady to join four young gentlemen on an extended visit to the wilds of Africa, unchaperoned, especially as her heart was deeply taken by the leader of the expedition, who was married and had two small children. But Mary Nicol was an unconventional young lady who smoked cigarettes, wore trousers and could pilot a glider. Her background and upbringing were unconventional too, and from them she had emerged as determined and ambitious as Louis Leakey himself, with an independence of spirit that uniquely complemented his.

Mary was an only child, born when her father was forty-five and her mother ten years younger. Her mother's maiden name was Frere. In 1797 John Frere, her great-great-great-grandfather, had been the first man ever to recognize that the curiously shaped flints found in gravel pits and the like were actually implements 'fabricated and used by a people who had not the use of metals', who lived at a time 'even beyond that of the present world' (Frere 1800: 204). Her father, Erskine Nicol, was a landscape painter, successful enough in the post-war years to maintain an enviable way of life. In the autumn, winter and spring, he travelled about Italy and southern France with his wife and daughter, painting stylish pellucid watercolours, which sold well at the exhibitions he held in London during the summer and financed the next trip to Europe. There was never any regular schooling for Mary. The family was always on the move in Europe and the schools in England were closed whenever they were there. None the less, she picked up French as they travelled, her father taught her the elements of arithmetic and the excitement of *Robinson Crusoe* read aloud by her parents encouraged her to read the book herself at the age of seven.

Erskine Nicol painted during the mornings only – strictly alone – and devoted the afternoons to his family. Mary remembers a series of afternoons when they were at Les Eyzies in France, near the famous caves where Cro-Magnon Man and the La Ferrassie remains had been discovered not many years before (see p. 18). Excavations were still going on and Mary visited the sites with her father. They talked to the archaeologists, she recalls, and rummaged through the debris from the caves, looking for stone tools – not as a kind of child's treasure hunt, Mary insists, but because of her father's interest. He was intrigued by the tools' aesthetic qualities, she says, and by the images they evoked of the men who had made and used them. Mary was eleven then, and doubtless the magic of those tangible links touched her too.

Erskine Nicol died unexpectedly of cancer in 1926. With the end of her father's life. Mary's idyllic childhood came to an abrupt end too. Her mother settled them in London, where Mary became an unhappy and rebellious teenager, quite unwilling to follow the path of formal education her mother planned. She persistently ran away from the convents she was supposed to attend, never completed a school course, never sat for an examination and never gained the slightest of academic qualifications. But this did not deter Mary Nicol from pursuing the only subject that really interested her: archaeology and Stone Age man.

At some point – she does not recall how, where or when – Mary learned that she could attend lectures at University College, London, without entrance qualifications and without having to endure the time-consuming tedium of a full undergraduate course. This discovery, she says, marked her 'return to sanity'. Such informal study could never qualify for a degree, but Mary was more interested in information than accolades and followed lectures in geology and archaeology as assiduously as any enrolled student.

In the summer of 1930 she was invited to join the excavations of an Iron Age fort at Hembury, Devon, under Dorothy Liddell, whose brother-in-law, Alexander Keiller, excavated the Avebury site (1924–39) and pioneered modern archaeological methods. In 1931 she worked under Dorothy Liddell again, at Stockbridge in Wiltshire, and she returned there in 1932 and 1933. The following year she ventured forth on her own and, with Kenneth Oakley handling the geological aspects, excavated a Stone Age site at Jaywick Sands near Clacton-on-Sea in Essex. Jaywick proved to be an important site which resolved some puzzling anomalies concerning the development of stone tool technology (Oakley and Leakey 1937). Mary was only twenty-one, but she was already an accomplished archaeologist with significant discoveries behind her.

Not surprisingly, Mary Nicol inherited a degree of artistic sensitivity and talent from her father. It lay dormant throughout her childhood and adolescence, but blossomed in 1932 at the instigation of a family friend who, possibly sympathetic to both the daughter's ambition and the mother's pecuniary plight, introduced Mary to the archaeologist Gertrude Caton-Thompson just when that lady needed some drawings of implements for her book, *The Desert Fayoum*. Mary was given the task and thus earned some money of her own for the first time. The drawings turned out splendidly. Then, whether by accident or design is not clear, Caton-Thompson introduced Mary to Louis Leakey just when he was in need of some drawings of stone tools for his book *Adam's Ancestors* (1934). The occasion was an informal dinner in London, and Caton-Thompson arranged that Louis should sit beside Mary. According to Mary the attraction was immediate and mutual, and given their shared interests this was perhaps not surprising.

Mary drew the tools for *Adam's Ancestors*; Louis visited the excavations at Jaywick. There was always a plausible professional reason for their meetings, but Mary's mother never approved of Louis. Perhaps in an attempt to forestall the inevitable she took her daughter to South Africa during the winter of 1934–5, but if her intention was that the study of prehistoric sites there should erase thoughts of Louis from Mary's mind, she was disappointed. Mary left her mother at Victoria Falls, flew to Tanganyika to join Louis on his fourth expedition to East Africa, and together they spent three months searching for stone tools and the remains of prehistoric man in the fossil beds of Olduvai Gorge.

Forty-five years later it can be said that their investigations have made Olduvai Gorge the longest, fullest and most revealing record of early man and his predicament yet found. Evidence is recorded from no fewer than 127 sites ranged along the length and breadth of the Gorge and throughout its geological sequence. From the base of Bed I up to the most recent deposits, the sites span nearly 2 million years. Artefacts and the fossilized remains of hominid meals have been collected in tens of thousands. Among them are stone anvils that have lain undisturbed since they were last used and tiny fish scales so perfectly fossilized that even their transparency is preserved. The sheer quantity is impressive enough, but the quality of the Olduvai evidence – and this is what distinguishes the Gorge from every other site mentioned in this book – lies in the glimpse it affords of man's earliest cultural activity and development at a single location during a known period of time. The stone tools littering the floor of Bed I are close to the beginnings of humanity, and the increasingly sophisticated tools in the higher beds are a clue to the evolution of skills ultimately responsible for the technological culture that surrounds and supports modern man.

Mary Leakey began the post-Zinj investigations at Olduvai in February 1960, with a full-time workforce of sixteen Kenyan labourers and the part-time assistance of visiting scientists, students and family. The first phase of the work, dealing primarily with the oldest deposits, was brought to a close at the beginning of 1964. In forty-six months only thirteen sites were excavated, but together they spanned 700,000 years from the base of Bed I (1.9 million years old) to the top of Bed II (1.2 million years). The excavations revealed forty-three distinct levels strewn with the evidence of hominid occupation. The total area of the occupational levels amounted to over 55,000 square feet and every square inch of it was mapped. The position, size and shape of every artefact, every stone and every fossil was plotted before its removal for study and analysis. In all, 37,127 artefacts and 32,378 fossils were recorded; and the latter figure does not include all the remains of birds, rodents, frogs and the like which occurred in prodigious quantities but were generally very small and fragmentary: 14,000 rodent fossils from one site, for instance, weighed less than fifteen pounds.

Mary Leakey's work at Olduvai (Leakey, M. D., 1971a) was roughly equivalent to recording the precise position and physical form of each stone and everything else encountered while digging a trench ten feet wide, ten feet deep and one mile long. Excavating procedures were simple enough. After the over-burden had been removed with pick and shovel, the fossil-bearing levels were marked in a grid of one-metre squares, each of which was excavated in ten-centimetre spits with a home-made chisel-like instrument. The matrix surrounding the fossils was removed more judiciously with a dental probe and paint brush before the specimen was coated with a preservative (many fossils were extremely friable). All the debris removed from the grid was sieved through a mesh one-sixteenth of an inch wide, and this is how most of the very small fossils came to light. And every artefact, fossil and stone was plotted on a map of the grid, numbered and recorded. But, though the procedures were simple, circumstances were not always favourable. At some sites the deposits were rock-hard when dry and slushy mud when wet; at others the sides threatened to crumble and had to be bolstered with sandbags; at yet others the overlying deposit tore away the fossil level beneath unless it was first thoroughly moistened to separate the two.

The work was tedious for the labourers, and tense for Mary Leakey. It fell upon her to manage the investigations in general and oversee the work at every site, ensuring, for instance, that the excavations proceeded vertically and that measurements in every plane, the relationship of different levels and any stratigraphic change were all recorded as well as every find plotted on the map of the site. These things were all crucial and if they were not recorded at the time of excavation, there would be no chance of recording them later on. Supervision, in fact, determined the speed of the investigations. Many more men could have been employed, but Mary Leakey had learned from previous experience that excavations are difficult to control when more than half a dozen people are working in the site at one time: detail tends to become blurred as speed increases, and detail is everything.

But to interpret the fine detail Mary Leakey's excavations were revealing at every site, the picture of their context had to be properly focused too. This task was performed by geologist Richard Hay, from the University of California at Berkeley, who undertook a geological survey of the entire Olduvai basin (Hay 1976). Hay collected substantial amounts of detailed data in the field, but no less effort was expended in the laboratory, where he analysed the rock samples and the data he had collected.

Hay's conclusions are revealing indeed. They are a fascinating insight into both the process of geological inquiry and the evolution of a natural landscape, quite apart from the importance of the supportive evidence they lend to Mary Leakey's investigations. In this latter respect Hay's prime objective was to correlate the deposits throughout the Gorge and determine the exact temporal sequence in which the sites occurred. This would be simple if each lay directly above the other in a neat geological sequence, but such is rarely the case. At Olduvai the sites are widely distributed in the horizontal plane, and the geological strata in which they occur are not always at the same height in the vertical plane; this may be because the thickness of the beds varies from point to point, or because they have been disturbed by erosion or by geological faulting. Five major faults associated with the formation of the Rift Valley are known at Olduvai, and there are many smaller ones that further complicate the picture.

Physical exploration and examination of the Gorge was essential, but complete understanding of its geology was finally achieved in the laboratory, where chemical and microscopic examination of the samples he had collected enabled Hay to determine the characteristics of each deposit and thus relate them to one another at all points along the Gorge. This in turn made it possible to state with certainty the sequence in which the archaeological sites had been occupied by early man.

The breadth and detail of Hay's study enabled him to provide a picture of the physical environments at Olduvai during the times that early man was living there. He showed that numerous small rivers and streams from the south-eastern highlands had maintained a sizeable lake in the Olduvai basin during Bed I and Lower Bed II times. It had measured roughly ten by five kilometres and persisted for several hundred thousand years, despite periodic inundation by showers of ash from the erupting Kerimasi and Olmoti volcanoes (Ngorongoro and Lemagrut, which dominate the scene today, were extinct before Bed I was laid down). The ash, of course, created the Olduvai deposits and preserved all the artefacts and fossil remains that are found within them.

Helped by the cumulative effect of rapid evaporation in a lake with no regular outflow, the ash was also responsible for the high alkalinity of the Olduvai lake, rendering the water suitable for both the microscopic algae which flourish in such conditions and the fish and birds which feed on them – tilapia and flamingoes, for instance. That such creatures lived in and around the Olduvai lake in large numbers is confirmed by their fossil remains, as indeed is the presence of their predators – crocodiles and man among them. Thus the volcanic ash not only preserved the remains of the early Olduvai inhabitants – that was simply fortuitous – but more fundamentally, because shallow alkaline lakes can support a far larger biomass than other bodies of water, the ash created the ecological circumstances that encouraged them to congregate there in large numbers.

At about 1·6 million years ago the lake shrank to a third of its earlier size. By 1·2 million years ago it was reduced to a series of seasonal pans dotted about an alluvial plain. One might imagine that volcanic ashes had filled the basin and were responsible for the demise of the lake they had previously made so productive, but there were other factors at work too. Foremost among them, perhaps, was geological faulting, which could have reduced the lake very rapidly and was certainly responsible for the eastward movement of the drainage sump until about 400,000 years ago, when it reached the Olbalbal depression, where it rests today.

But at the time the faulting was taking place, dramatic changes in climate also occurred. In Lower Bed I times, Olduvai was very wet, with perhaps even a groundwater forest standing around parts of the lake shore. By Upper Bed I times a much drier climate prevailed, but this reverted to wetter conditions again in Lower Bed II. These climatic changes are revealed by the evidence of fossil pollens that identify the vegetation, by the presence of animals that live exclusively in wet or dry habitats, and by the evidence of windblown and waterborne materials that Hay found in the sediments.

The distribution of the ancient stream channels in Beds I and II told Hay that the drainage pattern had been altered by the faulting and climatic changes too. He found that the streams and rivers from the highlands had merged into a large main stream flowing westward. With time, as the volcanoes continued to puff ash into the basin, laying down Bed III, drainage from the west joined this main stream. Ultimately, it turned and flowed eastward, as it does today. The stream began cutting the Gorge about half a million years ago; the deposition of volcanic ashes and lake sediments ceased only about 15,000 years ago, so that some of the younger deposits overlie earlier excisions, which makes the geology difficult to interpret in some places. The spot where Reck's Olduvai Man was found is a case in point.

Relating the positions of the occupation sites to the geology, Hay arrived at conclusions which, combined with Mary Leakey's findings, conjured up a picture of our ancestors at the beginning of humanity. Hay found very little evidence of hominid activity on the savannah and barren floodplains; it occurred principally in association with evidence of perennial freshwater, relatively abundant game and vegetation. All twenty campsites known from Bed I were situated around the lake margin, eighteen of them on the eastern side, where most of the streams flowed into the lake in those times. During the depositions of Bed II, when the lake dwindled away to nothing, hominid activity became much more widespread: of the sixty-three known sites, fifty were to the east of the lake basin and many were situated on the banks of watercourses. In Beds III and IV, the site pattern followed the change in drainage: forty out of forty-three sites were to the west of the basin.

Apart from establishing the geological and environmental circumstances of the sites, Hay's work also tells something of the tools that were found there, and the toolmakers. He identified the sources of nearly all the principal rocks used for making the stone tools. This is yet another point that makes Olduvai unique, for nowhere else are the sources of raw material so thoroughly known. This knowledge is particularly illuminating in that it offers clues to early man's growing awareness that some materials make better tools than others, and suggests his willingness to travel ever greater distances in search of the best. In Beds I and II, Hay found that most tools were made of lava obtainable within two kilometres of the campsite; other materials were used too, but the source was rarely more than four kilometres away. Higher in the sequence, however, the variety of material increases and more and more of it comes from further afield. Bed III assemblages include many tools made from rock found eight and ten kilometres away, and by Bed IV times the basin is criss-crossed with a veritable network of supply routes. Trachyte from Olmoti is found at sites fifteen kilometres distant; green phonolite from Engelosen occurs twenty kilometres from its source; Kelogi gneiss is found thirteen kilometres to the east. These are distances as the crow flies; on foot they were certainly greater.

Mary Leakey believes that it is unlikely that large blocks of raw material were carried over the entire distance by members of a single group. The various rocks have quite distinct properties, and perhaps the early hominids had equally distinct uses and preferences for them. Mary Leakey has suggested that the apparently random distribution throughout the basin could indicate some form of barter or exchange among the groups camped closest to the sources of the various rocks – a kind of trade in raw materials, known to have been well established during the later phases of the Stone Age, possibly just beginning at Olduvai one and a half million years ago (Leakey, M. D., 1979a: 76).

Mary Leakey's 1960 excavations began at FLK, where Zinj had been found. Given that the skull was relatively intact, there was some hope that the jaw might also be recovered, but it was not. This was regrettable, for the jaw would certainly have helped resolve the nagging question of Zinj's australopithecine affinities (Louis thought the jaw might also reveal whether or not Zinj could talk), but in the event the absence of fossils was inconsequential beside the wealth of detail that the site provided concerning the activities of the earliest known toolmakers, whether or not Zinj was one of them.

The Zinj living-floor occupied an area of 3,384 square feet. In the forty feet of deposits excavated from the hillside directly above it there were another twenty-one levels at which some evidence of hominid activity was found. The Zinj floor itself was remarkably well preserved and the material on it showed little or no sign of disturbance or weathering, probably because the site had been covered by a shower of ash soon after it was abandoned. It seems likely that the site had been in use for some time, for on it were found 2,470 artefacts, 3,510 fairly large fossils and literally thousands of bone fragments too small to be numbered.

But the major significance of the excavations at FLK lay not in their extent, nor in the quantity of material, nor its fine preservation, nor even in the skull of Zinj himself; it lay in the site's startling suggestion that nearly 2 million years ago the social structure of our ancestors already included the concept of a 'home'. Until then experts had doubted that man had reached this stage of social development so long ago, but the evidence at Olduvai suggested that he had been hunting, gathering in groups at a home-base and occasionally making shelters for at least 1.75 million years (Leakey, M. D., 1979a: 51).

The site plan of the Zinj living-floor shows a scattering of artefacts and faunal remains over the entire area, with a densely concentrated patch on one side surrounded by a narrow, barren zone. The concentration measures about twenty-one by fifteen feet and the assemblage within it is marked by a preponderance of lightweight artefacts and smashed animal bones; the surrounding areas, by contrast, contain mainly large artefacts and many large unbroken fossils. The two assemblages are so different that if they were found separately they would almost certainly be considered as two distinct cultures (Leakey, M. D., 1967: 417), yet at FLK they were together on the same living-floor. What is the explanation?

The site plan shows that the faunal remains within the concentrated area are almost exclusively the meat- and marrow-bearing bones of the carcass, while those outside are mostly jawbones, shoulderblades, hipbones, vertebrae, ribs and the like – all devoid of marrow. To Mary Leakey it seems probable that the concentrated remains marked a place where hominids had gathered to consume the animals they had caught. They would have sliced the meat from the carcass with small flake tools, she suggests, and then smashed the bones to extract the marrow. The large unbroken fossils scattered about the surrounding area would represent the rejects from their meals, and the barren zone in between the two assemblages is precisely where a brushwood shelter might have been erected to break a prevailing south-east wind. The skull of *Zinjanthropus*, incidently, had lain about fifteen feet from the patch of concentrated remains, on the lee side.

Excavations at two other sites revealed living-floors on which the distribution of cultural and faunal material was similar to that encountered at FLK, though at each of these there were not one but two patches of concentrated material; they were roughly circular and lay quite close together, reminiscent of the way nomadic Bushmen still arrange their camps in the Kalahari. At all three excavations the evidence of structures made by early man was entirely circumstantial, but then, it could hardly have been anything else. There was little chance of the brushwood windbreak itself being preserved, so only the bare ground in which it had stood could suggest its existence. At a fourth site, however, a group of hominids had camped where there was little or no soil into which branches could be thrust. Here the branches were supported with rocks instead and today a circle of small rocks remains, inviting interpretation as the earliest known of mankind's building efforts.

The site is known as DK (Donald McInnes's Korongo) and it lies immediately above a lava flow dated at 1·9 million years old. A profusion of flamingo bones and some fish remains indicate its proximity to the lake, and fossilized roots suggest that a bed of reeds or papyrus once grew there. The circle stands on a small hummock. The spot could have been chosen because it was conveniently close to the lake and the creatures that congregated there but drier than the surrounding areas; it might have been a small promontory.

The circle averages thirteen feet in diameter. It is little more than a ring of loosely piled lava blocks, with six small heaps spaced along the northern rim, where it is best preserved. Maximum height is about twelve inches. At first sight the circle is far from impressive, being little more than a jumble of rocks one might expect to find at the bottom of a gorge, but with a site plan to hand and given time for contemplation, the circle can evoke poignant images of our ancestors and their predicament nearly 2 million years ago.

DK is the earliest site at Olduvai and the tools found there are the simplest known, both in style and variety. None the less, they are tools, fashioned with some purpose in mind. The observation that removing a flake from a stone produces a useful sharp edge was almost certainly the result of natural accident. Rocks tumbling in a river or landslide occasionally break, and hurling stones about in a river bed can produce the same result. But such accidents are more infrequent than might be supposed: tumbling rocks are rounded more often than broken and hurled stones usually bounce. And besides, the edge formed by accident is entirely unpredictable. So a useful cutting edge must have remained rare until someone perceived the advantage of dependable supply and set about learning how the results of natural accident could be artificially reproduced.

Choppers are the simplest tools recognizable as manufactured artefacts. They are generally made from oblong, rounded, water-worn cobbles that fit comfortably in the hand, and the edge is formed by removing flakes alternately from either face along one side, or round one end. Deliberately turning a stone into a usable tool requires a surprising amount of skill. Even with our high level of general

Plan of the stone circle at site D K, Olduvai Gorge. The circle lies close to the 1·9 million year level and is the earliest known evidence of a man-made structure.

knowledge concerning technical and mechanical matters, very few people today could decide by themselves which stone is best and precisely where it should be struck to achieve the desired results. We know it can be done: there are many examples of beautiful and sophisticated stone tools to remind us that the effort is worthwhile. But the first toolmakers lacked this incentive. They acquired their skills in pursuit of an end, driven by a need, which means they had reached the conceptual threshold enabling them to identify a problem and appreciate the benefits of solving it. Crossing that threshold put our ancestors firmly on the path to *Homo sapiens*.

The simple tools at DK and elsewhere belong to the Oldowan Culture. The term was coined by Louis Leakey, who described its most common variety as 'a crude chopper varying in size from about the dimensions of a ping-pong ball to that of a croquet ball (Leakey, L. S. B., 1951: 34). He believed that the evolution of toolmaking skills at Olduvai could be traced in a direct line from the simple choppers at the base of Bed I to the fine handaxes at the top of Bed IV. Given the length of time spanned by the deposits, it was almost certain that some progress must have occurred, but Mary Leakey's excavations and analysis have revealed that it was by no means as straightforward as her husband had imagined. This is not to cast aspersions upon Louis's perspicacity: his pronouncements on the Olduvai tools merely reflected the current views of European experts, and these were based on the experiences of flint. There it was well known that the fine feather-flaking of an Acheulean handaxe (named after St Acheul in France, where they were first found) required far more skill than the deeply flaked Chellean pebble tools (from Chelles): in the latter, flakes were removed with a hammerstone; in the former a soft, broader hammer was used – wood or perhaps horn.

By experimentally reproducing known tools, the experts assessed the degree of skill needed to make each and established a stone tool chronology based entirely on the number and form of the flake scars. This was used to place sites in chronological order but could never be confirmed because no European deposits spanned enough time to reveal the development of manufacturing skills from one type of tool to another through ascending levels. But Olduvai spanned many ages. There were no flint tools in the Gorge, but perhaps it was natural that Louis Leakey should approach those made of other materials with the same ideas that were held in Europe. And it was natural too that as he collected and studied specimens from levels throughout the deposits he should seek what Europe's experts had said ought to be there. And he found it, or at least he believed he had found it. On the evidence of flake scars and presumptions of technique, Leakey carefully documented eleven stages by which, in his opinion, the technical skills used in the manufacture of Oldowan tools had evolved into those required for making Acheulean tools. The findings were well received in their day, but his wife's work has since rendered them out of date.

Louis Leakey's readiness to impose old ideas upon new evidence typifies the simplifying approach that science initially adopts towards discovery. It is generally the second round of investigation that takes the more circumspect view, that attempts to gather all available data and then subjects them to thorough analysis to see if any significant facts or trends emerge. So it was at Olduvai, where, with the acknowledged additional benefits of finance, time and patience not available to Louis, Mary Leakey has recorded the physical characteristics of all the 37,127 artefacts collected from Beds I and II at Olduvai. She noted the material of which the artefact was made, the number of flake scars it bore and, where visible, the angle of the striking platform, which is what determines the depth of the flake that is detached.

It was obvious from the start that the collection could be divided into a variety of tool categories, which might or might not provide clues to evolving skills. Mary Leakey eventually identified twenty quite distinct categories. Some of the terms she used to describe them relate to the form of the tool: spheroids, discoids, bifacial points, proto-bifaces, laterally trimmed flakes, polyhedrons, *outils écaillés* ('scaled tools') and debitage (flakes produced during manufacture of other tools but showing some sign of use themselves). Other terms suggest the function of the tool: awls, anvils, choppers, chisels, hammerstones, cleavers, picks, scrapers and punches. In addition she describes manuports (rocks foreign to the site but lacking any sign of modification) and utilized material (artefacts which defy closer description).

In the analysis of all these data, the relative proportions of the various raw materials and categories of tool occurring at each site were calculated. This was only one of several lines of inquiry but, relating the results to the position of the sites in the geological sequence, significant trends did emerge. We have already noted that raw materials seemed to be more specifically selected at sites through the ascending levels. This could reflect an increasingly complicated lifestyle, and the variety of materials, together with developing manufacturing skills, could indicate a growing ability to perceive and solve the problems of that lifestyle.

So what did the evidence show? The toolkit on relevant Bed I living-floors contained an average of only six different tools, but in Bed II the average had risen to just over ten different types. During the same period, the ratio of artefacts to faunal remains changed too: there were fewer bones on the younger sites and more tools. Why? Because the people in those times had developed the skill to catch larger animals than their predecessors had. At each of two butchery sites, for instance, the skeleton of an elephant was found strewn among a profusion of tools. Throughout the upper levels of Bed II the remains of giraffe, hippopotamus and rhinoceros were far more common than lower down. Obviously, one elephant would feed as many people as would a herd of antelope. These developments occurred over about 150,000 years. At the same time the simple chopper was supplanted by the proto-biface, which is the first known attempt to produce a tool with a point as well as a sharp edge, and the multi-faceted polyhedron, with its several cutting edges, probably evolved by progressive stages into the perfect spheroid – a stone ball which the Leakeys believed may represent a transition from passive tool to aggressive missile. They suggested that the spheroids were bolas, like those used in Argentina, where two or more are strung together on lengths of hide and flung at the legs of animals to entangle and halt them.

So among the wealth of detail there was a good deal of evidence suggesting that early man's technical skills developed considerably during the period of time spanned by the Olduvai deposits. The simple Oldowan Culture evolved into what Mary Leakey termed the Developed Oldowan Culture. Tools became more refined and the toolkit was enlarged by the addition of different types of tools and different raw materials.

But, while her work traced our ancestors' increasingly complex lifestyle and heightened conceptual perception, Mary Leakey uncovered an intriguing puzzle too: from the base of Bed I the Oldowan

Culture evolves into the Developed Oldowan A and thence into the Developed Oldowan B, but it does not evolve into the Acheulean handaxe culture, as Louis Leakey had surmised. The Developed Oldowan persists virtually unchanged through Beds II, III and IV, while the Acheulean arrives suddenly and fully fledged in the middle of Bed II. Thereafter the two cultures are contemporary, Mary Leakey says. In one part of the Gorge they are found within a few hundred metres of each other, on the same geological horizon, but there is no mingling. In Mary Leakey's view they remain culturally distinct despite such close proximity.

Since there is no sign of the Acheulean having evolved at Olduvai, it is presumed to have been intrusive. But where did it come from? No one knows. Its arrival coincides with the disappearance of the lake, when there was an abrupt change in climate, fauna and hominid activity in the basin. Perhaps another group migrated into the region at this time, bringing with them the superior skill of handaxe manufacture. But then, why did the Oldowan toolmakers already there not also acquire that skill and incorporate it into their own toolkit?

The primary factor that distinguishes the two cultures is the ability to remove from a boulder the large flakes essential to handaxe manufacture. This is not difficult once the idea is there, and one might expect that during the course of a few thousand generations the Oldowan people would have learned the trick, by example if not by instruction, for abandoned Acheulean handaxes were there to be picked up in their time just as in ours. With the skills they already possessed they surely could have copied them. But no, the Acheulean and the Developed Oldowan remain culturally distinct.

Another puzzle was encountered among the Acheulean handaxes themselves, though this one proved more susceptible to solution. There are two sites in Bed IV whose stratigraphic relationship is indisputable but appears to be contradicted by the evidence of the handaxes they contain. Site HEB is lower in the sequence and therefore must be older than WK, but its handaxes seem finer, more sophisticated and therefore more recent than those at WK. How is it possible that younger handaxes can occur on the older site? This apparent anomaly puzzled the experts, Mary Leakey included, and the fact that it was seen as an anomaly at all is an indication of the strength and persistence of the traditional views on stone tool manufacture.

The WK handaxes were considered to be primitive because very little flaking had been done on them while the HEB handaxes were flaked over most of their surface, and it was fine flat flaking at that, which everyone believed was a difficult and sophisticated technique that must have developed after the 'cruder' work at WK. The most plausible explanation of this apparent regression in manufacturing skill came from the work of Peter Jones, who assisted Mary Leakey at Olduvai for several years while pursuing his own researches into stone tool cultures.

Jones suggested that, far from denoting a regression in skills, the 'crude' WK handaxes actually represent a more sophisticated approach (Jones 1979). Like Louis Leakey sixty years before, Peter Jones was caught by the fascination of stone tools at an early age. But unlike Leakey he lived in England, became familiar with flint and developed more of an interest in making tools than in looking for them.

When Jones joined Mary Leakey in 1976 and began duplicating the Olduvai toolkit, he soon discovered that none of the various materials used by the early toolmakers behaved much like flint (except chert). Though the principle, of course, was essentially the same, different rocks required subtly different techniques. With hindsight this might not seem an especially surprising observation, but at the time it was noteworthy, for although Louis Leakey, for example, had made tools at Olduvai and even skinned goats with them, no one had set about duplicating the Olduvai toolkit in all the various materials, recording the best techniques and how much time each required.

In his experiments Jones found that some rocks were suitable for one class of tool and not for another, that techniques were not always interchangeable and that some tools could be made quickly while others took more time. Mary Leakey and Richard Hay had noted that the increasing variety of raw materials used at Olduvai was a significant development, but Jones showed that the development was more complex than they realized. The WK/HEB anomaly is a case in point. The WK handaxes can be made in less than a minute, because the material used produces a good, clean, sharp edge on the first flake struck from the boulder and requires a minimum of retouching. The material at HEB, however, is not suitable for this treatment: the edge has to be prepared by flaking all round and this can take between five and seven minutes. The WK handaxes, then, represented a considerable advance in manufacturing efficiency over those at HEB; their only drawback is that their fine edge cannot be retouched. Once a WK handaxe has been blunted in use, it is necessary to make a new one.

Jones began by simply copying the Olduvai tools, as he had copied the European specimens, but he discovered that actually using his results added an important new dimension to his perception of their purpose and of how they ought to be made. He quickly appreciated the advantages of a really heavy tool, for example, when he tried to skin a zebra with a light specimen; and he soon realized that the process of resharpening the right sort of large skinning tool produces numerous flakes perfectly suited for the subsequent task of disjointing the carcass, cutting the sinews and scraping the skin. It thus became obvious to Jones that the early toolmakers need only have carried a hammerstone and a few large tools to a butchery site in order to be fully equipped for every task that the job presented, a conclusion which explains the apparent superfluity of small tools at some sites that had previously puzzled many investigators.

Jones's work supports the contention that archaeological analysis has often been unduly biased by aesthetic considerations. Flint tools can be beautiful, and museum collections contain many outstanding examples, but do the aesthetic qualities we perceive today necessarily reflect the functional value of tools made 1 million years ago?

The discovery of lakeside living-sites at Olduvai Gorge, nearly 2 million years old and littered with stone tools and animal bones, contributed to a significant shift of opinion on what might be called the moral calibre of early man. The image of Man the Killer-Ape promoted by Raymond Dart (see Chapter 7) was replaced by the rather more attractive image of Man the Noble Hunter, and the dimensions of the new image were well demonstrated at a symposium on Man the Hunter held in 1966: '. . . in contrast to carnivores, human hunting . . . is based on a division of labour and is a social and technical adaptation quite different from that of other mammals. Human hunting is made possible by tools, but it is far more than a technique or even a variety of techniques. It is a way of life, and the success of this adaptation (in its total social, technical, and psychological dimensions) has dominated the course of human evolution for hundreds of thousands of years. In a very real sense our intellect, interests, emotions, and basic social life – all are evolutionary products of the success of the hunting adaptation' (Washburn and Lancaster 1968: 293).

The emphasis had moved from the killing aspect of hunting that tools had facilitated to the sharing aspects of social behaviour that underpinned the system. Studies of San Bushmen in the Kalahari showed that cooperative behaviour and altruism were essential aspects of the modern hunter-gatherer lifestyle, and Olduvai Gorge provided evidence of irrefutable antiquity, apparently affirming the presence of a similar hunter-gatherer lifestyle at a very early stage of human evolution. Before then, the ancestral hominids had been largely vegetarian, it was believed, and as uncooperative as modern primates. The addition of meat to the diet had fuelled both the enlargement of the brain and the development of the skills needed to catch meat, an interactive process that called for the establishment of home bases and an increasing degree of cooperation among the individuals occupying them. The sharing hypothesis was founded on these observations, its basic proposal being that although tools and hunting had facilitated access to a highly nutritious food source, it was the willingness to share labour and share food which had set our ancestors on the road to humanity (Isaac 1978).

Working under the auspices of the Leakeys' Olduvai research projects, Glynn Isaac (1938–85) made the archaeology of a Pleistocene living-site at Olorgesailie in Kenya the subject of his doctoral dissertation, and subsequently became a leading advocate of the sharing hypothesis.

The idea of a home-base was a vital component of the sharing hypothesis, but Isaac acknowledged that home-bases were not the only feasible explanation of the fossil and stone tool assemblages uncovered at Olduvai, Olorgesailie and (subsequently) East Turkana. The bones and stones could have been washed together by water currents; they could have accumulated independently at different times; or they could have been brought together by other agencies. During the last years of his life Glynn Isaac was involved with a number of research projects that were specifically designed to test the validity of the sharing/home-base hypothesis (Bunn 1982; Potts 1982; Toth 1982), and the results of these studies have begun to suggest that the hypothesis may not be valid.

Investigations at East Turkana have indicated that early hominids employed 'an opportunistic, least-effort strategy' (Isaac 1981: 185) of stone tool manufacture and use (as at Olduvai, see p. 173), and in 1981 Isaac acknowledged that evidence of sites used for only brief periods, rather than as home-bases, would radically alter the scheme of early hominid lifestyle that he proposed (Isaac 1981: 186–7).

In 1982, Richard Potts completed a re-evaluation of the evidence from Olduvai Gorge which led him to conclude that the assemblages of fossils and tools found in the Gorge do not represent home-bases but are evidence of an antecedent stage in hominid social evolution (Potts 1984). He suggested that even the famous stone circle at the D K site is likely to be the product of something other than hominid activity. Water flow could have been responsible for the accumulation of fossils and tools, and the stone circle itself could have been produced by the roots of a large tree – which are known to be capable of penetrating and breaking up bedrock. Other assemblages at Olduvai could be interpreted as stone caches, representing an energy-saving strategy of leaving a supply of stone tools and raw materials at convenient locations in the foraging area, to which the hominids would carry meat (and other foods) for further processing, away from the attention of competing carnivores (Potts 1984: 345).

But while Potts was working on the Olduvai fossils in Nairobi, taphonomist Pat Shipman was also examining the collection, and she found evidence which appeared to support the sharing/home-base hypothesis. Taphonomists study the processes affecting the nature of fossil assemblages, and Shipman was trying to establish a method of distinguishing between the bones which hominids had eaten from and those which had been gnawed on by other carnivores, tumbled in rivers or otherwise damaged. In the course of this work, she noticed what looked like cutmarks on one bone, and then on another. Alerted by Shipman, Potts found similar marks on the fossils he was studying, and another researcher, Henry Bunn, found them on fossils from East Turkana. Subsequent analysis convinced all three workers that the marks on the Olduvai and East Turkana fossils had been made by hominids cutting meat from the bones with stone tools (Bunn 1981; Potts and Shipman 1981). 'This direct evidence of early hominid diet allows us to dismiss models of human evolution which do not incorporate meat-eating as a significant component of early hominid behaviour ... [and] ... lends strong support to the food-sharing model proposed by Isaac,' concluded Bunn.

When Shipman came to analyse the body parts represented by the cutmarked bones, however, she was surprised to discover that more than 50 per cent were non-meat-bearing: lower limb bones, for instance, which have virtually no meat on them, only skin and tendon. Shipman was also startled to find no evidence of cuts indicating that the hominids had dismembered carcasses and cut meat from the bone for carrying and distribution, as the home-base/food-sharing hypothesis would demand (Shipman 1984a: 9–10). These observations might have seemed to discredit the suggestion that the cuts had been made by hominids, but Shipman drew other conclusions.

The prevalence of non-meat-bearing bones among the cutmarked specimens indicated that hominids must have indulged in skinning and tendon-removal as well as meat-eating, she observed, recalling an earlier suggestion that tendons would be useful for tying bundles (Shipman 1981). And if the hominids were not dismembering carcasses and carrying meat back to a home-base, they must have been eating it on the spot – scavenging, in other words. In this way, a lack of evidence confirming the home-base hypothesis actually became the basis of a scavenging hypothesis that found much favour in the early 1980s (Lewin 1981, 1984; Bower 1985). But while Shipman expanded this idea into the proposition that scavenging was the ecological niche from which the ancestral hominids evolved (Shipman 1984b), evidence suggesting an alternative explanation of the cutmarks on the fossil bones from East Africa was accumulating at the base of a small limestone cliff near Cheddar Gorge in Somerset, England.

A young cow fell over the cliff in January 1977 and died. Being valueless and lying on an unfrequented track, the dead cow was abandoned by its owner and thus provided two anthropologists with an opportunity to record the details of its progressive disintegration over a period of seven years (Andrews and Cook 1985). The carcass was only minimally utilized by foxes, badgers, dogs and crows, but as it broke up, bones were kicked about and trampled by cows using the rough track. Subsequent examination of these bones under a scanning electron microscope revealed scratches no different from the 'cutmarks' found on fossil bones from Olduvai and East Turkana, though

in this case, of course, no stone tools had been involved, only trampling.

Further affirmation of the significance of trampling in bone marking
has also resulted from controlled experiments in the United States
(Behrensmeyer *et al.* 1986). Clearly, trampling is just as likely to
produce interesting marks on bones as stone tools are, or any of the
other agencies that Potts, Shipman and Bunn considered; hominids
need not have been involved.

The home-base, food-sharing, cutmarks and scavenging episode is
an interesting example of palaeoanthropology in progress. Shipman
has drawn attention to the dangers of relying on negative evidence; the
food-sharing/home-base hypothesis remains unproven, but the science
is, perhaps, a little more open-minded on the subject.

10

Homo habilis

(1964)

We have seen (p. 148) that in order to accommodate *Zinjanthropus boisei* within his scheme of human evolution Louis Leakey subjected both the interpretation of the evidence and his own preconceptions to some distortion. He claimed that the specimen resembled modern man more closely than it resembled the South African australopithecines, which even the most casual observer might have disputed, and he accepted the unseemly creature as a direct ancestor of man – which must have offended his notion of the antiquity of the pure *Homo sapiens* line. How ironic, then, that not many months after Zinj was proclaimed man's earliest ancestor, the excavations funded by Leakey's publicity campaign should have produced a more worthy candidate: a series of fossils that could be accommodated much more readily than Zinj within the Leakey scheme of human evolution. The fossils in question were found together with tools, some of them on living-floors even older than that on which Zinj was found. They were more lightly built in tooth and bones, and estimates of cranial capacity suggested that the fossils represented a hominid whose brain was large relative to body size (Leakey, L. S. B., *et al.* 1964).

Without undue embarrassment, Louis Leakey embraced the new evidence and returned to the comfort of his former beliefs. He promptly demoted *Zinjanthropus boisei* to the status of non-toolmaking aberrant offshoot from the human line and hailed the new discovery as the true maker of the Oldowan tools – an entirely new species of human being from which *Homo sapiens* had evolved in Africa (by way of Kanjera man) before migrating to Europe. The discovery pushed man's origins back another 1·25 million years, he said, and would require many experts to rewrite their textbooks because it proved that *Australopithecus* was not an ancestor of man but simply another hominid lineage that had existed at the same time, just as he had said all along. The new species was called *Homo habilis* – 'handy man'.

Scientists of the day were quite willing to accept Leakey's latest discoveries as further proof that Olduvai Gorge was 'the finest prehistoric site on earth . . . geologically and archaeologically sensational', and they did not dispute the 'immense value of his discoveries', but they found his interpretations open to question (Campbell 1964). Controversy ensued.

Of the fossils now attributed to *Homo habilis*, the first to be discovered were a tibia and a fibula (the bones of the lower leg) found on the Zinj living-floor at FLK. Like Zinj, they lay outside the area of concentrated remains and were unbroken. They were found some distance from the skull, several yards apart. At first it was presumed they had belonged to Zinj himself, even though they seemed too lightly constructed for a creature with a skull of such large proportions. And indeed, the presumption had to be revised when remains of similarly light construction were found at other sites.

The first came from FLK NN, a few hundred metres north of FLK (another site, FLK N, lay in between). The site was discovered quite fortuitously by Leakey's eldest son, Jonathan, then nineteen, who had just finished school and was helping at Olduvai. Wandering away from the main excavations at FLK on a fossil hunt of his own one day in May 1960, Jonathan found an unusual lower jaw on a nearby slope. Though not immediately recognized as belonging to a sabre-toothed cat (a rare find), the specimen was deemed interesting enough to warrant a brief search for more remains of the creature. The surface soil of the slope was sieved. Nothing more of the cat turned up, but a solitary hominid tooth and a single fingerbone were compensation with far greater promise. To locate the level from which the tooth and fingerbone had come, a step-trench 1.53 metres wide and six metres long (in total) was cut into the slope. On 13 June Jonathan found a hominid collarbone, followed a few days later by several fragments of a very thin hominid skull, all lying on what was clearly an occupation floor.

As the excavations were extended to left and right (eventually an area seventeen by 12.3 metres was uncovered), an interesting collection of hominid remains, artefacts and debris was revealed. Erosion had removed most of the floor some time before Jonathan chanced upon the cat's jaw; only the outer limits were left and, as with the area surrounding the 'windbreak' at FLK, the remains found upon it were mainly of the non-marrow-bearing variety. Among a total of 2,158 fossils, there were the ribs, vertebrae, shoulderblades and jawbones of pig and bovid, six catfish skulls and seventeen tortoise shells. Artefacts were not plentiful (only forty-eight are recorded), but hominid remains were scattered about the entire floor.

They comprise a curious assortment of bones and they were curiously distributed. Twelve associated footbones, for example, were found among a variety of ribs, vertebrae and the sundry remains of horse and bird. Six metres away, twenty-one handbones lay beside a pig's skull, and nine metres from the handbones, a piece of lower armbone lay beside a pig's jaw. Towards the south-western edge of the site, one toebone and one fingerbone lay in splendid isolation more than six metres from both the hand and the foot to which they may – or may not – have belonged. In the vicinity of the trial trench that had produced the collarbone and skull fragments already mentioned, Jonathan found more skull fragments scattered over a wide area: 4·3 metres separated the most widespread, and a left and right parietal bone, which together formed the central arch of a skull, lay three metres apart. A solitary mandible completed the hominid collection: this important specimen was found about two and a half metres from the left parietal bone, where it lay with an unidentified rib between two tortoise shells.

The FLK NN living-floor posed several intriguing questions concerning the content and distribution of the fossil collection Jonathan Leakey found there. Why was there such a strange assortment of bones? Why were they spread across the floor in such a curiously random fashion? The answers so far available are neither complete nor absolutely conclusive, but they demonstrate that modern palaeoanthropology is a multi-disciplinary affair, with a variety of independent scientific investigations adding their findings to the growing knowledge of our ancestors' predicament.

Geologists identified the stratigraphic level of the FLK NN living-floor and geochronologists determined that it had been occupied at least 1·7 million years ago. Archaeologists found the distribution of fossils similar to that pertaining at FLK, and felt it likely that, before erosion, the FLK NN floor had also borne evidence of a crude shelter. Palaeontologists identified animals that the occupants must have killed and eaten. Anatomists concluded that three individuals were represented among the hominid remains: they found parts of two adult left feet and decided that the parietal bones, handbones and mandible had all come from a single young individual, though this could not be proved.

The hominids had died of natural causes, anthropologists believed, suggesting the bodies had been left outside the FLK NN encampment when the rest of the group moved on, a procedure that has been recorded among modern people. Taphonomists believed the corpses were almost entirely devoured by scavengers. Some skull fragments and some footbones bore characteristic teeth marks, and the wide-spread scattering of the few remains was typical of hyena activity, for instance.

At first glance the hominid fossils from FLK NN seem ill-assorted and not especially revealing of early man's physical form. But in fact, together with the legbones from FLK, they constitute an extraordinarily comprehensive collection which has supplied a good deal of new information — just about all of which lent strength to Louis Leakey's belief that the remains represented the earliest ancestor of true man. Among the handbones, anatomist John Napier found evidence of at least two hands (one juvenile and one adult), an opposable thumb and the physical capacity to manufacture the Oldowan tools found on the living-floor (Napier 1962). From the footbones another anatomist, Michael Day, reconstructed an almost complete adult left foot; it was entirely human, with no sign of the ape's divergent big toe and every indication that its owner had stood erect and walked with a bipedal and free-striding gait (Day and Napier 1964). This is a view which a third anatomist, Peter Davis, confirmed in an independent study of the tibia and fibula from FLK (Davis 1964). In the mandible, Leakey found the front teeth relatively large and the cheek teeth relatively small; this was quite different from the australopithecines, he said, and quite appropriate for a new and distinct type of early hominid (Leakey, L. S. B., 1961). From the parietal bones and other fragments yet another anatomist, Phillip Tobias, reconstructed a skull and estimated its cranial capacity as 680 cubic centimetres, which was nicely beyond the australopithecine average and approaching the *Homo* range (Tobias 1964).

So the scanty remains from FLK NN appeared to represent a hominid with a relatively large brain, thin human-like skullbones, *Homo*-like dentition, manipulative hands and the ability to make stone tools – evidence which, together with the age of the FLK NN living-floor, most persuasively suggested that the new fossils must represent man's earliest ancestor. It seemed likely that, contrary to Leakey's earlier belief, Zinj had been an intruder – or a victim – at the FLK campsite after all. The evidence was surely more compelling than much around which Louis Leakey had constructed theories in the past, but this time he did not rush to publish his conclusions.

Brief descriptive announcements appeared, but they did not assign the fossils to any particular genus or species. The new species was finally announced in April 1964 (Leakey, L. S. B., *et al.* 1964), by which time several more specimens had been found at Olduvai. Among them, the end joint of a big toe hardly affected the contentions, but two skulls, an upper and a lower jaw held considerable corroborative value. The skulls were broken, but the bone was indisputably as thin as the FLK NN specimen and the cranial capacity appeared equally large. The dentition of the new and earlier finds was very similar. Perhaps even more important, the finds were seen to range from the base of Bed I to the middle of Bed II, a span of about three-quarters of a million years, during which time there appeared to have been very little change in physical form, implying that *Homo habilis* had been a successful and enduring species.

Furthermore, to add to the significance of the *habilis* fossils, classic *Homo erectus* remains were found in Upper Bed II, making them about 1·2 million years old. The first of these was a skull found by Louis Leakey himself, the only hominid fossil he ever found. For many palaeoanthropologists, Leakey's discovery of a *Homo erectus* skull represented the last link in the Olduvai story of human evolution: the sequence *Homo habilis–Homo erectus–Homo sapiens* made a perfectly acceptable evolutionary continuum. Some have also suggested that the presence of *Homo erectus* in Upper Bed II could explain the puzzle of the Acheulean culture that appears so suddenly in slightly earlier deposits (see p. 172). Were the handaxes brought in by *Homo erectus*? The fact that only tools of the Oldowan culture have been found with *Homo habilis* and the discovery in 1970 of *Homo erectus* skeletal remains alongside Acheulean handaxes (Leakey, M. D., 1971b: 380–83) are two points that Mary Leakey interprets as suggesting that *Homo erectus* may have been responsible for the Acheulean culture of Bed II. But while the suggestion solves one puzzle it raises another, one in which the evidence of fossils and culture appear to contradict one another. The point is this: if it is accepted that man evolved from the primal stock via a lightly built toolmaker, then the *Homo habilis–Homo erectus–Homo sapiens* continuum is eminently reasonable. But if *Homo habilis* with Oldowan tools evolved into *Homo erectus* with Acheulean tools, why do the two cultures not show a similar connection? Why should the Oldowan and Acheulean cultures be contemporary and quite separate in the Olduvai deposits if they are the products of an evolving hominid lineage?

The puzzle is still unsolved, but for Louis Leakey it never even arose. He had described *Homo erectus* as an aberrant offshoot from the human line long before the discovery of *Homo habilis*. In his view, the apparently conflicting evidence of the new skull (which was especially thick-boned) simply proved that three hominid lineages had existed at Olduvai: that is, the robust australopithecines (now that he had assigned Zinj to that group); *Homo erectus*, as represented by the latest find; and the species he regarded as the true ancestor of man, *Homo habilis*.

The advent of *Homo habilis* marked the first time that an assortment of fossil bones was used to define a new hominid species. Most, if not all, species until then were founded on the evidence of skulls or teeth demonstrably belonging to just one individual. The mandible from FLK NN could have supported the definition, but Leakey and his co-authors, Napier and Tobias, decided that the skull and handbones should be included, since they believed that the fossils all represented the same individual (something which could never be proved and therefore remains in doubt). So the remains 'of a single juvenile individual from site FLK NN Olduvai, Bed I' were presented as the holotype, or defining specimen, of *Homo habilis* (Leakey, L. S. B., *et al.* 1964). The footbones and other fossils were listed as paratypes, or examples of the same species included in the reference sample.

Leakey and his co-authors believed that *Homo habilis* represented a hitherto unknown stage in the course of human evolution, so they felt obliged and entitled to revise the standing definition of the genus *Homo* in accordance with their new evidence. This may seem an audacious step, but in fact the genus had never been more than provisionally defined (Clark 1964a: 86), and Leakey's proposals were more an extension than a revision of those already existing.

Most authorities believed that absolute brain size was the distinguishing feature of the evolving *Homo* genus and had variously proposed cranial capacities from 700 to 800 cubic centimetres as the size beyond which a hominid brain could be termed human. Leakey and his co-authors scrapped this notion. The *Homo* brain was highly variable in size, they said, and they proposed relative brain size as a more accurate indication of generic status. The most important factor, in their view, was that the evolving *Homo* brain was large in relation to body size. In respect of the other evidence, the new generic definition accepted skull shape, facial form and bipedal gait as previously given, while extending the list of dental characteristics and adding the opposable thumb as distinguishing features of the genus.

Following publication, *Homo habilis* was subjected to frequent reappraisal. It has been suggested that one of the handbones is a vertebral fragment, for example, that two may have belonged to an arboreal monkey, and that six came from some unspecified non-hominid (Oxnard 1972; Day 1976). But despite such inquiries, the evidence remains valid. Its significance, in fact, was never doubted; it was Leakey's interpretation that caused problems, mainly because he chose to stress differences rather than similarities and created a new species rather than squeeze the specimens into one that already existed. And then, most provocative of all, he reinforced his own conception of human evolution by calling the new specimen *Homo* instead of *Australopithecus*, which most others believed had stood on the path of human evolution at that point. His critics responded with complaints that the conventions of classification had been flouted (Campbell 1964); some said that the distinctiveness of the new species had been inadequately demonstrated (Clark 1964b; Robinson 1965); and others claimed there was insufficient 'morphological space' for another species between *Australopithecus* and *Homo erectus* (Campbell 1964). But at the same time, critics and supporters alike accepted the association of stone tools as evidence that the hominid Leakey had discovered was responsible for the Oldowan Culture and therefore qualified as a human ancestor; and all agreed that the enlarged brain was a significant step in the direction of *Homo sapiens*.

In essence, then, it was agreed that *Homo habilis* was an ancestor of man and, for those who believed *Australopithecus* had stood on the human line, the controversy had more to do with name than status. Was *habilis* the most advanced *Australopithecus* or the lowliest *Homo*, they asked? Given the difficulty of determining when one species becomes another on a lineage where evolution is presumed to be gradual, this purely academic question could never be answered. As the debate reached the correspondence columns of *The Times* even the anatomists Tobias and Napier confessed that the association of stone tools was the most convincing evidence of the affinities of *habilis* to the genus *Homo* (Tobias and Napier 1964). But such an assertion was hardly adequate. Classification is determined by morphology, not by inferred behaviour (Oakley 1964). And besides, Leakey had offered exactly the same argument as evidence that *Zinjanthropus* was an ancestor of mankind, and that claim had proved to be incorrect.

Acknowledging that the fossils needed a label, most authorities would probably have accepted *Australopithecus habilis*. Indeed, that label was applied (Pilbeam 1972: 135). But for Louis Leakey, of course, such a name was a contradiction in terms: he had never believed that *Australopithecus* was a human ancestor, while he had known since a boy that stone tools were made by the ancestor of man, who would be called *Homo*. Therefore in his view *Homo habilis* was the only name that could be applied.

More than a dozen specimens from Olduvai Gorge were attributed to *Homo habilis* in the twenty years following its description in 1964, and others were described from Sterkfontein and Swartkrans in South Africa, from the Omo in Ethiopia, and from the excavations directed by Louis Leakey's son Richard at East Turkana in Kenya (Wood 1987). The expanding collection did not resolve the issue of the species' status, however. Indeed, the stream of discoveries and attributions has been a major factor in delaying completion of the definitive monograph on the species which Phillip Tobias began working on in the late 1960s and which at the time of writing still awaits publication.

Meanwhile, commentators seemed to have agreed that *Homo habilis* as originally defined was too variable to be a sound species, though they differed on just how it should be split (Wood 1987). There were also differences of opinion concerning the functional abilities of *Homo habilis*. Morphological analysis of the legbones, footbones and handbones from Olduvai convinced Randall Susman and Jack Stern of the University of New York at Stony Brook, for instance, that although *Homo habilis* shared modern man's ability to walk upright and make stone tools, the species also shared the apes' characteristic of being able to climb trees with ease (Susman and Stern 1982: 933). This interpretation was greeted with some scepticism (not least because it was questionable that the hand and the foot they examined had come from the same individual), but the combination of ancient and modern features they defined was ideally suited to a species postulated as the link between the generalized morphology of an ancestor and the more specialized characteristics of a descendant.

At that time (1982), a majority of commentators agreed that *Australopithecus afarensis*, as described by Johanson and White in 1979 (see Chapter 12), stood close to the beginning of the hominid line, that *Homo erectus* was the most recent ancestor of modern humans and that *Homo habilis* was probably a link between the two. The fossils attributed to *Australopithecus afarensis* dated from 3.75 to 3 million years ago, and those of *Homo erectus* from 1.8 million to about 200,000 years ago, so there was a gap of some 1.2 million years in the fossil record during which it was assumed that *Australopithecus afarensis* had evolved into *Homo habilis*. A hominid that made tools and walked upright but still climbed trees to sleep, feed and escape from predators, as Susman and Stern conjectured, fitted this scheme of things perfectly. It was another case of evolutionary speculation filling a stretch of time from which morphological evidence was absent (see p. 156).

Mary Leakey continued to live and work at Olduvai Gorge through the 1970s and into the 1980s, but by 1984 life at the Gorge had become a battle for survival. Provisions were difficult to obtain and petrol supplies extremely erratic; at the age of seventy-one she handed over the camp and its facilities to the Tanzanian Department of Antiquities and moved permanently to the house she had kept in Nairobi (Leakey, M. D., 1984: 210).

Barely one year later, the Olduvai camp was occupied by a team of Tanzanian and United States researchers led by Donald Johanson and Tim White, two protagonists in the *Australopithecus afarensis* debate for whom Mary Leakey had very little sympathy indeed (see p. 215). The irony of Johanson and White taking over the Olduvai excavations from the Leakeys hardly needs comment, though it has generated plenty among observers in private. The team returned for the 1986 season, and on the third day of surface survey, Tim White picked up a piece of hominid armbone just off the track leading to the Zinj site. Subsequent excavations and sifting recovered nearly 18,000 fragments of fossil bone and tooth, including antelope, giraffe, hippopotamus, pig, baboon, reptiles, birds and hominids.

In total, 302 pieces of hominid fossil were recovered: fragments of skull, jaw and limbs representing a single individual who had died about 1·8 million years ago. In their announcement of the discovery (Johanson *et al.* 1987), the authors attributed the partial skeleton to *Homo habilis* on the basis of its skull and teeth, but pointed out that its postcranial anatomy was strikingly similar to that of *Australopithecus afarensis*. 'There's no doubt that it is *Homo habilis*,' Johanson commented later (Johanson 1987). 'This is the first time that limb bones and cranial material of *Homo habilis* have been found in definite association,' he went on. 'The result is a big surprise.'

The surprise was that the hominid represented by the new find, though indisputably adult and female, stood only thirty-six inches high, with hands hanging to her knees – just like the apes and the famous Lucy discovered by Johanson and his co-workers in Ethiopia thirteen years before (see Chapter 12). But the *Australopithecus afarensis* species to which Lucy belonged was at least 3 million years old, while the new *Homo habilis* dated from just 1·8 million years ago. This meant that the primitive ape-like characteristics of *Australopithecus afarensis* must have remained a distinctive and unchanging feature of the ancestral hominid for a very long time. The earliest humans were more like apes than had been supposed, it seemed, and if they had remained unchanged for so long, the subsequent adaptation to *Homo erectus* must have been completed between the time of the youngest *Homo habilis* and the oldest *Homo erectus* – just 200,000 years. White interpreted this implication of long-term stasis and abrupt change as evidence of stability in the *Australopithecus afarensis* adaptation. '*Australopithecus afarensis* was not poised on a razor edge between apes and humans,' he said; 'this adaptation lasted at least 2 million years, right up to the origin of *Homo erectus*.' According to Tim White, the new *Homo habilis* raised problems of interpretation only because 'people have viewed human evolution through the glasses of gradualistic change. Well,' he said, 'this fossil has smashed those glasses. The change was obviously abrupt, with a big modification in body form and between *Homo habilis* and *Homo erectus*' (White 1987).

Susman and Stern greeted the new Olduvai specimen as welcome proof of their contention that *Homo habilis* had been an accomplished tree-climber, but, whatever the specimen might do for the arboreal status of habilines, other assessments suggested that it confused rather than clarified the status of *Homo habilis* in the unfolding saga of human evolution. One authority believed that Johanson and White should have named a new species of hominid around the specimen and others from East Turkana (Hill 1987). Another asked 'Who is the "real" *Homo habilis*?', and said that 'the new find rudely exposes how little we know about the early evolution of *Homo*' (Wood 1987: 187).

It seems that more than twenty years of accumulating evidence and discussion have left *Homo habilis* more insecure than it ever was. While the species stood alone, a box of fossils separated from their putative ancestors and descendants by respectable distances in both time and morphology, its intermediate status seemed perfectly secure. Further evidence has filled in the temporal gaps and intensified discussion of the species' morphological characteristics, but it has yet to produce the basis of unequivocal fact on which a secure species must be founded. *Homo habilis* remains more of an idea in an evolutionary scheme than an example of anatomical fact linking one species to another. Only more evidence, and more rigorous analysis of early hominid variation, can resolve the question of its status.

During the 1970s, palaeoanthropology became less the pursuit of individuals, calling more and more for the collaboration of expert specialists. But at the same time, the public and the media continued to demand their scientific heroes. Richard Leakey was described as 'the organizing genius of modern paleoanthropology' (Pilbeam 1977). The research he initiated at East Turkana in northern Kenya was carried out by a large number of invited specialists. As scientist, Leakey played only a minor role, but undoubtedly he directed the investigations with extraordinary success. His background (some say his birthright) may have contributed to the East Turkana project's initial impetus, but its subsequent success was entirely due to Richard Leakey's ambition, determination and impressive administrative skill.

By 1979, Richard Leakey's ambitions extended beyond the search for early man (Leakey, R. E. F., 1979a) and he wanted the East Turkana Research Project to become less his personal enterprise. In this he hoped to promote a more impersonal trend in the science, whereby the predispositions of a discoverer (or expedition leader) could be lost, or at least diffused, while the fossils were studied by the appropriate experts.

But Richard Leakey was a public figure by then, and his public statements tended to overshadow his scientific utterances. He expounded his views fluently and frequently in magazines, newspapers, books and on television, so that despite his avowed conviction that less public and more impersonal scientific procedures should prevail, Richard Leakey personally became a celebrated champion of the theory of man's distant ancestry.

Like his father, Richard Leakey always believed that the ancestry of mankind is very long indeed, and that *Australopithecus* has played no direct part in it since the two lines split from the common ancestor about 6 or 7 million years ago (Leakey, R. E. F., 1979a). Others have championed the opposite view, saying that *Australopithecus* was the ancestor of mankind, and that the *Homo* and *Australopithecus* lineages split from a common ancestor little more than 2 million years ago. The primary evidence used to support the two theories was basically the same: fossils found at East Turkana and in Ethiopia. Each side interpreted the evidence differently, but the arguments were united by familiar undertones: each reflected preconception as much as interpretation and each revealed as much of the scientist as of science.

The field base-camp of Richard Leakey's East Turkana Research Project is situated on the shores of Lake Turkana, near a sandy spit called Koobi Fora. It is an oasis of comfort in a hot and windy wilderness. Water is the most important attraction. Only 100 metres or so separate the camp buildings from the lake, and from the shore, water extends to the horizon. The water is unpalatable and slimy to the touch because of its extremely high alkalinity, and it has to be shared with hippos and crocodiles. The cool sandy shore stretches away in the distance; flamingoes, pelicans and plovers congregate in large numbers. Zebras, antelopes and gazelles gather on the flats, the sun sets across the lake, the wind drops – it is a place of exceptional beauty.

The camp buildings are constructed with flagstones from the lakeshore and kept cool by the draught that circulates beneath the low thatched roofs. In the dining area there is always squash available, large pint glasses, ice in the fridge and a canvas watercooler hanging in the breeze. Essential supplies are brought by a lorry which constantly plies the rough five-day, 800-kilometre 'road' to and from Nairobi. Richard Leakey flies in for a few days whenever he can, bringing with him fresh meat, fruit and lettuce.

Leakey has made Koobi Fora a most desirable place, but it is only a base-camp. Scientists are likely to spend only the weekends here, a well-earned respite in which to soak up water, wash clothes and hair, after a week of work conducted from satellite camps where conditions are less congenial and where meals consist monotonously of corned beef.

Working conditions on the distant landscapes where the East Turkana fossils are found are probably among the most testing on earth. For an hour or so each morning and evening, when the shadows are long and the sky is a saturated blue, the temperature is comfortable.

For the rest of the day, however, the heat is overwhelming: bleached sky, burned vegetation, glaring reflections from burnished lava cobbles. And then there is the wind. An easterly gale blows most of the day, most days, and the best to be said of it is that conditions are far more uncomfortable when it drops. Everything radiates heat, and without the wind tiny sweat bees and midges cluster on the exposed damp skin. They whine about the ears and irritate body and mind.

In these circumstances it might be imagined that stress would arise between individuals. In fact, the sun and wind do not so much shorten tempers as exhaust everyone, creating silences around the tea table and in the casual moments when people usually chatter and gossip after a day's work. Scientists working from the satellite camps often feel unusually vulnerable: one said that he needed a long thick book to preserve his serenity.

Most of the East Turkana hominid fossils have been found by a group of Kenyans known familiarly as the Hominid Gang. Generally there are six of them and they scour the exposures six hours a day, six days a week, six months a year. They cover virtually every square metre of 800 square kilometres every year. In the eleven years up to 1979 (aided by the scientists who have occasionally accompanied them) they brought back more than 5,000 fossils. Of these, some 200 were hominid, of which less than twenty are whole bones, nine are reasonably complete skulls, thirty or so are mandibles in varying states of preservation and the rest are isolated teeth, skeletal and mandibular fragments. Hominid hunting is hard work.

Finding fossils at places like East Turkana is also an expensive business. In ten years Richard Leakey channelled more than $800,000 into his East Turkana Research Project. Government institutions and the more august bodies that fund scientific research do not rate the search for fossil evidence of human evolution very highly among their priorities, and initially Leakey found all his money elsewhere. The National Geographic Society gave him $25,000 in 1968; in succeeding years other foundations have contributed too and, all along, participating scientists have been required to find some independent funding for their travel and research. The East Turkana Research Project has shown that money is available for a wide range of investigations associated with the search for the origins of mankind. In some seasons a total of up to fifty specialists have worked at East

Turkana and for most of them the research was part of a personal academic programme. Their results have contributed significantly to the overall investigations at East Turkana, but dependence upon such individual research and piecemeal funding has hindered the development of the long-term programme.

If grants totalling $800,000 had been guaranteed when the project began, there can be no doubt that both research and results would have benefited. But such long-term planning was impossible. Grants were made irregularly and ran for just a few years; the National Geographic Society, for example, decided upon its contribution annually. Thus funding was most readily encouraged by short-term results and the prospect of more to come. In this respect hominid fossils were the most valuable result of the research at East Turkana, even though their scientific value depended heavily upon other, less colourful, investigations. So the search for more hominids became fundamental to each year's research programme at East Turkana, and Richard Leakey was obliged to find something interesting to say about each new discovery.

All scientists are obliged to report upon their investigations and most would like to reach the widest audience possible, but few are so fortunate in their subject as those studying the evolution of man. For one thing, the very nature of their investigations, *human* evolution, is bound to arouse popular interest; and palaeoanthropologists have not hesitated to take advantage of this.

The 'Missing Link' was a flag they waved for many years. There are enough 'Missing Links' in the popular record to merit their classification as a distinct species, but during the sixties and seventies they were superseded by the 'Oldest Man' as the image of palaeoanthropology that best caught the public attention. The advent of potassium/argon dating was the primary cause of the demise of the 'Missing Link'. The new process enabled scientists to determine the absolute age of fossils from suitable deposits and, since they turned out to be much older than anyone had thought likely, it was not surprising that the press releases stressed their age before the significance of any discernible evolutionary context.

Richard Leakey's 1968 season at Lake Turkana produced fossil remnants of extinct pigs and elephants 'about 4 million years old', and a few fragments of australopithecine jaw, poorly preserved but enough to strengthen Leakey's application for more funds with the suggestion that 'near-man had lived along the eastern shore of Rudolf [the nàme was changed to Turkana in 1974] between two and three million years ago' (Leakey, R. E. F., 1970a: 723). Further investigations 'would turn up further evidence of man's ancestry', he said, and the National Geographic Society responded with funds for another year.

The ages Leakey had attributed to these fossil fauna were educated guesses based on the evidence of other sites. The pigs, for instance, seemed older than those from Olduvai. In 1969, he determined that the age of his finds should be more accurately assessed as part of a geological and stratigraphical survey of the 800-square-kilometre deposits that would be undertaken by Kay Behrensmeyer, a graduate student of geology at Harvard University. Early in her endeavours, Behrensmeyer found some stone tools. She selected samples of the volcanic ashfall in which they appeared to have been embedded and dispatched them to Cambridge University for potassium/argon dating by Frank Fitch and Jack Miller. The first results included an age of 2·4 million years, which was enthusiastically celebrated at Koobi Fora (Leakey, R. E. F., 1970a: 725). Subsequently, further tests of additional samples caused Fitch and Miller to reverse their first estimate to a 'more accurate date of very close to 2·6 million years, plus or minus 260,000 years' (Fitch and Miller 1970).

Meanwhile, Leakey had found a complete hominid skull about fifty kilometres north of the tool site, and one of his Kenyan assistants found fragments of another – but different – skull nearby. According to Behrensmeyer's stratigraphic work, the hominid site lay below the geological horizon on which the tools had been found. In Leakey's estimation, the fossil fauna confirmed her correlation and so, he deduced, the tools and the hominids must all be at least 2·6 million years old. The oldest evidence of toolmaking known before had come from Olduvai, as we have seen, from beds dated at close to 1·9 million years old. So after his second season at East Turkana Richard Leakey could claim to have pushed the toolmaking phase of mankind back nearly three-quarters of a million years. Furthermore, his expedition had discovered two skulls as well – one magnificent, the other mysterious. The first was an undistorted version of Zinj, a wonderful specimen that was found, incidentally, ten years almost to the day after Richard's mother had found the original at Olduvai. There could be no doubt about its affinities: robust australopithecine. The second was incomplete, puzzling and, in the short term, more useful for that very reason.

Leakey referred to the mystery skull in *Nature* (Leakey, R. E. F., 1970b) and *National Geographic* (Leakey, R. E. F., 1970a: 731–2). Although the skull was too fragmentary to permit conclusive interpretation, certain things, wrote Leakey, were clear. There was not much of *Australopithecus* to be seen in it, and not much of *Homo* either; but he believed the slight morphological evidence of the latter was strengthened by the associative evidence of stone tools. It was generally agreed, he pointed out, that australopithecines had not made tools. Therefore a second hominid species must have existed at East Turkana. Was this it? If so, then the remarkable repetition of events at Olduvai might have seemed sufficient precedent, and *Homo habilis* might have seemed the obvious candidate for the East Turkana toolmaker as well. But Leakey could see little of *habilis* in the mystery skull either.

If not *habilis*, what was it? Could it be a prototype of *Homo erectus*, he wondered, making tools at East Turkana over 2 million years before appearing in Java and Peking? Richard Leakey believed it was quite possible. 'We will find the answer, I am sure,' he told *National Geographic* readers, 'for among the strata of the East Turkana desert lies a fascinating volume of prehistory, holding untold chapters of the origin of mankind . . . we have scarcely turned the first page, and I am eager to get on with the reading.'

Funds flowed, fossils too. In 1970 sixteen hominids were found, followed by another twenty-six in 1971. Among these were some important mandibles, a fragmentary half-skull (subsequently described as a female of the robust australopithecine lineage), some skeletal parts and some isolated teeth. Preliminary reports were published in *Nature* (Leakey, R. E. F., 1971, 1972a), but the 'mystery skull' was finally classified in the pages of *Social Biology*, where it was assigned to the *Australopithecus* lineage (Leakey, R. E. F., 1972b).

The next major discovery from East Turkana was the famous 1470 skull. The first scraps of it were found on 27 August 1972 by Bernard Ngeneo. Richard Leakey and Bernard Wood, an anatomist with the research project, joined the search and within days they had collected and assembled enough pieces to satisfy themselves that Ngeneo's find was the oldest, most complete hominid skull with a relatively large brain-case ever found. Many believe that large brain equals *Homo*; therefore 1470 was the 'Oldest Man'. An extensive area surrounding the discovery site was carefully sieved to ensure that all pieces that might belong to the skull were recovered. Richard's wife, the zoologist Meave Leakey, continued the reconstruction. Later she was joined by Alan Walker, another of the three anatomists on the project, and together they built a respectably complete skull out of about 150 pieces of the pile that had been recovered. There was a great deal left over. The reconstruction confirmed the first predictions: undeniably 1470 was a large-brained hominid. But Alan Walker saw affinities to the gracile australopithecines that he found equally undeniable. Large brain, yes; *Homo*, no. As far as Walker was concerned, 1470 was a large-brained representative of the *Australopithecus* line (Walker 1978).

Richard Leakey did not agree; nor did Bernard Wood. They acknowledged the distinctive australopithecine attributes of the specimen, but 1470, Leakey announced to *National Geographic* readers, represented the 'earliest suggestion of the genus *Homo*' (Leakey, R. E. F., 1973a).

Richard Leakey showed the skull to his father shortly before he died. The meeting was by way of a reunion that Richard remembers fondly. Relations between father and son had been strained for some time. 'He [Louis] was a sick old man at the end of his career,' Richard has said (Leakey, R. E. F., 1977), 'and he found my successes very difficult. I was not old enough or mature enough to respond to that adequately.' By unspoken agreement, they preferred not to meet. 1470 brought them together again and, indeed, showed that in science as in spirit there was never much separating them. Louis was tremendously excited by the skull. He believed it confirmed his views on the antiquity of true man, vindicated his Kanam find (see p. 139) and dismissed *Australopithecus* from the human line once and for all. If 1470 really was, as Richard believed, about 2·6 million years old, then, together with a robust australopithecine Richard had found at the same level in 1969, it seemed to prove that at least two hominid lines had existed at East Turkana well before the days of Zinj and *habilis* at Olduvai. Louis was certain there would be more. 1470 was one thing, he told Richard, the robust australopithecines were another and *Homo erectus* was yet something else; there will be others, he said, and you will find them.

But some of Leakey's contemporaries, notably Alan Walker, could not accept 1470 as *Homo*. This difference of opinion gives rise to two crucial questions. First, if both the large brain of *Homo* and the demonstrable affinities to *Australopithecus* are recognizable in a skull 2 million years old, does this not suggest that the two lineages are more closely linked than the Leakey theory of two distinct lines evolved from a very distant common ancestor allows? Perhaps there was only one line after all, along which *Australopithecus* evolved into *Homo* with 1470 representing an intermediate stage. Secondly, if *Homo* and *Australopithecus* were indeed two separate lineages, as Leakey claimed, and assuming human evolution was gradual and proceeded at a regular pace, then does not 1470's blend of distinctive *Homo* and *Australopithecus* features imply that the two genera had diverged from a common ancestor a relatively short time before, as the believers in mankind's more recent ancestry have proclaimed?

1470 is an outstanding specimen, and there can be little doubt that in an earlier scientific era it would have been presented as the archetypal 'Missing Link' and not many would have disputed its credentials. By September 1973, when Richard Leakey called a meeting in Nairobi to discuss the formal scientific description of the fossil, he had already introduced 1470 to the world as the 'Oldest Man', bolstering his personal belief in mankind's unique antiquity.

Foremost among those attending the Nairobi meeting were the three anatomists Bernard Wood, Alan Walker and Michael Day. In private conversation scientists have described the meeting as one distinguished by emotion and lack of harmony; the fact that different participants give different accounts of the proceedings must lend credence to this. The following is a synthesis.

As the anatomist most involved with the reconstruction of the skull, Alan Walker had undertaken and already completed the detailed, technical description of the specimen when the meeting was convened. He opened the discussions with a proposal that the title and preamble of the published paper should mention the australopithecine affinities he saw in the skull. Although all acknowledged that these existed (and the anatomists could all have made a case for them), Leakey and Wood insisted that the large brain was pre-eminent. 1470 was *Homo*, they said. Day remained non-committal.

In the ensuing debate Walker detailed the australopithecine affinities

(Walker 1973) and insisted that they merited nomenclatural acknowledgement regardless of brain size. Furthermore, the skull had been distorted during fossilization, he said, and the configuration of the right
side of the vault had been squashed into a deceptively *Homo*-like form.
But for Leakey and Wood, brain size was all that counted. As the debate warmed to argument with no concession from either side, Walker
resorted to persuasion of a more personal nature. If the published
description of 1470 was to include *Homo* attribution, he said, then his
name must be removed from the paper. This was no mean threat,
given Walker's academic standing and contributions to the science,
but it did not bring the capitulation he sought. Quite the contrary, in
fact, for the threat drew from across the table the injudicious remark
that his withdrawal might be welcomed. At this Walker picked up the
fossil and left the room.

After his departure, Richard Leakey decided to resolve the conflict
in the following manner: if Walker stayed away then 1470 would be
attributed to *Homo* without qualification; if he returned then Walker's
views would be accommodated, to some degree, in the paper. Walker
did return, and the paper was published with his name beneath the
innocuous title: 'New Hominids from East Rudolf, Kenya' (Day *et al.*
1975). The preamble refers to the preliminary accounts in which
Leakey – personally – had attributed the specimen to *Homo*, while
making it clear that detailed comparative studies (which would determine what the skull should be called) were not yet complete.

The worldwide admiration and congratulation that greeted the
twenty-eight-year-old Richard Leakey and his two-and-a-half-million-
year-old 1470 were not entirely unanimous. Within the science, there
was serious doubt about the fossil's age. On the basis of palaeontological evidence, Canadian geologist Basil Cooke suggested that
1470 was not as old as Leakey claimed; that it might, in fact, be only
1·8 million years old and therefore no older than *Homo habilis* from
Olduvai Gorge. Cooke's suggestion (Cooke 1973) was widely supported. By September 1973, when Richard Leakey convened the
meeting at which the fossil's attribution was discussed, he was beginning to realize that interpreting the significance of 1470 seemed to
depend more upon accurate determinations of its geological, stratigraphical and geochronological status than upon its anatomical
detail.

It is particularly difficult to achieve absolute accuracy when dating hominid fossil levels. This is partly because the deposits in which hominid fossils are found are, in geological terms, relatively young. They are therefore nearer the surface and much more likely to be contaminated with extraneous material of a quite different origin – and age.

The intrinsic problems of dating young deposits were further compounded at East Turkana by the manner in which the fossil beds had been formed, and re-formed. The ash and pumice originally came from volcanoes and fissures; they variously settled in the ancient lake, were eroded or were transported by streams and rivers. The lake level rose and fell; geological faulting uplifted some parts and caused others to subside. The sequence of deposition (the stratigraphy) is nowhere easy to determine, and relating the stratigraphy of one area to another is even more difficult.

All in all, then, giving an accurate absolute date for the East Turkana fossils was fraught with problems: there was room for error at every turn. Nowhere was this more clearly demonstrated than in the case of the KBS tuff (KBS stands for Kay Behrensmeyer Site, the spot where the tools were found), a layer of solidified volcanic ash designated as a 'marker' in the stratigraphic determinations and a reference-point against which many of the important fossils are dated, including 1470.

Fitch and Miller's tests on the first samples of the KBS tuff that Leakey sent to Cambridge actually gave an average age of 221 million years (Fitch and Miller 1973: 132). Such an age was impossible: clearly the sample must have been contaminated, so Leakey sent more samples. From these the scientists selected crystals that seemed fresher than others (Hall 1974) and produced an age of 2·4 million years. Later they adjusted this to 2·6 million plus or minus 260,000 years (Fitch and Miller 1970). But the work on the KBS tuff did not stop there. Fitch and Miller subsequently tested many more samples (including some they had collected themselves) and their results ranged from a minimum of 290,000 years to a maximum of 19·5 million.

The scientists were not embarrassed by this apparent imprecision. They were perfecting a complicated technique and developing another that they hoped would give greater accuracy. They expected discrepancies and endeavoured to identify the cause; that is how experimental science proceeds. The trouble is that palaeoanthropology is an interpretative science which depends upon expensive research and publicity-conscious palaeoanthropologists found the 'Oldest Man' a most valuable asset in their quest for funds. So when a fossil appeared to have achieved that status, the potassium/argon date upon which it was based tended to receive far greater emphasis than the experimental techniques justified.

The potassium/argon process is undoubtedly an important aid to the study of fossil man, but it is not a final arbiter. Its validity is very much contingent upon other factors: geology, stratigraphy and chemistry, for example. And furthermore, it is only one of several ways by which the antiquity of fossils can be assessed, and its concordance with other assessments is fundamental to the validity of any particular potassium/argon date. Where it conflicts there is likely to be something wrong.

The KBS date conflicted with certain palaeontological evidence, which cast doubt upon the 'Oldest Man' status of 1470. And naturally enough, perhaps, the East Turkana research team was at first more concerned with defending the antiquity of the fossil than with objectively investigating the question of its age. Palaeomagnetic investigations (relating the shifts of the earth's magnetic field as revealed by the magnetic properties of the rocks to a geochronological scale) were instigated to support the evidence for 1470's age, and the fossil thereby acquired an age of close to 3 million years (Brock and Isaac 1974: 344–8). But more objective observers were unconvinced. Opposition grew, especially among palaeontologists familiar with the faunal evidence of the region, and when Cooke presented his report on the fossil pigs of the Turkana Basin (Cooke 1973), the counter-evidence became irresistible.

Cooke had studied the pig fossils from the Omo and East Turkana. The sites are only about 150 kilometres apart; the fossil fauna is generally similar, so it would be reasonable to expect that the sequence of fossils found in the beds at one site would be the same as the sequence found at the other. And indeed it was: Cooke was able to trace an identical line of evolutionary development in the pigs at both the Omo and East Turkana. Now, according to the precepts of palaeontology, it should follow that identical ages could be attributed to the beds in which the identical fossils had been found. But when he came to place the evolving pig lineages side by side on the scale of their potassium/argon dating, Cooke found that identical fossils seemed to differ substantially in age. For instance, the data on one of the pigs, *Mesochoerus*, suggested that the KBS tuff at East Turkana should be about the same age as the bed known as Member F at the Omo, whereas the radiometric date said it was 600,000 years older. 'The discrepancy is considerable and cannot be ignored,' wrote Cooke (1973: 261).

The implications of the discrepancy were serious. If the KBS tuff was 600,000 years younger than had been deduced from the Fitch and Miller age determinations, then everything dated in relation to it was that much younger too. The tools, for instance, were no older than those found at Olduvai, and 1470 was no longer the 'Oldest Man' but simply an extremely well-preserved contemporary of *Homo habilis*.

Some responded to Cooke's findings, naturally enough, with the suggestion that the Omo dating must be wrong. However, this was hard to support, since the Omo sequence is particularly well defined. Furthermore, both the potassium/argon dates and the fossil fauna (including the pigs) agreed with the ages given for Olduvai Gorge, which are exemplary.

Leakey and his supporters soon realized that if their belief in the unique antiquity of 1470 and other finds associated with the KBS tuff was to stand, then the inconvenient evidence of the pigs had to be accommodated. Pig-proof helmets were an early suggestion which raised a laugh. Some mirth also greeted the more seriously intended proposition that although the fossil pigs at first seemed 'an embarrassing discrepancy between geophysics and palaeontology', they might turn out to be 'an exciting glimpse of the existence of prehistoric mosaics of spatial and ecological differentiation between the faunas of adjacent but environmentally contrasting regions' (Isaac 1976: 6).

In plain language, this proposal suggested that perhaps the Omo and East Turkana pigs had evolved quite independently and at different rates. Having inherited the identical evolutionary impetus from their common ancestor, the two populations were somehow completely isolated from one another and, for some reason, proceeded along their identical paths of evolutionary development at quite different rates. Thus, the idea went, the East Turkana pigs could have reached the *Mesochoerus* stage 600,000 years before their cousins 150 kilometres away at the Omo. This process would conveniently account for the age difference between identical specimens, but the barrier that kept the pigs apart for so long and evolving at such different rates was not so easy to envisage. The problem exercised the imaginations of several very earnest scientists. Islands were proposed, both aquatic and ecological, which arose very suddenly and trapped the East Turkana pigs in unique conditions that hastened their evolutionary development.

Though these attempts to explain the pigs' age discrepancy were not as frivolous as they may seem, Richard Leakey quickly realized that something more substantial was required. The 2·6-million-year date for the KBS tuff had meanwhile received another blow from Garniss Curtis at the University of California, Berkeley, a pioneer of the potassium/argon process whose tests on KBS samples confirmed Cooke's assertions and contested the findings of Fitch and Miller. Curtis dated the KBS tuff at 1·8 million years (Curtis *et al.* 1975).

While noting that critics of the East Turkana research team's age estimates were willing to believe a single report from Curtis before a whole series from Fitch and Miller, and were prepared to accept the word of one geologist, Basil Cooke, before that of an entire multi-disciplinary research team, Richard Leakey countered the attack on the dates he and his collaborators preferred with another, grander study of the fossil pigs of Africa. Leakey hoped the results would prove Cooke wrong (Leakey, R. E. F., 1979a) and the study was instigated with that objective in mind, but even were it to dismiss the estimate of 2·6 million years or more for the KBS tuff, he preferred to be proved wrong by his own efforts rather than by someone else's (Leakey, R. E. F., 1979a).

The new study was undertaken by palaeontologist John Harris and physical anthropologist Tim White, and amounted to a complete review of all the fossil pigs from fifty African sites south of the Sahara (White and Harris 1977). They reduced the number of genera from twenty-three to seven and the number of species from seventy-seven to sixteen. They recognized the evolutionary trends shown especially well in some species and confirmed the value of these fossils in correlating geological sequences.

They then applied their finds to the evidence of the Omo, East Turkana and Olduvai. The results confirmed all Cooke's conclusions. In their view as well as his, the pigs convincingly showed that the age

assigned to the KBS tuff was 600,000 years older than the palaeontological evidence implied. Discussing the implications of their
findings on the study of fossil hominids, Harris and White concluded
that the pigs showed that 1470 was 'essentially' the same age as *Homo
habilis* at Olduvai (1977: 20).

In the light of further age determinations from a number of laboratories using a variety of methods, Richard Leakey conceded that
earlier pronouncements on the age of 1470 (and the other fossils dated
by the KBS tuff) were wrong. He suggested 1·8 million years as the
age of the tuff itself, and something between 1·8 and 2 million years as
the age of 1470, which was found below it. But if the earlier estimates
were wrong, what caused the error? Richard Leakey blamed the dating
procedures employed by Fitch and Miller (Leakey, R. E. F., 1979a);
Fitch, on the other hand, wondered if the material his team had dated
was actually representative of the KBS tuff (Fitch 1979). Repeated
tests on the samples confirmed the older dates, he said, suggesting
that they may have been collected from a tuff thought to be part of the
KBS but actually part of an older level. Leakey and others denied this,
arguing that the KBS tuff was unmistakable.

The KBS tuff dating controversy showed that modern palaeoanthropologists are no less likely to cling to erroneous data that
support their preconceptions than were earlier investigators (both
Dubois and Leakey dismissed objective assessment in favour of the
notions they wanted to believe), but more significantly, perhaps, it
showed that dating discrepancies are as likely to reflect errors of
geology as of geochronology, and underlined the observation that
accurate geological and stratigraphic determinations are crucial to the
interpretation of fossil evidence.[¹]

This work has since been completed at Lake Turkana. A series of
reports on the geology, stratigraphy and chronology of the Turkana
basin has correlated the sequence and age of the deposits at Koobi
Fora, Omo and West Turkana (Brown *et al.* 1985), and the KBS tuff
has been firmly dated at 1·88 plus or minus 0·02 million years (Mc-
Dougall 1985).

The relevance of 1470 in the study of fossil man transcends the
controversy that flared around determinations of its age, and the
significance of the East Turkana fossil collection is not touched by the
interpretations that have been imposed upon them. In the first eighteen

years of work at East Turkana, researchers assembled a large and diverse assortment of hominid (and other) fossils – skulls, jaws, teeth, limb bones (Leakey, M. G. and R. E. F., 1978) – from a discernible timespan and expanded the context of the science beyond recognition. Some cherished beliefs have been demolished. The simple and appealing single species hypothesis, for instance, expired on the eastern shores of Lake Turkana in 1973 (Cartmill *et al.* 1986: 416), when fossils unquestionably belonging to *Homo* were found in deposits which had also contained *Australopithecus* remains (Walker and Leakey, R. E. F., 1978). *Homo erectus* (see p. 49) and *Australopithecus boisei* (see p. 155) specimens found on the west side of Lake Turkana have both provoked reconsideration of long-standing ideas about their species' status in the story of human evolution. The work goes on, gradually confirming a view that the story of early hominid evolution is probably a good deal more complex than has been thought.

Australopithecus afarensis

(1978)

If a medal were struck commemorating achievements in palaeo-anthropology during the 1970s and 1980s it should have the head of Richard Leakey on one side and that of Donald Johanson on the other. Such close proximity separated by a few millimetres of solid metal would illustrate their achievements, their affinities and their mutual antipathy admirably. They are both ambitious, clever and energetic men who achieved success in their late twenties and early thirties, that time of life when energy and ambition are most aggressively combined. They both directed expeditions which discovered important hominid fossils, but they hold opposing views on the status of those fossils in human evolution. This difference of opinion is suffused with personal animosity, which television and the popular press have whipped up into a grand old scrap. The 'Battle of the Bones', *Life* magazine called it (Kern 1981), though it is entirely a battle of personalities. The bones have been passive throughout.

While Richard Leakey was working at East Turkana, Donald Johanson contributed substantially to the success of international expeditions that between 1973 and 1977 found 250 hominid fossils in deposits exposed along the ravines and tributary valleys of the Hadar river in the Afar region of north-eastern Ethiopia. More fossils might have been found in following years, but Ethiopia's internal strife made further exploration impossible.

The Afar fossils are all about 3 million years old and the extraordinary variety of bones and teeth is said to represent a minimum of thirty-five and a maximum of sixty-five individuals. The most famous has become known as 'Lucy' and comprises roughly 40 per cent of a complete skeleton. Another large collection of bones from a single site, known by its museum reference number, 333, and sometimes referred to as 'The Family', includes a minimum of thirteen adults and juveniles. This is the first discovery of fossils that might represent a 'population' of early man. In the first announcements of these remarkable discoveries, Johanson and his colleagues suggested there were three species of hominid among the Afar fossils: a small one, which they thought might be *Australopithecus africanus*; a large one, which could have been *Australopithecus robustus*; and a third, which they thought might represent *Homo* (Johanson and Taieb 1976). And, of course, fossil remains of *Homo* dated at 3 million years old would also represent the 'Oldest Man'.

The fossil deposits of the Afar region were first noted by the French geologist Maurice Taieb in 1967, while he was working there on research for his doctoral dissertation. The Afar, a fractured depression in the earth's crust, is of great interest to geologists because it links the African Rift Valley to the rift systems of the Red Sea and the Gulf of Aden. It is known as a geological hotspot and has supplied important information on plate tectonics and the origins of the continents.

Part of the Afar depression is below sea level. Here and there hot sulphur springs bubble as active reminders of the earth's internal stirrings, which about 4 million years ago caused lava to erupt from surface fissues and flooded basalt across the Afar. The basalt subsequently became the floor of a lake basin, which in turn filled with the clays, sands, gravels and silts brought down by rivers and streams from the surrounding highlands. These sediments settled and consolidated on the lake beds at a rate of about one centimetre every ten years, filling the entire basin in the relatively short period of barely 1 million years and presenting Taieb with a rugged terrain to explore in 1967. By then, of course, the sediments had been tilted and broken by geological faulting and rivers had sliced through them. One such river is the Hadar, which, as it carries the seasonal flood from the high land down to the larger Awash river, has gouged a meandering channel up to 140 metres deep through the sediments, exposing in its banks and ravines the fossilized remains of the many creatures which lived and died on the shores of the ancient lake.

In 1971 Taieb and Johanson worked together on the joint French, American and Kenyan expedition to the Omo, from which Richard Leakey defected to East Turkana (see p. 154). They talked of the Afar and in 1972 Taieb took Johanson there to assess the palaeontological potential of the region. It was a brief trip, squeezed between their commitments to that year's Omo expedition, but none the less, Johanson and Taieb found substantial quantities of splendidly preserved fossils of extinct animals suggesting that the beds were up to 3 and perhaps even 4 million years old, predating Olduvai Gorge and East Turkana and therefore a likely repository of fossils representing earlier stages of mankind's evolution. Johanson realized immediately that the Afar presented a unique opportunity in the search for human origins. 'It was like a dream within reach,' he has said. He drew up plans with Taieb for a major research expedition to explore the region in 1973.

Don Johanson was born in Chicago in 1943; his parents were immigrants from Sweden, his father a barber, his mother a cleaning lady. In 1966 he completed his undergraduate course with a distinction in anthropology and embarked upon a study of chimpanzee teeth for a master's degree. Simultaneously, he began teaching anthropology and set his mind upon the search for early man as an ultimate ambition. 'But the fossil man game is like being an astronaut,' he recalls; 'there aren't many of them. Actually finding the fossils is only for very few, and when you're a graduate student in Chicago the prospects seems as far away as Jupiter' (Johanson 1978). And indeed, while Maurice Taieb was discovering the fossil beds of the Afar in 1967, Don Johanson was in Alaska, helping to measure teeth for someone else's anthropological study. But fossils and human evolution drew closer. He undertook an *Odontological Study of the Chimpanzee with some Implications for Hominid Evolution* for his Ph.D and in 1970 was invited to join the Chicago group on that summer's Omo Research Expedition.

Johanson's job on the Omo expedition in 1970 (and again in 1971 and 1972) was palaeontological excavation. He and his co-workers cleared up to eight metres of overburden from over 500 square metres of fossil-bearing deposits. Most of the excavations were inspired by the discovery of hominid fragments on the surface, but none fulfilled the initial promise. Of the 11,781 vertebrate fossils the team found, fewer than forty were hominid (Johanson *et al.* 1973). There was one mandible, one lower armbone, four matching skull fragments and twenty-four isolated teeth. Most of the Omo fossils, in fact, were of baboons, crocodiles and ruminants. None the less, Johanson gained valuable experience in the Omo, and a valuable introduction to Maurice Taieb.

The first International Afar Research Expedition (IARE) under the joint leadership of Yves Coppens, Donald Johanson and Maurice

Taieb began work in the late summer of 1973. At first it seemed destined to follow the familiar pattern: weeks of mapping geology and stratigraphy; collection and cataloguing of nearly 6,000 fossils of some forty different vertebrate species – but no hominids, not even a single tooth. Until 30 October when, late in the afternoon, as his party was completing the survey of a small gully, Johanson found four pieces of hominid legbones, two of which belonged together and formed a perfect knee joint. The fossils came from deposits over 3 million years old. The individual of whom they formed a part had been a small adult, but unquestionably he or she had been fully capable of walking upright. Johanson had found the earliest conclusive evidence of mankind's bipedalism.

The promise of this discovery was confirmed the following year (1974). Within a week of the I A R E establishing its camp on the banks of the Awash, Alemeyhu Asfaw (seconded from the Ethiopian Antiquities Department) found a fragment of hominid jawbone with two teeth still in place. The next day Alemeyhu found another, more complete specimen, and then another. And the day after that the site foreman, Melissa, found yet another. 'Unbelievable,' Johanson later reported, 'in three days, four hominid specimens, representing four individuals' (Johanson 1976: 801). The most remarkable of these was a palate with all sixteen teeth still in place. It was remarkable not only because of its splendid preservation but also because of its combination of primitive and modern features. The front teeth were large relative to the back teeth, as in modern man, but there was a gap between the canines and the incisors, as in the apes; the teeth rows were parallel rather than curved and the palate was shallow, all primitive features reminiscent of the chimpanzee, in Johanson's view. He believed that such a combination of ape- and man-like features had not been encountered before and arranged to announce the discovery at a press conference in Addis Ababa.

The fossils were introduced to representatives of the world press as 'an unparalleled breakthrough in the search for the origins of man's evolution'. In a prepared statement the I A R E team claimed: 'We have in a matter of merely two days extended our knowledge of the genus *Homo* by nearly 1·5 million years. All previous theories of the origins of the lineage which leads to modern man must now be totally revised. The genus *Homo* was walking, eating meat and probably using tools to kill animals' 3 to 4 million years ago and probably already had 'some kind of social cooperation and some sort of communication system', the statement declared (Johanson 1974).

The Addis announcement read rather more into the evidence of one and a half palates, two half mandibles and a knee joint than most authorities were willing to accept; and the IARE's claim that they had discovered the 'Oldest Man' was soon countered by Richard Leakey, who pointed out that evidence of a relatively large brain was required before fossils could be assigned to the genus *Homo*.

Johanson returned to the field. Around midday on 24 December he noticed a fragment of armbone poking from a slope he was casually exploring with a colleague, Tom Gray. At first sight it could have been a monkey bone but, though small, it lacked the characteristic flange of the comparable part of a monkey. 'My pulse was quickening,' Johanson later wrote: 'suddenly I found myself saying, "It's hominid".' There were more fragments higher up on the slope and then: 'the realization struck us both that we might have found a skeleton. An extraordinary skeleton . . . The searing heat was forgotten. Tom and I yelled, hugged each other, and danced, mad as any Englishman in the midday sun' (Johanson 1976: 793).

The slope was sieved extensively during the following three weeks. Many more pieces of hominid bones were recovered, including skull fragments (but not enough to reconstruct a brain-case), a mandible, most of a left and right arm, several vertebrae, a number of rib fragments, the sacrum, the left pelvic bone, the left thighbone and some pieces of the right lower leg. In all, about 40 per cent of an entire skeleton. The form of the pelvic bones showed that the individual had been female, and erupted wisdom teeth suggested she had been about twenty years old, but the size of the thighbone made it clear that she had been very small – no more than 122 centimetres tall, and perhaps as short as 107 centimetres.

The Afar skeleton features in the IARE field collection specimen list as: A.L. 288–1 Partial Skeleton. But this formal title extends only to the academic journals; everywhere else – in conversation and in print – the specimen is known as Lucy, from the Beatles song 'Lucy in the Sky with Diamonds', which the camp tape recorder frequently broadcast across the Afar deposits, though the name chosen by

Ethiopians working with the expedition is a better token of the fossil's status: 'Denkenesh', meaning 'you are wonderful'.

Lucy was the star of a press conference held in Addis Ababa at the end of the 1974 season. But Johanson was cautious on the question of her attribution, saying only that she was either 'a small *Homo* or a small australopithecine', which inspired a reporter from the *Washington Post* to comment that Johanson's team 'refused deliberately to say that the skeleton belonged to the genus *Homo* . . . They are trying to avoid further controversy with Richard Leakey . . . who has contested their claims to have found specimens of early man in the absence of crania' (Ottoway 1974b).

Given the success of the IARE in 1973 and 1974, the following year might have been expected to be an anti-climax, but in fact 1975 was no less successful. 'I felt I was moving through a dream,' Johanson recalls; 'each day produced more remains', including some of the oldest remains of the genus *Homo* ever unearthed. And not just a few fragments, but pieces enough to identify men, women and children – perhaps a family – who had died together 3 million years ago. The find was unprecedented: the earliest group of associated individuals ever found (Johanson 1976: 801).

In all, the trove comprised 197 hominid fossils – jaws, teeth, legbones, scores of handbones and footbones, vertebrae, ribs, adult skull fragments and part of an infant's skull. It was a disproportionate collection, but a minimum of thirteen individuals, young and old of both sexes, appeared to have been buried together at the site. Maurice Taieb speculated that they had died together too, perhaps caught in a flash flood while sleeping in a riverbed. This explanation has been repeated by Johanson on several occasions (Johanson 1979; Johanson and Edey 1981), but it is not popular with other experts. Richard Leakey has suggested that the band may have succumbed to a particularly virulent disease (Leakey, R. E. F., and Lewin 1977: 90); Alan Walker has proposed a carnivore assemblage wherein the bones were remnants of a leopard's meals, perhaps, dropped from a tree into a waterhole below, where they sank into the mud and were fossilized (Walker 1978). But however the bones arrived where the IARE found them, Johanson was certain they represented the genus *Homo*, were over 3 million years old and were conclusive evidence, therefore, of the 'Oldest Man'.

In a *National Geographic* article entitled 'Ethiopia Yields First "Family of Man"', Donald Johanson described the Afar fossil hominids as 'discoveries that are writing new chapters in the annals of early man research'. He resigned Lucy to her australopithecine affinities, but quite unequivocally assigned the 'family' fossils to the genus *Homo*. And upon what evidence was his judgement based? Well, there was the dental evidence already noted, and in general the bones were larger than Lucy's, said Johanson, and there were features among them that were very much like *Homo*. The footbones, for instance, closely resembled those of modern man, and the handbones could be combined with modern bones to reconstruct a completely modern hand. Unhappily, there were no skulls to provide the evidence of a relatively large brain that critics might call for; but among the Afar fossils Johanson did find a lower jaw that he was certain would fit 1470 (Johanson 1976: 809) – Leakey's claimant to the title of 'Oldest Man'.

In 1974, while the IARE were still gathering their evidence of *Homo* in the Afar, apparent confirmation of the attribution came from a distant and perhaps unexpected source. During a Christmas picnic that year, Mary Leakey and her son Philip found a number of hominid fossils at Laetoli, the fossil beds near Olduvai she and Louis had visited many years before. The new fossils were from deposits over 3·5 million years old; they included several isolated teeth, a juvenile mandible and one adult mandible which bore a striking resemblance to the specimens found at Afar, 2,000 kilometres away and at least half a million years younger.

At an early opportunity Mary Leakey and Donald Johanson met to compare the Afar and Laetoli specimens side by side. Given the distance separating the fossils in both space and time their overall similarity was astonishing. Mary Leakey and Johanson agreed that among the larger specimens, *Homo* affinities were dominant. In her *Nature* report (Leakey, M. D., *et al.* 1976) on the Laetoli discoveries, Mary Leakey wrote: 'preliminary assessment . . . suggests placement of the Laetoli specimens among the earliest dated members of this genus.' Some critics preferred to emphasize the specimen's australopithecine affinities (which undeniably are present), but Mary Leakey argued that since *Australopithecus* became extinct while *Homo* survives, any fossils with distinct *Homo* features must be assigned to the surviving lineage: *Homo*. The inference, of course, is that the Laetoli specimens represent the 'Oldest Man'.

Because Mary Leakey considered herself an archaeologist and not qualified to write the formal description of fossils for publication, she asked Tim White, the physical anthropologist who had worked at Laetoli, to undertake the task. White knew Johanson, who was then similarly engaged with the description of the Afar material. Because of the general similarity between the two collections some discussion between White and Johanson was obviously helpful to both, and perhaps rendered it inevitable that the Laetoli and Afar fossils were subsequently grouped together in a publication (Johanson *et al.* 1978; Johanson and White 1979) which assigned all the material to a new hominid species.

When she invited White to describe the Laetoli material, Mary Leakey was confident there were two species to be named. The Laetoli specimens were all *Homo* in her view, and even her critics seemed to agree that the large and small specimens from Afar must represent two distinct species. However, when Johanson, White and their French associate, Yves Coppens, began to analyse the fossils and compare them with other collections, they found themselves forced to reject conclusions that had previously seemed obvious in favour of 'exciting new possibilities', as Johanson has written in a popular report (Johanson 1979). To cite one among several points: although Lucy was small enough to be a representative of *Australopithecus africanus*, equally small individuals among the 'family' would stand out as anomalies if she were classified as such. Clearly it was unlikely that two distinct species would have existed within the confines of one family group. The anomaly disappeared, however, when Johanson, White and Coppens concluded from their analytical studies that only one species had existed at Afar and at Laetoli. The individuals from both sites were morphologically identical, they said, and the size variation was due entirely to sexual dimorphism – very large males and very small females – within a single species. But the degree of sexual dimorphism seemed quite exceptional, remarked other commentators; how could it be explained?

In living primates sexual dimorphism is least among the smallest species and most among the largest – which is the gorilla. The Afar hominids were demonstrably smaller than the larger living primates, yet their sexual dimorphism as proposed by Johanson and White appeared to exceed that of the gorilla, a point raised at an informal seminar in Nairobi when White presented the conclusions of the I A R E studies to members of the East Turkana Research Project.

ALAN WALKER (anatomist): If the degree of sexual dimorphism is outside the modern range, then you must justify your reasoning.

TIM WHITE (physical anthropologist): It's simplest to have only one species in the family collection, so . . .

WALKER: Numerical simplicity is not necessarily the truth.

RICHARD LEAKEY (Director, Kenya National Museums): Have you done sufficient study and measurements to convince us?

WHITE: Our scheme elucidates . . .

ANDREW HILL (palaeontologist): Obscures!

WHITE: We recognize a significant . . .

HILL: How do you know it's significant if you haven't quantified?

WHITE: From my experience!

WALKER: You need to be just a little more precise . . .

LEAKEY: It's my feeling that you are guilty of imposing what you think is right upon the fossils.

WALKER: It might be nice to put the numbers down.

WHITE: Sure! There'll be someone with red-hot water-cooled calipers to provide the measurements you want, but we're trying to understand the evolution and biology – not just catalogue the fossils.

LEAKEY: Well, we think that chances are that you've got it wrong.

(Reader 1978)

In their understanding of the evolutionary significance of the Afar and Laetoli fossils, Johanson and White concluded that the blend of *Homo* and *Australopithecus* they found within the single species must imply that it had been ancestral to both. So what should it be called? At the generic level they might have been inclined to call it *Homo*, as Johanson had done originally, and as Mary Leakey preferred. But there was no evidence of the relatively large brain that distinguishes the genus *Homo*, while the fossils did have many characteristics in common with the gracile australopithecines.

The evidence, they concluded, demanded attribution to the genus *Australopithecus*. At the specific level, they felt several features (the more primitive teeth, for instance) merited distinction from the known species of *Australopithecus*, so they created a new one for their fossils:

Australopithecus afarensis (Johanson *et al.* 1978). As type specimen of
the new species Johanson and White chose the adult mandible from
Laetoli, which, though less well preserved than a similar specimen
from Afar, had already been described by White (1977), and thus
Australopithecus afarensis acquired a maximum age of about 3·7
million years. The evolutionary scheme that Johanson and White
presented with the new species was a single, straight and slender stem
with *Australopithecus afarensis* at the bottom and *Homo sapiens* at
the top. One short truncated branch was provided along which
Australopithecus africanus evolved from the main stem into
Australopithecus robustus and subsequent extinction. Johanson and
White believed that *Australopithecus* was the only hominid line for a
very long time, from which the *africanus* stock diverged about 2·5
million years ago, while the genus *Homo* arose even more recently
with the advent of *Homo habilis* about 1·9 million years ago. The new
scheme, though simple, was all-embracing. Within it, *Australopithecus
afarensis* became not just the ancestor of *Australopithecus* and
mankind but also of virtually every hominid fossil ever found.
Australopithecus and *Homo*, *africanus* and *robustus*, *habilis*, *erectus*
and *sapiens* – all owed their origin to *Australopithecus afarensis*, including, of course, the most important example of large-brained *Homo
habilis*: 1470.

'Yippee,' wrote White to Johanson with the final draft of their
afarensis manuscript, 'tell them to start up their armchairs and fasten
their seat-belts. We're on our way!' This exhortation referred to
members of the scientific community, who White felt were likely to
question the validity of the new species.

Australopithecus afarensis was the first new hominid species to be
created around original fossils since Louis Leakey had named *Homo
habilis* fourteen years before; Johanson and White gave careful
thought to the question of where and how it should be announced.
For a while Johanson favoured a carefully coordinated press campaign, but in the end he reserved the announcement for the occasion
of a Nobel Symposium on Early Man held in Sweden under the
auspices of the Royal Swedish Academy during May 1978, and
Australopithecus afarensis remained a close secret until Johanson read
his paper. The new species was hardly better known when he had
finished. The paper was long and not easily followed; its import

probably escaped most of the audience. The invited authorities on early man noticed *afarensis*, of course, but their response was not clamorous. As the assembly adjourned for tea Richard Leakey remarked that he did not like it very much, and Phillip Tobias suggested that perhaps sub-specific distinction would have been adequate – something like *Australopithecus africanus tanzanensis* ... Subsequently, however, response to the new species was considerable and sustained. Comment was favourable at the popular level, where *afarensis* inspired a book, a television 'special' and several articles, but less favourable within the science.

Apart from quibbles about taxonomy and the flouting of convention (Day *et al.* 1980) that seem to greet the naming of every new species, the scientific criticism centred around two points: first, the validity of grouping the Afar and Laetoli material together as one species – many felt the fossils represented at least two species; and second, the question of whether or not the material was distinctive enough to justify a new species – could it not have been assigned to existing species of *Homo* or *Australopithecus*?

After due consideration, anatomist Phillip Tobias concluded that *Australopithecus afarensis* was invalid on both counts (Tobias 1981). At least fifteen cranial, mandibular and dental features that Johanson *et al.* had cited as diagnostic of the new species were also present in *Australopithecus africanus*, he told a meeting of the Royal Society in March 1980, and therefore were not diagnostic at all. *Australopithecus afarensis* should be formally suppressed, Tobias demanded, and the fossils renamed with no more than sub-specific distinction based on geographical distribution: *Australopithecus africanus aethiopicus* for the Afar fossils and *Australopithecus africanus tanzanensis* for the Laetoli specimens (Tobias 1981: 47). In the ensuing discussion, however, Tobias was reminded that the International Code of Zoological Nomenclature prohibited such suppression. Once in existence, *Australopithecus afarensis* could not be simply wished away.

Mary Leakey's reaction to the new species was restrained on the whole (1984: 180–84). She did not agree with the White and Johanson conclusions, and when told that the announcement of the new species would include her name among its authors she demanded that it be removed (Leakey, M. D., 1978). At the Royal Society meeting, she questioned the validity of assigning specimens from localities more than 1,000 miles apart to the same species, and said that including the Laetoli hominid specimens in a new species of *Australopithecus* did 'nothing to clarify one of the most important issues in the study of man's evolution' (Leakey, M. D., 1981: 102). Informally, she reiterated her conviction that the Laetoli fossils and the large specimens from Afar should be assigned to *Homo*, and expressed deep regret that 'the Laetoli fellow was now doomed to be called *Australopithecus afarensis*'.

Richard Leakey did not agree with the new species either. With Alan Walker he attacked the scheme of hominid evolution that Johanson and White had constructed (Leakey, R. E. F., and Walker 1980) and in his personal capacity insisted that Johanson had been correct in his very first interpretation of the Afar fossils as *Homo* and should not have changed his mind (Leakey, R. E. F., 1979b). There were two distinct species among the Afar and Laetoli collections, he said, one of them an ancestor of *Homo* and the other an ancestor of *Australopithecus*. Which in Leakey's view proved that the two hominid lineages had co-existed in the Afar basin 3 million years ago, just as they had at East Turkana one and a half million years ago. Richard Leakey, in fact, regarded the evidence of Johanson's Afar fossils as proof of his belief that *Homo* and *Australopithecus* are no more closely related than cousins who shared an ancestor in the very distant past, some 6 or 7 million years ago (Leakey, R. E. F., 1979a).

Just as Leakey's fossils from East Turkana could support Johanson's belief that mankind had recently evolved from *Australopithecus*, so Johanson's fossils from the Afar could support Leakey's belief that *Homo* and *Australopithecus* had been distinct lineages for a very long time. Each, it appeared, had found the evidence to substantiate the other's theory. The fact that the evidence could sustain alternative interpretations raises another point: where would the science stand today if, for argument's sake, Leakey had worked at Afar as well as East Turkana? Or if Johanson had likewise worked at both sites? With the same fossils to hand, one or other of them would presumably claim his beliefs doubly affirmed, and the quantitative value of the fossils from two widely separated sites might persuade many that the evidence substantiated those beliefs.

During the early 1980s, the science has accepted *Australopithecus afarensis* as a valid species. Detailed analysis of the dental morphology of the Laetoli and Hadar material published by Tim White (1985: 138–52) has convinced many authorities that the fossils represent one and the same species of hominid, but not all agree. Yves Coppens, a co-author of the original *afarensis* paper, now believes there are two species (and possibly more) represented at Hadar and Laetoli (Coppens 1983); Todd Olson, of the City University of New York, takes a similar view (Olson 1985).

An account of the Leakey, Johanson and Lucy saga (Lewin 1987c) concludes with a comment from David Pilbeam of Harvard University which also makes a fitting conclusion to this chapter: 'no position [in the argument] is overwhelmingly strong, which probably means that there simply isn't enough fossil material available to allow a fully objective assessment.' Pilbeam goes on to point out that as discoveries and analysis bring palaeoanthropologists closer and closer to the point in time at which the ape and hominid lines diverged, it will become increasingly difficult to distinguish the human ancestor from the other (or others) that evolved from the split on the basis of their morphology, simply because they will all look very much alike. It is when such objective uncertainty arises that subjective preconceptions exert their greatest influence (Pilbeam 1987: 299).

Whatever its ambiguities, the evidence from Afar, East Turkana and Laetoli tidily confirmed the hypothesis that hominids had stood up and walked erect long before the brain achieved any great size (Leakey, M. D., and Hay 1979). Just when brain expansion began and what its precise significance was during the early stages of man's evolution from the ancestor he shares with the apes were matters of speculation, though the majority had long believed that bipedalism came first. Now this was confirmed. The new evidence showed that while the brain of *Australopithecus afarensis* was barely larger than that of an ape of comparable body size (a chimpanzee, for example), the creature was fully capable of walking upright. Thus, if *Australopithecus afarensis* represented the ancestor of man, the habitual bipedal gait had assuredly preceded brain expansion in man's divergence from the common ancestor. It would seem that contrary to the assertions of Grafton Elliot Smith and others (see Chapter 4), it was not the brain but the feet which had led the way after all.

Of course, the claim that man's bipedal gait was an early acquisition had been around for some time before then. In the eighteenth century Jacob Bontius, a Dutch doctor living in Java, even credited the orang-utan with this peculiarly human trait. These creatures, he observed, 'generally walk upright and behave much like other people'. And, as we have seen (Chapter 3), the name *Pithecanthropus erectus* reflects Dubois's belief that the Java Man he discovered in 1891 had stood erect. Similarly, in 1925 Raymond Dart deduced from the evidence of the Taung skull that *Australopithecus* was capable of erect posture and bipedal gait; and in the 1930s and 1940s Robert Broom found fossils which, he claimed, fully confirmed Dart's deduction. Peking Man and his relations from Java were eventually named *Homo erectus*. In 1960 Louis Leakey claimed that *Zinjanthropus* possibly held his head 'even more erect than in man's carriage today' (Leakey, L. S. B., 1960b: 434) and in 1964 the *Homo habilis* footbones from Olduvai

Gorge were said to possess 'most of the specializations associated with the plantigrade propulsive feet of modern man' (Leakey, L. S. B., *et al.* 1964).

But while these assertions may have reflected a common belief that the early ancestors of mankind had been able to stand erect and move about on two legs, the belief was not unqualified. A curious reluctance to believe in the *perfection* of early man's bipedal gait persisted for a long time. For many years the misinterpretation of Neanderthal Man's arthritis, for example, contributed to the idea that although early man may have walked upright, he could do so only in a shambling bow-legged fashion. This view was reinforced by the pronouncements of Boule and Elliot Smith, and without evidence to contradict the eminent gentlemen such notions became points of faith to their followers. Even the skeletal remains found by Robert Broom brought no complete change of attitude. The trouble with Broom's fossils was that although their overall appearance indicated an upright stance and bipedal gait, the detail was uncertain, lost in the peculiarities and the distortions of the fragmented fossils. And where the evidence was uncertain, even scientists appeared predisposed to believe that the mode of locomotion was not entirely human. In reviewing the evidence of the South African fossils the anatomist Wilfred le Gros Clark, for instance, concluded that erect bipedalism in the australopithecines 'had not been developed to the perfection shown in *Homo sapiens*' (Clark 1964a: 162).

The *Homo habilis* legbones and footbones were much more complete than the evidence Broom had offered, but even they were said to be less than adequate to propel their owner in a fully modern human manner. The structure of the *habilis* foot fell somewhere between that of man and gorilla in its weight-bearing capabilities, the preliminary report said, and certain peculiarities of the anklebone in particular suggested that 'the unique striding gait of *Homo sapiens* had not yet been achieved' (Day and Napier 1964). The size and shape – the form – of the Olduvai anklebone was subsequently compared with 131 other human, ape and fossil anklebones in an exhaustive study which took the measurements of seven angles and indexes of functional significance, combined them in a computer and analysed the results. This study (Day and Wood 1968) was a notable example of the then popular canonical analysis, a multivariate statistical technique exploiting recent advances in computer technology. Its results precisely confirmed the earlier conclusions based solely on personal experience and contemplation of the evidence: 'whilst the Olduvai Hominid 8 foot is the foot of a biped,' the new report said, 'the striding gait of modern man had not yet been achieved.' Meanwhile, another anatomist, P. R. Davis, was analysing the 'functional implications' of the *habilis* legbones. The tibia and fibula (the lower legbones) were preserved and although the upper parts were missing, the evidence of the remainder – the robusticity factor, for example – suggested that the adaptation to bipedalism was well advanced at the ankle but less so at the knee. This study also concluded that 'while the fossil form was clearly an habitually bipedal plantigrade primate, its gait may well have differed considerably from that of modern man' (Davis 1964).

These conclusions on the bipedal status of *Homo habilis* echo views expressed by Wilfred le Gros Clark, who believed that as the ancestor of mankind had evolved from quadruped to biped, the adaptation would have commenced at the foot and ended at the hip (Clark 1967b: 43), so that fossils representing an intermediate stage of mankind's evolution could be expected to demonstrate intermediate adaptation to bipedalism. And *Homo habilis*, therefore, could be expected to have stood with ankles 'somewhat flexed, suggesting a rather bent-kneed posture', as one authority surmised (Pilbeam 1972: 140).

But if early man did not employ the bipedal plantigrade propulsive gait of modern man, how did he walk? The fossils themselves could not provide the answer to this question, for although measurement and comparative analysis could indicate competence in certain known functions, they could not define a completely unknown function, even where scientists may have believed the fossils were capable of performing one.

Pondering the nature of this unknown function, Sherwood Washburn suggested that perhaps the ancestors of mankind *ran* on two legs before they were able to walk easily that way, and subsequently acquired the efficient bipedal striding gait only in response to a need to cover long distances (Washburn 1960). And Richard Leakey envisaged that several methods of bipedalism must have arisen in the course of human evolution, quite apart from the modern variety. He did not define them, however, and confined them to *Australopithecus*

(Leakey, R. E. F., 1978), who, he believed, employed 'a locomotor pattern unique and distinctive' to himself during the Lower Pleistocene times, while the true ancestors of mankind were already as fully upright and bipedal as *Homo sapiens* (Leakey, R. E. F., 1972c:387).

In the absence of conclusive evidence, speculation on the nature of early man's gait proliferated, but it was halted by new evidence of an unusual but wholly appropriate kind – evidence of function rather than form: fossil footprints rather than fossil feet or legs. These earliest-known footprints of man were discovered in 1977 during the course of Mary Leakey's expedition to Laetoli in search of more fossils. Natural erosion had exposed a trail of five prints set in a cement-like volcanic tuff laid down at least 3.6 million years ago. The trail was not as clear and conclusive as it might have been. Only two prints were fully exposed and some experts argued that they were not hominid prints at all. Mary Leakey herself was '75% certain' they represented the tracks of mankind's earliest ancestor; but by emphasizing the non-human quality of the ancestor's stance and stride, announcements of her discovery demonstrated a continuing reluctance to accept the antiquity of bipedalism. *Time*, for example, reported that the creature 'probably walked with what Leakey calls "a slow rolling gait", like a chimpanzee's' (*Time* 1978).

But while one group of experts sought to deduce the gait of early man from the logic of evolutionary theory, and another from the evidence of fossils , yet a third approached the subject from a related but essentially different direction: biomechanics, a discipline which attempts to assess the limits and potential of the skeletal frame and musculature and define the mechanical requirements of movement and locomotion. And here the work of an American anatomist and anthropologist, Owen Lovejoy, is especially relevant.

Early in his career Lovejoy worked on the excavations of an Amerindian (American Indian) burial site about 1,000 years old, and the study of the skeletons that were recovered there has been an important component of his researches ever since. The collection is unique. It represents over 1,300 individuals and spans burials during a period of between 200 and 250 years. The remains of males and females of all ages are preserved, including several foetuses, one of which fits on the palm of the hand. Some skeletons demonstrate strange physical deformities, others appear to exceed the 'normal' limits of the human form. In all, the collection presents a convincing example of the extraordinary degree of variation to which the human skeletal frame is susceptible; in particular, it shows very clearly that living bone is a plastic material which can be moulded to suit the demands of behaviour and anatomy. Where anatomy is normal and behaviour is not unusually demanding, the skeletal frame functions in a consistent manner, subject only to the variations of size and muscular development. But disease or broken or distorted bones may force the skeletal frame to function quite differently; and the bones may assume unusual shapes as they grow and are moulded to suit the abnormal function. Thus, although the style and mechanics of man's movement and locomotion are potentially consistent throughout the species, the detail may vary considerably. It therefore follows that morphological variations in the form of the bones are not necessarily indicative of functional variation. Nor are they necessarily indicative of taxonomic distinction. The Amerindian collection on which Lovejoy works undoubtedly represents a population belonging to the species *Homo sapiens*, yet it includes many unusual bones that would probably have been assigned to a different species, or even a different genus, if they had been discovered as individual fossils.

This apparent contradiction lies close to Lovejoy's belief that shape and form are not enough to reconstruct the pattern of function. Isolated features of the components vary much more in their shape and size, he says, than does the function they perform. Feet, ankles, shinbones, knees, thighbones, hip joints, and pelvises may vary enormously, together and individually, but whether the variation actually prevents the body they support from walking with the bipedal propulsive plantigrade gait of *Homo sapiens* is another question. And to find the answer Lovejoy and his associates have sought to place the fossil evidence of the early hominids' lower limbs in their biomechanical perspective, seeking to discover not how closely they resemble the *form* of modern man but rather to what extent they were capable of performing the *function* of walking like him.

The answer, to summarize the published results (Lovejoy 1973; Lovejoy *et al.* 1973; Lovejoy 1975), is that the early hominids were probably better adapted to bipedalism than modern man. The biomechanical pattern of their lower limb skeleton differs in one significant respect: the articular ball of the hip joint in *Australopithecus* exerts only half the pressure on the joint that was the average for the *Homo sapiens* sample. This is a considerable mechanical advantage, reflecting the manner in which body weight and the stresses of bipedal locomotion are distributed in the australopithecine pelvis. The distance of the hip joint from the centre of gravity is the most important feature, and in *Australopithecus* the distance is such that it permits a smaller femoral head (the ball of the hip joint) than in *Homo*, and a longer femoral neck (the extension at the top of the thighbone which carries the femoral head), which in turn provides a more efficient lever arm for the muscles that operate the hip joint. Both the small femoral head and the longer femoral neck of *Australopithecus* have been cited as evidence that the physical form of *Australopithecus* was not fully adapted to the upright bipedal gait (Leakey, R. E. F., 1973a:828). Lovejoy's work now shows that these features were integral components of a pelvic structure that was stronger and functionally more efficient than the pelvis of modern man. But if our ancestors really were more advantageously adapted to bipedalism, how did we lose the advantage? According to Lovejoy, the regression of bipedal efficiency was inevitably combined with the advance of the other most critical factor in mankind's evolution: the development of a large brain.

As the brain and the innovative processes it inspired (the manufacture of stone tools, perhaps) brought survival advantages to those best able to use it, enlargement of the brain through successive generations was constrained only by the size of the pelvic opening, the birth canal. Clearly, there would have been immediate natural selection against the combination of large-brained infant and small birth canal (both mother and child would have died during birth) and in favour of females with large birth canals through which large-brained offspring could pass into the world. For a time the progressive enlargement of the brain could have been accommodated by a progressive broadening of the hips, but there is a limit to the total pelvic breadth that can be maintained in a biped of any given stature, beyond which rapid locomotion becomes awkward and striding efficiency is lost (Lovejoy *et al.* 1973: 777). So as babies with increasingly large heads were conceived, their birth was most satisfactory − both in terms of maternal ease and species evolution − where the size of the birth canal had increased while the overall breadth of the pelvis remained unchanged. This adjustment could be achieved only by the shortening of the femoral neck, thus disturbing the structural and mechanical efficiency of the pelvis, doubling the weight stress on the articular ball of the hip joint and rendering modern man less favourably adapted to bipedalism than his ancestors.

The large brain may have become the survival tool of the species, but far from leading the way to our present status, as many have surmised, its development actually appears to have compromised our earlier and more fundamental evolutionary asset: the habitual upright stance and striding bipedal gait. The compromise is evident in several aspects of modern life: the greater incidence of hip joint failure in women than men demonstrates their closer proximity to the limits of pelvic structural and functional capability. By comparison with the foetal development of other mammals the human infant is born six months early so that the relatively large head may pass through the birth canal. Even so, the head is severely squashed during birth, and the bones of the skull may overlap as it is squeezed through the pelvic opening. And of course many difficult births, especially among those achieved by Caesarian section or with the aid of forceps, are instances of the evolutionary conflict between brain size and bipedalism that natural selection would resolve more drastically in the absence of modern medical practice.

Lovejoy investigated the biomechanics of the lower limb in the early 1970s, at a time when the available fossil evidence was limited to specimens from South Africa and Olduvai Gorge. His hypothesis was essentially complete by 1973, when, in March, Richard Leakey announced the discovery at East Turkana of an almost complete fossil left leg (Leakey, R. E. F., 1973b, c) and, in October, Donald Johanson found a knee joint at Afar. The anatomical evidence of the 1·8 million-year-old East Turkana fossils and the 3-million-year-old specimen from Afar supported Lovejoy's biomechanical deductions, but it was equivocal. The evidence undoubtedly proved that hominids had walked erect at those times, but Richard Leakey, for instance, claimed that the East Turkana specimens were proof that only the ancestor of man 'walked erect as his normal mode of locomotion'. *Australopithecus* had walked differently, he said, its longer femoral neck implying that although the creature was capable of walking upright, it did so only for short periods (Leakey, R. E. F., 1973a:828).

This assertion underlines the inadequacy of fossil *form* as conclusive evidence of bipedalism. Proof of Lovejoy's assertion concerning bio-mechanical *function* was ultimately supplied by the fossil footprints discovered by Mary Leakey's Laetoli expedition – not so much by the trail already mentioned as by another uncovered in 1978 which inspired Mary Leakey to ask: 'Now who needs fossil bones to substantiate bipedalism? They're superfluous. Absolutely superfluous.'

The preservation of fossil prints at Laetoli is due to an unusual and possibly unique combination of climatic, volcanic and mineralogical conditions (Leakey, M. D., and Hay 1979; Leakey, M. D., and Harris 1987). Not less than 3·6 million years ago a series of light ash eruptions from a volcano called Sadiman coincided with a series of rain showers, probably at the onset of the rainy season. The eruptions contained a significant amount of natrocarbonatite, which yielded carbonate on contact with the rain. This substance then cemented the ash layer quite solidly as it dried in the sun. Evidently a profusion of animals crossed the ash layers while they were still wet, leaving their tracks to be preserved and then protected by further showers of ash and rain. The succession of showers created at least six distinct surfaces on which prints are preserved; all together they are no more than 15·6 centimetres thick. Raindrops are clearly defined on some surfaces, hare prints are present on virtually all of them, guinea fowl prints are numerous, as are the prints of small antelopes and gazelles. In all, over twenty different animals have been identified, including giraffe, elephant, rhinoceros, pig, hyena, baboon, the three-toed horse and, of course, bipedal hominids.

The fossil footprints at Laetoli were not recognized until the end of Mary Leakey's 1976 expedition, even though scientists and research workers had regularly walked across some of them on their way to and from the fossil beds during two full seasons. But, of course, those expeditions were inspired by the hominid fossil discoveries mentioned in Chapter 12, and the participants were intent on looking for fossils and defining the geology and stratigraphy of the region. The fossil beds were dated at between 3·59 and 3·77 million years during that time; a good collection of vertebrate fossils was assembled, but hominids were few. Some mandibular fragments and isolated teeth were found in 1975, and fragments of a juvenile skeleton in 1976 – but that was all. After a promising start it seemed as though the Laetoli potential was exhausted. The deposit in which the fossils are preserved is extremely hard and specimens that do erode from it are often fragmented by the sun and rain, especially the delicate hominid fossils, But, as already noted, the beds were uniquely suited to the preservation of footprints.

In a manner which matches the fortuity, if not the consequence, of Archimedes' bath and Newton's apple, the fossil footprints were eventually noticed one evening in September 1976 by the palaeontologist Andrew Hill, who fell while avoiding a ball of elephant dung hurled at him by the ecologist David Western. The two were paying a visit to the Laetoli camp at the end of the season; their walk that sunny evening took them along a dried river bed in which an expanse of solidified fine-grained volcanic tuff was exposed. Elephants apparently frequented the area, and the ecologist's familiarity with the evidence of their passing thus lent a new angle to the palaeontologist's eye. While on his knees, Hill noticed a curious spattering of tiny indentations in the flat grey surface. These were later identified as raindrop prints but, having attracted Hill's attention that day, they led him to examine the surface and other indentations very closely. Among them he recognized a quite unmistakable series of animal tracks.

Thereafter, Hill's fortuitous fall imposed a new outlook upon the Laetoli expeditions. During the final weeks of the 1976 season, footprints of birds and mammals ranging from elephant and rhinoceros to carnivores and hares were identified. In 1977 and 1978 seven sites were found where the footprint-bearing surfaces were well exposed by natural erosion and weathering. Mammal and bird prints occurred everywhere, including the first inconclusive hominid trail (which was actually close to where Hill had suffered his fall), and another, undeniably hominid trail which was uncovered in 1978 and 1979.

The latter discovery comprised not just one but two trails. The first evidence of them was found in July 1978, when a biochemist, Dr Paul Abell, noticed a hominid heel print at the broken edge of an erosion gully. Skilful excavations that season and the following year uncovered two trails nearly fifty metres long, transected by other mammalian trails, fractured by subsidence here and there, but traceable throughout. The trails are parallel and about twenty-five centimetres apart, too close for the individuals to have been walking abreast. In any case, there is a noticeable difference in the clarity and condition of the two trails which suggests that the individuals had crossed the ash at different times as it was drying. The prints of one trail are smaller and more splayed than the other; at one point the smaller individual seems to have paused and made a half turn to the left. Where the trail is exceptionally well preserved, yet another series of hominid prints seems to be set in those of the larger trail, as though a third individual had walked in the other's footsteps.

The Laetoli footprints are entirely human. Unlike the form of the ape footprint, they show a well-developed arch to the foot and no divergence of the big toe. The size of the feet and stride suggests the larger individual stood about 140 centimetres tall, and the smaller about 120 centimetres. They were slight figures in the ancient land-scape, but whether they be called *Australopithecus* or *Homo*, there can be no doubt that the Laetoli hominids had already acquired the habitual, upright, bipedal, free-striding gait of modern man 3·6 million years ago. The hypothesis of bipedal precedence was confirmed. No one could argue against the Laetoli evidence of function quite as easily as they had against the evidence of fossil form, though they would have to think again about the function and development of culture in the earliest stages of human evolution.

Ever since Darwin's day, commentators had supposed that once man's hands were free to develop manipulative skills, stone tools would have been an immediate consequence of bipedalism (immediate on the evolutionary scale, that is). It was said that tools were probably a critical factor in the initial divergence of the hominid line from the ancestral stock of man and ape. Yet although hominids were bipedal and free to develop manipulative skills at Laetoli 3·6 million years ago, not a single artefact or introduced stone has been found anywhere among the eighty-square-kilometre deposits. The earliest tools known to date are about 2 million years old. Hominids, it seems, were walking erect with their hands free for at least 1·6 million years before the advent of stone tools. For the greater part of our evolutionary history the human ancestor was no more advantageously endowed to cope with the vagaries of nature than any other creature.

We can conclude from this that for millions of years the com-bination of zoological inheritance and environmental circumstance was quite enough to ensure the survival of those small, lightly-built animals of erect posture. Then some among their number perceived the value of the cutting edge and discovered how to reproduce the rare accident that created it. They began making stone tools. That event marked the beginning of culture, no less a product of inheritance and circumstance than any other development in the 3,000 million years that life has existed on earth, but one that distinguishes man from every other creature and has led us so far from the pristine world that we can even look back and contemplate our origins.

ACKNOWLEDGEMENTS

Two people inspired the first edition of this book. The first was Mary Leakey, who advised and encouraged me when I was planning it. The concept changed somewhat during the two and a half years I worked on the book, but Mary remained a constant source of information and advice throughout. She read the first draft, and contributed to the improvement of the second. Her help, kindness and hospitality, at Olduvai Gorge and at Laetoli, are very much appreciated.

The second source of inspiration was my wife, Brigitte, who sought and collected papers both obscure and recent, translated some technical French and German, maintained a system of filing and retrieving information and occasionally displayed more confidence than I secretly thought the project deserved. Such special support was invaluable.

Delving into the science again for this expanded and updated edition of the book has been a pleasant as well as a productive experience, assisted to no small extent by conversations and correspondence with David Pilbeam, Andrew Hill, Sally McBreaty, Chris Stringer, Robert Kruszynski, Peter Andrews, Chris Dean, Tim Bromage, Bernard Wood, Andrew Chamberlain and Roger Lewin. My thanks to all.

I also remain indebted to the organizations and individuals listed below, without whose assistance and cooperation the original research and photography could not have been contemplated. I imposed myself upon some institutions for several weeks, on some individuals for no more than a cup of tea – but every contact contributed to the book in some way, and I am especially grateful for the kind patience with which my inquiries were treated. I have tried to be accurate and to ensure that my own opinion, where expressed, is clearly distinguishable from that of the relevant authority. If I have failed in any instance the responsibility is entirely mine, and I offer my apologies.

American Museum of Natural History, New York.
Bernard Price Institute, Johannesburg.
British Museum (Natural History), London.
Cleveland Museum of Natural History, Laboratory of Physical Anthropology.
Dubois Collection, Rijksmuseum van Natuurlijke Historie, Leiden.

Geologisch-Paläontologisches Institut der Universität, Heidelberg.
The International Afar Research Expedition.
Koobi Fora Research Project, Kenya.
Laboratoire de l'Anthropologie, Musée de l'Homme, Paris.
Laetoli Research Project, Tanzania.
The London Library.
National Geographic Society, Washington.
National Museums, Kenya.
Olduvai Gorge Research Project, Tanzania.
Palaeontological Institute, Uppsala.
Rheinisches Landesmuseum, Bonn.
The Royal Society, London.
The Royal Swedish Academy of Sciences.
Senckenberg-Museum, Frankfurt-am-Main.
Transvaal Museum, Pretoria.
*University of California: Department of Anthropology and Department of
    Geology and Geophysics*, Berkeley.
University of the Witwatersrand Medical School: Department of Anatomy.

Paul Abell
Jim Aronson
Kay Behrensmeyer
Birger Bohlin
Karl Bolt
Bob Brain
L. Brongersma
Mike Bush
Ms Carmean-Dubois
Russ Ciochon
Ron Clarke
Yves Coppens
Harvey Croze
Andrew Cruikshank
Garniss Curtis
Raymond Dart
Hilary Davies
Michael Day
Bob Drake
Jean M. F. Dubois
Peter Faugust
Ian Findlater

Frank Fitch
Hod French
Gatenby-Davies family
Alan Gentry
Bob Ginna
Chris Gow
Tom Gray
John Harris
Sidney Haughton
John Hawkins
Hawthorne family
Ralph Holloway
The Hominid Gang
C. R. Hooijer
Adrian House
Alun Hughes
Hans Joachim
Don Johanson
Peter Jones
Trevor Jones
Mac Kamoya
Bill Kimbel

James Kitching
Lars-Köning Königsson
Reinhart Kraatz
Björn Kurten
Misia Landau
Dr Meave Leakey
Philip and Valerie Leakey
Richard Leakey
Owen Lovejoy
Brian and Judy Maguire
Henry McHenry
Carl-Axel Moberg
Theya Molleson
Mike Norton-Griffiths
Emma Nzuki
K. P. Oakley
Alan Ogot
Melvin M. Payne
David Pilbeam
Hazel Potgieter
Rick Potts
Louis Robbins
Pat Shipman

Elwyn Simons
Bill and Ginny Smith
Chris and Sylvia Smith
Mary Griswold Smith
Solveig Stuenes
Ian Tattersall
Teutsch family
J. Thackeray
Phillip Tobias
Eric Trinkhaus
P. van Helsdingen
G. H. R. von Koenigswald
Elizabeth Vrba
Alan Walker
Priscilla Ward
Steve Ward
Sherwood Washburn
Ron Watkins
Tim White
James and On-Ke Wilde
Bernard Wood
Otto Zdansky

PHOTOGRAPHS

The photographs were taken by the author, courtesy of:
1: Rheinisches Landesmuseum, Bonn; 2 and 3: Musée de l'Homme, Paris; 5: Dubois Collection, Rijksmuseum van Natuurlijke Historie, Leiden; 6 and 7: Trustees of the British Museum (Natural History); Illustrated London News Picture Library; 8: Department of Anatomy, University of the Witwatersrand Medical School, Johannesburg; 9: Transvaal Museum, Pretoria; 10: Dr M. D. Leakey, Olduvai Gorge Research Project; 11: National Museum of Tanzania, Dar es Salaam; 12: Professor G. H. Curtis, Department of Geology and Geophysics, University of California, Berkeley; 13: Dr M. D. Leakey, Olduvai Gorge Research Project; 14: R. E. F. Leakey and National Museum of Kenya, Nairobi; 15: Dr D. C. Johanson, Cleveland Museum of Natural History on behalf of The National Museum of Ethiopia, Addis Ababa; 16: Dr M. D. Leakey, Laetoli Research Project.

GLOSSARY

Acheulean   Stone tool culture characterized by pointed or almond-shaped handaxes. Type site: Saint Acheul, Amiens (Somme), France.

Adaptation   The evolution of features that make a group of organisms better suited to live and reproduce in their environment; a feature of structure, physiology or behaviour which aids an organism in its environment.

Analogous   Applied to structures similar in function but different in evolutionary origin (e.g. the wing of a bird and the wing of an insect).

Anthropoid   A member of the Anthropoidea; pertaining to the Anthropoidea.

Anthropoidea   The zoological sub-order of primates which includes monkeys, apes and humans.

Artefact (artifact)   An object made or fashioned by man.

Aurignacian   A culture of worked stone, bone and antler found in association with Cro-Magnon remains. Type site: Aurignac, Haute Garonne, France.

Australopithecinae   The zoological sub-family which contains the fossil 'ape-men', 'man-apes' and 'near-men'.

Australopithecine   A member of the Australopithecinae; pertaining to the Australopithecinae.

Bipedal gait   Two-legged walking.

Chronology, absolute   A temporal sequence expressed in exact years.

Chronology, relative   A temporal sequence based on the relationship of artefacts and cultures to each other or to natural events.

Cladistics   A system of taxonomic classification that determines evolutionary relationships according to identifiable points of divergence in evolutionary lineages.

Clonal   Pertaining to the reproductive or replicative process by which a population of identical individuals or cells (a clone) is derived from a single ancestor.

Collagen   A fibrous protein in bones, tendons and other connective tissues.

Cranium   The part of the skull that forms the brain-case.

Cytoplasm   The substance within a cell, excluding that found within the nucleus.

DNA   Deoxyribonucleic acid: the molecule carrying hereditary genetic information in cells, composed of two complementary strands wound in a double helix, and capable of self-replication.

Ecology The study of the interactions of organisms with their physical environment and each other.

Ecosystem The totality of organisms, physical environment and the factors (climate, etc.) with which they interact.

Endocast A cast of a cavity (e.g. a fossil cranium) which shows internal surface features in relief.

Family A taxonomic grouping of related genera.

Fossil (from the latin *fossilis*, meaning dug up) The remains of an organism, or direct evidence of its existence (such as tracks). May be an unaltered hard part (tooth or bone), a mould in rock, petrification (wood or bone), unaltered or partially altered soft parts (a frozen mammoth).

Gene The basic hereditary unit of living organisms.

Generic Pertaining to genus.

Genus (pl. genera) A taxonomic grouping of closely related species.

Habilis (meaning able, handy) The specific name given to a group of fossil hominids from the Lower Pleistocene.

Habitat The place in which individuals of a particular species can usually be found.

Heredity The transmission of characteristics from parent to offspring.

Hominid A member of the zoological family Hominidae; pertaining to the Hominidae.

Hominidae The zoological family which includes fossil and modern man, and the australopithecines.

Hominoid A member of the zoological super-family Hominoidea; pertaining to the Hominoidea.

Hominoidea The zoological super-family which contains fossil apes, the australopithecines and fossil man, as well as the living great apes and modern man.

Homo The genus in which the hominids including fossil and modern man are grouped.

Homology Similarity in structure and/or position assumed to result from common ancestry regardless of function (e.g. the wing of a bird and the foreleg of a mammal).

Lapilli In geological terms refers to the fragments of stone ejected from volcanoes.

Matrix In palaeontology, the mass of rock or other material in which a fossil is embedded.

Mitochondrion A self-replicating organelle (small cytoplasmic structure) involved in energy production.

Morphological Pertaining to the form and structure of organisms.

Morphology The study of the form and structure of organisms.

Mousterian A stone tool culture most frequently associated with Neanderthal remains, consisting principally of simple choppers, scrapers and points. Type site: Le Moustier, Dordogne, France.

Mutation An inheritable change in an organism's DNA sequence.

Obsidian Volcanic glass capable of producing sharp flake tools.

Oldowan An Early Palaeolithic stone tool culture consisting of crudely flaked implements. Type site: Olduvai Gorge, Tanzania.

Ontogeny The history of the individual's development from egg to adult form.

Organic Pertaining to organisms and living things generally; compounds formed by living organisms.

Organelle Structured parts of a cell's cytoplasm responsible for specific functions.

Organism Any living creature.

Palaeoanthropology The study of man in past geological times.

Palaeontology The study of the life of past geologic times, principally by means of fossils.

Paranthropus (meaning beside, or equal to, man) Generic name given to a group of South African Pleistocene hominids.

Phylogeny The evolutionary history of a taxonomic group. Phylogenies are often depicted as evolutionary trees.

Pithecanthropus (meaning ape-man) Generic name given to a group of Asian Middle Pleistocene hominids.

Plantigrade Walking upon the soles of the feet.

Population Any group of individuals of one species that occupies a given area at the same time; in genetic terms an interbreeding group of individuals.

Post-cranial Refers to all bones of the skeleton except the skull.

Potassium/Argon Method A technique by which the age of volcanic deposits can be determined.

Primate A member of the zoological order that includes anthropoids and prosimians.

Prosimian The sub-order of primates that includes fossil and modern lemurs, lorises, tariers and tree shrews.

Protoplasm The substance within a cell, including the nucleus.

Punctuated equilibrium The process of evolutionary change described as long periods during which no change occurs (stasis), punctuated by spells of rapid speciation (*q.v.*).

Quadrumana (meaning four-handed) The primates whose hind feet as well as fore feet have an opposable digit and can therefore be used as hands: monkeys, apes, baboons and lemurs.

Sinanthropus (meaning Chinese-man) The generic name given to Middle Pleistocene hominids found near Beijing.

Skull The bony skeleton of the head, including the lower jaw.

Speciation The formation of two or more species from a single existing one.

Species A taxonomic grouping of morphologically similar individuals capable of interbreeding which is reproductively isolated from all other such groups.

Stratigraphy A branch of geology concerned with the formation, constituents and sequence of stratified deposits.

Taxon (pl. taxa) Any group of organisms which is sufficiently distinct from all others to be accorded a scientific name (i.e. species, family, class, etc.).

Taxonomy The study of the classification of organisms.

Territory An area or space occupied and defended by an individual or a group; may be a breeding, nesting or food-gathering site, or any combination thereof.

Tuff A consolidated deposit of volcanic ash, often laid down in water.

Vertebrate Animal having a skull and backbone.

Zinjanthropus (meaning East African Man) The generic name given to an East African hominid from the Lower Pleistocene.

BIBLIOGRAPHY

Abel, W. 1931: 'Kritische Untersuchungen über *Australopithecus africanus* Dart', *Morphol. Jahrb.* 65 (4): 539–640.

Andersson, J. G. 1934 London: *Children of the Yellow Earth.*

Andrews, P. 1984 Frankfurt: 'On the characters that define *Homo erectus*', pp. 167–78 in: Andrews, P., and Franzen, J. L. (editors) 1984 Frankfurt: 'The early evolution of man, with special emphasis on Southeast Asia and Africa', *Courier Forschungsinstitut Senckenberg* 69.

Andrews, P. 1986: 'Fossil evidence on human origins and dispersal', *Cold Spring Harbor Symposia on Quantitative Biology* 51: 419–28.

Andrews, P., and Cook, J. 1985 London: 'Natural modifications to bones in a temperate setting', *Man* N.S. 20: 675–91.

Andrews, P., and Cronin, J. 1982 London: 'The relationships of *Sivapithecus* and *Ramapithecus* and the evolution of the orang-utan', *Nature* 297: 541.

Andrews, P., and Franzen, J. L. (editors) 1984 Frankfurt: 'The early evolution of man, with special emphasis on Southeast Asia and Africa', *Courier Forschungsinstitut Senckenberg* 69.

Andrews, R. C. 1932 New York: 'Natural history of Central Asia. A narrative of the explorations of the Central Asiatic expeditions in Mongolia and China 1921–30', Volume One, *The New Conquest of China.*

Anon. 1862 London: *Medical Times and Gazette*, 28 June.

Anon. 1864 London: 'Notes on the antiquity of man', *Anthropological Review.*

Anon. 1912 London: 'The earliest known Englishman', *Illustrated London News* 140: 442, 446–7.

Anon. 1926 Manchester: 'News report on Peking Man', *Manchester Guardian*, 17 November.

Anon. 1928 London: Leader comment on *Hesperopithecus* in *The Times*, 25 February.

Anon. 1953 London: Parliamentary report comment on *Piltdown* in *The Times*, 27 November.

ApSimon, A. M. 1980 London: 'The last Neanderthal in France?', *Nature* 287: 271–2.

Ardrey, R. 1961 London: *African Genesis.*

Ashton, E. H., and Zuckerman, S. 1950 London: 'Some quantitative dental characters of fossil anthropoids', *Philosophical Transactions of the Royal Society* B 234: 485.

Behrensmeyer, A. K., Gordon, K. D., and Yanagi, G. T. 1986 London: 'Trampling as a cause of bone surface damage and pseudo-cutmarks', *Nature* 319: 768–71.

Beynon, A. D., and Wood, B. A. 1987 London: 'Patterns and rates of enamel growth in the molar teeth of early hominids', *Nature* 326: 493–496.

Bilsborough, A., and Wood, B. A. 1986 Cambridge: 'The nature, origin and fate of *Homo erectus*', pp. 295–316 in: Wood, B. A., Martin, L., and Andrews, P. (editors) 1986 Cambridge: *Major Topics in Primate and Human Evolution*.

Binford, L. R., and Stone, N. M. 1986 New York: 'Zhoukoudian: A closer look', *Current Anthropology* 27: 453–75.

Bishop, W. W., and Clark, J. D. (editors) 1967 Chicago: *Background to Evolution in Africa*.

Black, D. 1926a London: 'Tertiary man in Asia: The Chou K'ou Tien discovery', *Nature* 118: 733–4.

Black, D. 1926b Washington: 'Tertiary man in Asia: The Chou K'ou Tien discovery', *Science* 64: 586–7.

Black, D. 1927 London: 'Further hominid remains of Lower Quaternary age from the Chou K'ou Tien deposit', *Nature* 120.

Black, D. 1929: Quoted in: Hood, D. 1964 Toronto: *Davidson Black. A Biography*: 100.

Blake, C. C. 1862 London: 'On the crania of the most ancient races of men', *Geologist* 5.

Blake, C. C. 1864 London: 'On the alleged peculiar characters and assumed antiquity of the human cranium from the Neanderthal', *Journal of the Anthropological Society* 2.

Blinderman, C. 1986 Buffalo: *The Piltdown Inquest*.

Bohlin, B. 1978 Uppsala: Personal communication. Interview with author.

Boule, M. 1911–13 Paris: 'L'Homme fossile de La Chapelle-aux-Saints', *Annales de Paléontologie* 6, 7, 8.

Boule, M. 1921 Paris: *Les Hommes Fossiles*; 1923 Edinburgh: *Fossil Men*.

Boule, M., and Vallois, H. V. 1957 New York: *Fossil Men*.

Boswell, P. G. H. 1935 London: 'Human remains from Kanam and Kanjera, Kenya Colony', *Nature* 135: 371.

Bower, B. 1985: 'Hunting ancient scavengers', *Science News* 127: 155–7.

Bower, B. 1988: 'An earlier dawn for modern humans?' *Science News* 133: 138.

Brace, C. L. 1964: 'The fate of the "classic" Neanderthals: A consideration of hominid catastrophism', *Current Anthropology* 5.

Brain, C. K. 1975 Amsterdam: 'An introduction to the South African australopithecine bone accumulations', *Archaezoological Studies* (editor Clason, A. T.): 109–19.

Brain, C. K. 1977 New York: Quoted in: 'Puzzling out man's ascent', *Time*, 7 November: 53.

Brain, C. K. 1981 Chicago: *The Hunters or the Hunted? An Introduction to African Cave Taphonomy.*

Brauer, G. 1984a New York: 'A craniological approach to the origin of anatomically modern *Homo sapiens* and implications for the appearance of modern Europeans', pp. 327–410 in: Smith, F. H., and Spencer, F. (editors) 1984 New York: *The Origins of Modern Humans: A World Survey of the Fossil Evidence.*

Brauer, G. 1984b Frankfurt: 'The Afro-European *sapiens* hypothesis, and hominid evolution in Asia during the late Middle and Upper Pleistocene', pp. 145–66 in: Andrews, P., and Franzen, J. L. (editors) 1984 Frankfurt: 'The early evolution of man, with special emphasis on Southeast Asia and Africa', *Courier Forschungsinstitut Senckenberg* 69.

British Museum 1814 London: *Philosophical Transactions.*

Brock, A., and Isaac, G. Ll. 1974 London: 'Paleomagnetic stratigraphy and chronology of the hominid-bearing sediments east of Lake Rudolf, Kenya', *Nature* 247: 344–8.

Bromage, T. G., and Dean, M. C. 1985 London: 'Re-evaluation of the age at death of immature fossil hominids', *Nature* 317: 525–7.

Broom, R. 1885 Edinburgh: 'On the volume of mixed liquids', *Proceedings of the Royal Society of Edinburgh* 13: 172–4.

Broom, R. 1888 Glasgow: 'On a monstrosity of the common earthworm, *Lumbricus terrestris*', *L. Trans. Nat. Hist. Soc.* 2: 127–130.

Broom, R. 1895 Glasgow: 'On the comparative anatomy of the organ of Jacobson', unpublished M.D. thesis.

Broom, R. 1915 London: 'On the organ of Jacobson and its relations in the "Insectivora"', Part I. Tupaia and Gymnura, Part II. Talpa, Centetes, and Chrysochloris, *Proceedings of the Zoological Society of London*: 157–62, 347–54.

Broom, R. 1925a: Quoted in: Findlay G. 1972 Cape Town: *Dr Robert Broom, F.R.S.*

Broom, R. 1925b London: 'Some notes on the Taungs skull', *Nature* 115: 569–71.

Broom, R. 1933 London: *The Coming of Man – Was it Accident or Design?*

Broom, R. 1936a London: 'A new fossil anthropoid skull from South Africa', *Nature* 138: 486–8.

Broom, R. 1936b London: 'On a new ancestral link between ape and man', *Illustrated London News* 189: 476–7.

Broom, R. 1938a London: 'More discoveries of Australopithecus', *Nature* 141: 828–9.

Broom, R. 1938b London: 'The missing link is no longer missing', *Illustrated London News* 193: 3101.

Broom, R. 1939 Johannesburg: 'On evolution', *Star*, 18 August.

Broom, R. 1942a London: 'The hand of the ape-man Paranthropus robustus', *Nature* 149: 513–14.

Broom, R. 1942b London: 'An ankle-bone of the ape-man Paranthropus robustus', *Nature* 152: 689–90.

Broom, R. 1946 Quoted in: Wells, L. H. 1966 Johannesburg: The Robert Broom Memorial Lecture, *South African Journal of Science*, September 1967: 365.

Broom, R. 1950 London: *Finding the Missing Link.*

Broom, R., and Schepers, G. W. H. 1946 Pretoria: 'The South African fossil ape-men. The Australopithecinae', Part I. The occurrence and general structure of the South African ape-men, *Transvaal Museum Memoir* 2.

Broom, R., Robinson, J. T., and Schepers, G. W. H. 1950 Pretoria: 'Sterkfontein ape-man, Plesianthropus', *Transvaal Museum Memoir* 4.

Brown, F. H., McDougall, I., Davies, T., and Maier, R. 1985 New York: 'An integrated Plio-Pleistocene chronology for the Turkana Basin', pp. 82–90 in: Delson, E. (editor) 1985 New York: *Ancestors: The Hard Evidence.*

Bunn, H. T. 1981 London: 'Archaeological evidence for meat-eating by Plio-Pleistocene hominids from Koobi Fora and Olduvai Gorge', *Nature* 291: 574–6.

Bunn, H. T. 1982 Berkeley: 'Meat-eating and human evolution', Ph.D diss., Univ. of California.

Bunney, S. 1986 London: 'Did Neanderthal babies have bigger brains than ours?', *New Scientist*, 29 May: 29–30.

Busk, G. 1864a Bath: Report on British Association Meeting, *Bath Chronicle*, 22 September.

Busk, G. 1864b London: 'Pithecoid Priscan Man from Gibraltar', *Reader*, 23 July.

Busk, G., and Falconer, H. 1865 London: 'On the fossil contents of the Genista cave, Gibraltar', *Q. J. Geol. Soc.* 21: 364–70.

Campbell, B. 1964 London: 'Just another "man-ape"?', *Discovery* 25 (June): 37–8.

Campbell, B. 1965 London: 'The nomenclature of the Hominidae', *Occasional paper of the Royal Anthropological Institute* 23.

Cann, R. L., Stoneking, M., and Wilson, A. C. 1987 London: 'Mitochondrial DNA and human evolution', *Nature* 325: 31–6.

Carnot, A. 1893 Paris: 'Recherches sur la composition générale et la teneur en fluor des os modernes et des os fossiles de différents âges', *Ann. Min.* (9, Mem.) 3: 155–95.

Cartmill, M., Pilbeam, D., and Isaac, G. Ll. 1986: 'One hundred years of Paleoanthropology', *American Scientist* 74: 410–19.

Cave, A. J. E., and Straus, W. L. Jnr 1957: 'Pathology and posture of Neanderthal Man', *Quarterly Review of Biology* 32.

Chambers, R. 1844 London: *Vestiges of the Natural History of Creation.*

Chase, P. G., and Dibble, H. L. 1987: 'Middle Paleolithic symbolism: a review of current evidence and interpretations', *J. Anthrop. Archeo.* 6: 263–296.

Clark, W. E. le Gros, 1946 London: *Nature* 157: 863–5.

Clark, W. E. le Gros, 1964a Chicago: *The Fossil Evidence for Human Evolution.*

Clark, W. E. le Gros, 1964b London: 'The evolution of man', *Discovery*, 25 (July): 37.

Clark, W. E. le Gros, 1967a London: 'Hominid characters of the australopithecine dentition', *Journal of the Royal Anthropological Institute* 80: 37.

Clark, W. E. le Gros, 1967b New York: *Man-apes or Ape-Men?*

Cole, S. 1975 London: *Leakey's Luck.*

Constable, G. 1973 New York: *The Neanderthals.*

Cooke, H. B. S. 1973 Nairobi: 'Suidae from Plio-Pleistocene strata of the Rudolf Basin', in: Coppens, Y., Howell, F. C., Isaac, G. Ll., and Leakey, R. E. F. (editors) 1976 Chicago: *Earliest Man and Environments in the Lake Rudolf Basin*: 251–63.

Coppens, Y. 1983: 'Les plus anciens fossiles d'Hominides', *Pontif. Acad. Scient. Scripta Varia* 50: 1–9.

Coppens, Y., Howell, F. C., Isaac, G. Ll., and Leakey, R. E. F. (editors) 1976 Chicago: *Earliest Man and Environments in the Lake Rudolf Basin.*

Costello, P., 1985–6 London: 'The Piltdown hoax reconsidered', *Antiquity* 49: 167–83; 60: 145–7.

Curtis, G. H., Drake, R., Cerling, T. E., and Hampel, J. E. 1975 London: 'Age of KBS tuff in Koobi Fora Formation, East Rudolf, Kenya', *Nature* 358: 395–8.

Cuvier, G. 1808: *Mineral Geography and Organic Remains of the Neighbourhood of Paris.*

Cuvier, G. 1812 Paris: *Recherches sur les Ossemens Fossiles*, 4 vols.

Daniel, G. 1975 London: *A Hundred and Fifty Years of Archaeology*.

Dart, R. 1925 London: 'Australopithecus africanus: The Man-Ape of South Africa', *Nature* 115: 195–9.

Dart, R. A. 1948 Philadelphia: 'The Makapansgat proto-human *Australopithecus prometheus*', *Am J. Phys. Anthrop.* NS 7: 259–84.

Dart, R. A. 1953: 'The predatory transition from ape to man', *Internat. Anthrop. and Ling. Review* 1: 201–18.

Dart, R. 1955 London: 'The first australopithecine fragment from the Makapansgat pebble culture stratum', *Nature* 176: 170.

Dart, R. A. 1957 Pretoria: 'The osteodontokeratic culture of *Australopithecus prometheus*', *Transvaal Museum Memoir* 10.

Dart, R. 1959 London: *Adventures with the Missing Link*.

Dart, R. 1978 Johannesburg: Personal communication. Interview with author.

Dart, R., and Keith, A. 1925 London: 'On the Taungs skull': An exchange of letters, *Nature* 116: 462.

Darwin, C. 1871 London: *The Descent of Man*; second edition, 1882.

Darwin, C. 1888 London: *The Origin of Species*: Historical Sketch.

Davis, P. R. 1964 London: 'Hominid fossils from Bed I, Olduvai Gorge, Tanganyika', *Nature* 201: 967–70.

Dawson, C., and Woodward, A. S. 1913 London: 'On the discovery of a Palaeolithic human skull and mandible in a flint-bearing gravel overlying the Wealden (Hastings Beds) at Piltdown, Fletching, Sussex', *Quarterly Journal of the Geological Society* 69: 117–44.

Day, M. H. 1976 California: 'Hominid postcranial material from Bed I, Olduvai George', in: Isaac, G. Ll., and McCown, E. R. (editors) 1976 California: *Human Origins: Louis Leakey and the East African Evidence*.

Day, M. H. 1986 London: *Guide to Fossil Man*.

Day, M. H., Leakey, M. D., and Olson, T. R. 1980 Washington: 'On the status of Australopithecus afarensis', *Science* 207: 1102–3.

Day, M. H., Leakey, R. E. F., Walker, A. C., and Wood, B. A. 1975 Philadelphia: 'New hominids from East Rudolf, Kenya, I', *American Journal of Physical Anthropology* 42: 461–76.

Day, M. H., and Napier, J. R. 1964 London: 'Fossil foot bones', *Nature* 201: 969–70.

Day, M. H., and Wood, B. A. 1968 London: 'Functional affinities of the Olduvai Hominid 8 talus', *Man* (new series) 3: 440–55.

Dean, M. C. 1987: 'Growth layers and incremental markings in hard tissues and fossil hominid enamel', *Journal of Human Evolution* 16: 157–72.

Delson, E. (editor) 1985 New York: *Ancestors: The Hard Evidence*.

Delson, E. 1985 London: 'Palaeobiology and the age of African *Homo erectus*', *Nature* 316: 762–3.

Delson, E. 1986 London: 'Human phylogeny revised again', *Nature* 322: 496–7.

Delson, E. 1987 London: 'Evolution and palaeobiology of robust *Australopithecus*', *Nature* 327: 654–5.

Dubois, E. 1891 Batavia: 'Paleontologische onderzoekingen op Java', *Verslagen van het Mijnwezen*, fourth quarter.

Dubois, E. 1892 Batavia: *Verslagen van het Mijnwezen*, third quarter.

Dubois, E. 1894 Batavia: *Pithecanthropus erectus, eine menschenähnliche Uebergangsform aus Java*.

Dubois, E. 1898 Cambridge: 'The brain-cast of Pithecanthropus erectus', *Proceedings of the International Congress of Zoology*.

Dubois, E. 1920 Amsterdam: 'The proto-Australian fossil man of Wadjak, Java', *Koninklijke Akademie van Wetenschappen; proceedings* 13.

Dubois, E. 1933 Amsterdam: 'The shape and size of the brain in Sinanthropus and in Pithecanthropus', *Koninklijke Akademie van Wetenschappen; proceedings* 36.

Dubois, E. 1935 Amsterdam. 'On the gibbon-like appearance of Pithecanthropus erectus', *Koninklijke Akademie van Wetenschappen; proceedings* 38.

Dubois, E. 1940 Amsterdam: 'The fossil human remains discovered in Java by Dr G. R. H. von Koenigswald and attributed by him to Pithecanthropus erectus, in reality remains of Homo sapiens soloensis', *Koninklijke Akademie van Wetenschappen; proceedings* 43: 494–6, 842–51, 1268–75.

Dubois, J. M. F. Unpublished manuscript, *Trinil: A Biography of Professor Dr Eugene Dubois, the discoverer of Pithecanthropus erectus*.

Eiseley, L. 1958 New York: *Darwin's Century*.

Eldredge, N., and Tattersall, I. 1975 Basel: 'Evolutionary models, phylogenetic reconstruction, and another look at hominid phylogeny', in: Szalay, F. S. (editor) 1975 Basel: *Approaches to Primate Paleobiology*.

Ellesmere, Lord, 1849 London: *A Guide to Northern Antiquities*.

Falconer, H. 1864 London: Letter to Busk of 27 August 1864, quoted by Keith, A. 1911 London: 'The early history of the Gibraltar Cranium', *Nature* 87: 313.

Findlay, G. 1972 Cape Town: *Dr Robert Broom, F.R.S.*

Fitch, F. J. 1979 London: Personal communication. Interview with author.

Fitch, F. J., and Miller, J. A. 1970 London: 'Radioisotopic age determinations of Lake Rudolf artefact site', *Nature* 226: 226–8.

Fitch, F. J., and Miller, J. A. 1973 Nairobi: 'Conventional potassium-argon and argon-40/argon-39 dating of volcanic rocks from East Rudolf', in: Coppens, Y., Howell, F. C., Isaac, G. Ll., and Leakey, R. E. F. (editors) 1976 Chicago: *Earliest Man and Environments in the Lake Rudolf Basin*: 132.

Frere, J. 1800 London: *Archaeologia* 13: 204.

Garrod, D. A. E., and Bate, D. M. A. 1937 Oxford: *The Stone Age of Mount Carmel*.

Gorjanovic-Kramberger, K. 1906 Wiesbaden: *Der diluviale Mensch von Krapina in Kroatien*.

Haeckel, E. 1868 Berlin: *Natürliche Schöpfungsgeschichte*; 1876 London: *The History of Creation* (2 vols.).

Haeckel, E. 1879 London: *The Evolution of Man* (2 vols.).

Haeckel, E. 1899 London: *The Last Link*.

Haeckel, E. 1906 London: *Last Words on Evolution*.

Haldane, J. B. S. 1974: Quoted in: Terry, R. 1974 Johannesburg: 'Raymond A. Dart: Taung 1924–1974', *The Museum of Man and Science*.

Hall, E. T. 1974 London: 'Old bones – but how old?', *Sunday Telegraph*, 3 September.

Halstead, L. B. 1978 London: 'The cladistic revolution – can it make the grade?', *Nature* 276: 759–60.

Harding, R., and Teleki, G. (editors) 1981 New York: *Omnivorous Primates*.

Haughton, S. H. 1920 Cape Town: 'On the occurence [*sic*] of a species of baboon in deposits near Taungs', Abstract in *Transactions of the Royal Society of South Africa* 12, 1925: lxviii.

Hay, R. L. 1976 Berkeley: *Geology of the Olduvai Gorge*.

Hennig, W. 1966 Urbana: *Phylo-genetic Systematics*.

Hill, A. 1987 New Haven: Personal communication. Interview with author.

Hood, D. 1964 Toronto: *Davidson Black. A Biography*.

Howell, F. C., and Coppens, Y. 1976 Chicago: 'An overview of hominidae from the Omo Succession, Ethiopia', pp. 522–32 in: Coppens, Y., Howell, F. C., Isaac, G. Ll., and Leakey, R. E. F. (editors) 1976 Chicago: *Earliest Man and Environments in the Lake Rudolf Basin*.

Howells, W. W. 1976: 'Explaining modern man: Evolutionists *versus* migrationists', *J. Hum. Evol.* 5: 477–95.

Hrdlicka, A. 1919 Philadelphia: 'Physical anthropology, its scope, and aims, history and present status in the United States ', quoted p. 17 in: Spencer, F. (editor) 1982 New York: *A History of American Physical Anthropology 1930–1980*.

Hrdlicka, A. 1927 London: 'The Neanderthal phase of man', *J. Roy. Anthrop. Inst.* 57: 249–74.

Hrdlicka, A. 1930 Washington: 'The skeletal remains of early man', *Smithsonian Miscellaneous Collections* 83: 65–90.

Huxley, T. H. 1863 London: *Man's Place in Nature*; Ann Arbor edition, 1959 Michigan.

Huxley, T. H. 1864 London: 'Further remarks upon the human remains from the Neanderthal', *Natural History Review* 1: 429–46.

Isaac, G. Ll. 1976 Chicago: p. 6 in: Coppens Y., Howell, F. C., Isaac, G. Ll., and Leakey, R. E. F. (editors) 1976 Chicago: *Earliest Man and Environments in the Lake Rudolf Basin.*

Isaac, G. Ll. 1978 New York: 'The food-sharing behavior of protohuman hominids', *Scientific American* 238 (4): 90–106.

Isaac, G. Ll. 1981 London: 'Emergence of human behaviour patterns', pp. 177–88 in: Young, J. Z., Jope, E. M., and Oakley, K. P. (editors) 1981 London: 'The emergence of man', *Phil. Trans. R. Soc.* B.292: 3–5.

Isaac, G. Ll., and McCown, E. R. (editors) 1976 California: *Human Origins: Louis Leakey and the East African Evidence.*

Jia Lanpo 1980 Beijing: *Early Man in China.*

Johanson, D. C. 1974 Addis Ababa: Quoted in: Ottoway, D. B. 1974 Paris: '3-million-year-old human fossils found', *Herald Tribune,* 28 October.

Johanson, D. C. 1976 Washington: 'Ethiopia yields first "Family" of early man', *National Geographic,* December.

Johanson, D. C. 1978 Cleveland: Personal communication. Interview with author.

Johanson, D. C. 1979 Chicago: 'Our roots go deeper', in: *Science Year* 1979; Worldbook Childcraft International Inc.

Johanson, D. C. 1987 Washington: quoted in: Lewin, R. 1987b Washington: 'The earliest "humans" were more like apes', *Science* 236: 1061–3.

Johanson, D. C., and Edey, M. A. 1981 New York: *Lucy: The Beginnings of Humankind.*

Johanson, D. C., Masao, F. T., Eck, G. C., White, T. D., Walter, R. C., Kimbel, W. H., Asfaw, B., Manega, P., Ndessokia, P., and Suwa, G. 1987 London: 'New partial skeleton of *Homo habilis* from Olduvai Gorge, Tanzania', *Nature* 327: 205–9.

Johanson, D. C., Splingaer, M., and Boaz, N. T. 1973 Nairobi: 'Paleontological excavations in the Shungura Formation, Lower Omo Basin, 1969–73', in: Coppens, Y., Howell, F. C., Isaac, G. Ll., and Leakey, R. E. F. (editors) 1976 Chicago: *Earliest Man and Environments in the Lake Rudolf Basin:* 402–20.

Johanson, D. C., and Taieb, M. 1976 London: 'Plio-Pleistocene hominid discoveries in Hadar, Ethiopia', *Nature* 260: 293–7.

Johanson, D. C., and White, T. D. 1979 Washington: 'A systematic assessment of early African hominids', *Science* 203: 321–30.

Johanson, D. C., White, T. D., and Coppens, Y. 1978 Cleveland: 'A new species of the genus *Australopithecus* (Primates: Hominidae) from the Pliocene of Eastern Africa', *Kirtlandia* 28: 1–14.

Jones, P. R. 1979 Washington: 'Effects of raw material on biface manufacture', *Science* 204: 835–6.

Jones, T. 1978 Pretoria: Personal communication. Interview with author.

Keith, A. 1894 London: *Journal of Anatomy* 28.

Keith, A. 1912a London: *The Human Body*.

Keith, A. 1912b Dundee: 'Modern problems relating to the antiquity of man', *Report of the British Association*.

Keith, A. 1913a London: 'The human skull etc. from Piltdown', discussion, *Quarterly Journal of the Geological Society* 69.

Keith, A. 1913b London: Report in *The Times*, 11 August.

Keith, A. 1913c London: 'The Piltdown skull and brain cast', *Nature* 92: 197.

Keith, A. 1914 London: 'The reconstruction of fossil human skulls', *Journal of the Royal Anthropological Institute* 44: 12.

Keith, A. 1915 London: *The Antiquity of Man*.

Keith, A. 1917 London: 'Second skull from Piltdown gravel', discussion, *Quarterly Journal of the Geological Society* 73.

Keith, A. 1925a London: *The Antiquity of Man*; second edition.

Keith, A. 1925b London: 'The Taungs skull', *Nature* 116: 11.

Keith, A. 1931 London: *New Discoveries Relating to the Antiquity of Man*.

Keith, A. 1942 London: *The Rationalist Annual*.

Keith, A. 1948a London: In a foreword to Woodward, A. S., *The Earliest Englishman*.

Keith, A. 1948b London: *A New Theory of Human Evolution*.

Keith, A. 1950 London: *An Autobiography*.

Keith, A., Smith, G. E., Woodward, A. S., and Duckworth, W. J. H. 1925 London: 'The fossil anthropoid from Taungs', *Nature* 115: 234–6.

Kern, E. P. H. 1981 New York: 'Battle of the bones', *Life* 4 (12): 109–20.

King, W. 1864 London. 'The reputed fossil man of the Neanderthal', *Quarterly Journal of Science* 1: 88–97.

Koenigswald, G. H. R. von. 1938 Amsterdam: 'Ein neuer Pithecanthropus-Schädel', *Koninklijke Akademie van Wetenschappen; proceedings* 41.

Koenigswald, G. H. R. von, and Weidenreich, F. 1939 London: 'The relationship between Pithecanthropus and Sinanthropus', *Nature* 144: 926–9.

Kramer, L. M. J. 1953 London: Letter to *The Times*, 28 November.

Lartet, E., and Christy, H. 1866–75 Paris: *Reliquiae Aquitanicae: Being Contributions to the Archaeology and Palaeontology of Périgord*.

Lartet, L. 1869 Paris: 'Une sépultre des troglodytes du Périgord', *Annales des Sciences naturelles*, 5th Series, vol. 10.

Lartet, L., and Chaplain-Duparc 1874 Paris: 'Une sépultre des anciens troglodytes des Pyrénées', *Matériaux* 9.

Leakey, L. S. B. 1931 London: Article in *The Times*, 3 December.

Leakey, L. S. B. 1932a London: Article in *The Times*, 9 March.

Leakey, L. S. B. 1932b London: Article in *The Times*, 19 April.

Leakey, L. S. B. 1934 London: *Adam's Ancestors*.

Leakey, L. S. B. 1936 London: 'Fossil human remains from Kanam and Kanjera, Kenya Colony', *Nature* 138: 643.

Leakey, L. S. B. 1937 London: *White African*.

Leakey, L. S. B. 1951 Cambridge: *Olduvai Gorge: A Report on the Evolution of the Hand-axe Culture in Beds I–IV*.

Leakey, L. S. B. 1954 London: 'The giant animals of prehistoric Tanganyika, and the hunting grounds of Chellean man . . .', *Illustrated London News* 244: 1047–51.

Leakey, L. S. B. 1958a London: 'Recent discoveries at Olduvai Gorge, Tanganyika', *Nature* 181: 1099–103.

Leakey, L. S. B. 1958b London: 'A giant child among the giant animals of Olduvai? A huge fossil milk molar which suggests that Chellean man in Tanganyika may have been gigantic', *Illustrated London News* 232: 1104–5.

Leakey, L. S. B. 1959a London: *Nature* 185: 408.

Leakey, L. S. B. 1959b London: 'A new fossil skull from Oldvuai', *Nature* 184: 491–3.

Leakey, L. S. B. 1959c London: Quoted in *The Times*, 4 September.

Leakey, L. S. B. 1960a London: 'From the Taung skull to "Nutcracker Man": Africa as the cradle of mankind and the primates . . .', *Illustrated London News* 236: 44.

Leakey, L. S. B. 1960b Washington: 'Finding the world's earliest man', *National Geographic* 118: 420–35.

Leakey, L. S. B. 1961 London: 'New finds at Olduvai Gorge', *Nature* 189: 649–50.

Leakey, L. S. B. 1965 Cambridge: *Olduvai Gorge 1951–1961*. Vol. I.

Leakey, L. S. B. 1969 California: Public Lecture. Recording in possession of Leakey, M. D.

Leakey, L. S. B., Evernden, J. F., and Curtis, G. H. 1961 London: 'Age of Bed I, Olduvai Gorge, Tanganyika', *Nature* 191: 478–9.

Leakey, L. S. B., Hopwood, A. T., and Reck, H. 1931 London: 'Age of the Oldoway bone beds, Tanganyika', *Nature* 128: 724.

Leakey, L. S. B., Reck, H., Boswell, P. G. H., Hopwood, A. T., and Solomon, J. D. 1933 London: 'The Oldoway human skeleton', *Nature* 131: 397–8.

Leakey, L. S. B., Tobias, P. V., and Napier, J. R. 1964 London: 'A new species of the genus *Homo* from Olduvai Gorge', *Nature* 202: 7–9.

Leakey, M. D. 1967 Chicago: 'Preliminary survey of the cultural material from Beds I and II, Olduvai Gorge, Tanzania', in: Bishop, W. W., and Clark, J. D. (editors) 1967 Chicago: *Background to Evolution in Africa* 417.

Leakey, M. D. 1971a Cambridge: *Olduvai Gorge, volume 3, Excavations in Beds I and II*.

Leakey, M. D. 1971b London: 'Discovery of postcranial remains of *Homo erectus* and associated artefacts in Bed IV at Olduvai Gorge, Tanzania', *Nature* 232: 380–83.

Leakey, M. D. 1978: Quoted p. 285 in: Lewin, R. 1987 New York: *Bones of Contention: Controversies in the Search for Human Origins.*

Leakey, M. D. 1979a London: *Olduvai Gorge: My Search for Early Man.*

Leakey, M. D. 1979b Olduvai: Personal communication. Interview with author.

Leakey, M. D. 1981 London: 'Tracks and tools', pp. 95–102 in: Young, J. Z., Jope, E. M., and Oakley, K. P. (editors) 1981 London: 'The emergence of man', *Phil. Trans. R. Soc.* B.292, 3–5.

Leakey, M. D. 1984 London: *Disclosing the Past.*

Leakey, M. D., and Harris, J. M. (editors) 1987 Oxford: *Laetoli: A Pliocene Site in Northern Tanzania.*

Leakey, M. D., and Hay, R. L. 1979 London: 'Pliocene footprints in the Laetoli beds at Laetoli, northern Tanzania', *Nature* 278: 317–23.

Leakey, M. D., Hay, R. L., Curtis, G. H., Drake, R. E., Jackes, M. K., and White, T. D. 1976 London: 'Fossil hominids from the Laetoli Beds', *Nature* 262: 460–66.

Leakey, M. G., and Leakey, R. E. F. (editors) 1978 Oxford: *The Fossil Hominids and an Introduction to Their Context.* Volume 1 of: Leakey, R. E. F., and Isaac, G. Ll. (editors) 1978– Oxford: *Koobi Fora Research Project Monograph series.*

Leakey, R. E. F. 1970a Washington: 'In search of man's past at Lake Rudolf', *National Geographic* 137: 712–33.

Leakey, R. E. F. 1970b London: 'Fauna and artefacts from a new Plio-Pleistocene locality near Lake Rudolf in Kenya', *Nature* 226: 223–4.

Leakey, R. E. F. 1971 London: 'Further evidence of Lower Pleistocene hominids from East Rudolf, North Kenya', *Nature* 231: 241–5.

Leakey, R. E. F. 1972a London: 'Further evidence of Lower Pleistocene hominids from East Rudolf, North Kenya, 1971', *Nature* 237: 264–9.

Leakey, R. E. F. 1972b: 'New evidence for the evolution of man', *Social Biology* 19: 99–114.

Leakey, R. E. F. 1972c London: 'Man and sub-men on Lake Rudolf', *New Scientist* 56: 385–7.

Leakey, R. E. F. 1973a Washington: 'Skull 1470', *National Geographic* 143: 819–29.

Leakey, R. E. F. 1973b London: 'Further evidence of Lower Pleistocene hominids from East Rudolf, North Kenya, 1972', *Nature* 242: 170–73.

Leakey, R. E. F. 1973c London: 'Evidence for an advanced Plio-Pleistocene hominid from East Rudolf, Kenya', *Nature* 242: 447–50.

Leakey, R. E. F. 1977 New York: Quoted in: 'Puzzling out man's ascent', *Time*, 7 November.

Leakey, R. E. F. 1978 Nairobi: Personal communication. Interview with author.

Leakey, R. E. F. 1979a London: Personal communication. Interview with author.

Leakey, R. E. F. 1979b Pittsburgh: Quoted in: Rensberger, B. 1979 New York: 'Rival anthropologists divide on "Pre-human" find', *New York Times*, 18 February.

Leakey, R. E. F., and Lewin, R. 1977 London: *Origins*.

Leakey, R. E. F., and Walker, A. C. 1976 London: '*Australopithecus, Homo erectus* and the single species hypothesis', *Nature* 261: 572–4.

Leakey, R. E. F., and Walker, A. C. 1980 Washington: 'On the status of Australopithecus afarensis', *Science* 207: 1103.

Leakey, R. E. F., and Walker, A. C. 1985 Washington: '*Homo erectus* unearthed', *National Geographic* 168: 625–9.

Lee, R. B. 1968 New York: 'What hunters do for a living, or, how to make out on scarce resources', pp. 30–48 in: Lee, R. B., and DeVore, I. 1968 New York: *Man the Hunter*.

Lee, R. B., and DeVore, I. 1968 New York: *Man the Hunter*.

Leroi-Gourhan, D. 1975 Washington: 'The flowers found with Shanidar IV, a Neanderthal burial in Iraq', *Science* 190: 562–4.

Léveque, F., and Vandermeersch, B. 1980 Paris: 'Les découvertes de restes humains dans un horizon Castelperronien de Saint-Césaire (Charente-Maritime)', *Bull. Soc. préhist. fr.* 77: 35.

Lewin, R. 1981 Washington: 'Protohuman activity etched in fossil bones', *Science* 213: 123–4.

Lewin, R. 1984 Washington: 'Man the scavenger', *Science* 224: 861–2.

Lewin, R. 1986 Washington: 'New fossil upsets human family', *Science* 233: 720–21.

Lewin, R. 1987a Washington: 'Debate over emergence of human tooth pattern', *Science* 235: 748–50.

Lewin, R. 1987b Washington: 'The earliest "humans" were more like apes', *Science* 236: 1061–3.

Lewin, R. 1987c New York: *Bones of Contention: Controversies in the Search for Human Origins*.

Lorenz, K. Z. 1966 London: *On Aggression*.

Lovejoy, C. O. 1973 Philadelphia: 'The gait of australopithecines', *Yearbook of Physical Anthropology* 17: 147–61.

Lovejoy, C. O. 1975 The Hague: 'Biomechanical perspectives on the lower limb of early hominids', in: Tuttle, R. H. (editor) 1976 The Hague: *Primate Morphology and Evolution*: 291–326.

Lovejoy, C. O., Heiple, K. G., and Burstein, A. H. 1973 Philadelphia: 'The gait of Australopithecus', *American Journal of Physical Anthropology* 38: 757–80.

Lubbock, J. 1865 London: *Prehistoric Times*.

Lyell, C. 1830–34 London: *Principles of Geology*, 3 vols.

Lyell, C. 1863 London: *The Antiquity of Man*.

Lyne, C. W. 1916 London: 'The significance of the radiographs of the Piltdown teeth', *Proceedings of the Royal Society of Medicine* 9 (3 Odont. Sect.): 33–62.

Manchester Guardian 1926: News report on Peking Man, 17 November.

Mann, A. 1975 Philadelphia: *Paleodemographic Aspects of the South African Australopithecines*.

Mann, A. 1987 Washington: Quoted in: Lewin R. 1987a Washington: 'Debate over emergence of human tooth pattern', *Science* 235: 748–50.

Mann, A. 1988 Washington: p. 41 in Fisher, A. 1988 Washington: 'On the emergence of humanness', *Mosaic* 19 (1): 35–42.

Marston, A. T. 1936 London: 'Preliminary note on a new fossil human skull from Swanscombe, Kent', *Nature* 138: 200–201.

Marston, A. 1937 London: 'The Swanscombe skull', *Journal of the Royal Anthropological Institute* 67: 394.

Mayer, F. 1864 Leipzig: 'Ueber die fossilen Ueberreste eines menschlichen Schädels und Skeletes in einer Felsenhöhle des Düssel – oder Neander – Thales', *Arch. Anst. Physiol.* 1864: 1–26.

Mayr, E. 1944: 'On the concept and terminology of vertical subspecies and species', *Nat. Res. Council Bull.* 2: 11–16.

Mayr, E. 1951: 'Taxonomic categories in fossil hominids', *Cold Spring Harbor Symposia on Quantitative Biology* 15: 109–18.

Mayr, E. 1976 London: *Evolution and the Diversity of Life*.

McBreaty, S. (in prep.) London: 'The origin of modern humans', *Man*.

McDougall, I. 1985: 'k-Ar and ^{40}Ar/^{39}Ar dating of the hominid-bearing Plio-Pleistocene of Koobi Fora, Lake Turkana, northern Kenya', *Geol. Soc. Am. Bull.* 96: 792–4.

Mellars, P., and Stringer, C. B. (in prep.) Edinburgh: *The Origin and Dispersal of Modern Humans: Behavioural and Biological Perspectives*.

Middleton, J. 1844 London: 'On fluorine in bones, its source, and its application to the determination of the geological age of fossil bones', *Proceedings of the Geological Society* 4.

Miller, G. S. 1915 Washington: 'The jaw of Piltdown man', *Smithsonian Miscellaneous Collections* 65: 1–31.

Moir, J. Reid, 1912: 'The occurrence of a human skeleton in a glacial deposit at Ipswich', *Proceedings of the Prehistory Society of East Anglia* 1.

Mortillet, G. de 1869 Paris: 'Essai de classification des cavernes et des stations sous Abri', *Comptes rendus de l'Académie des Sciences*.

Mortillet, G. de 1883 Paris: *Le Préhistorique*.

Napier, J. R. 1962 London: 'Fossil hand bones from Olduvai Gorge', *Nature* 196: 409–11.

National Museum, Copenhagen 1836: *Ledetraad til Nordisk Oldkyndighed*.

Newsweek 1988 New York: *The African Eve*, 11 January.

Nuttall, G. H. F. 1904 Cambridge: *Blood Immunity and Blood Relationships*.

Oakley, K. P. 1956 London: 'The earliest toolmakers', *Antiquity* 30: 4–8.

Oakley, K. P. 1964 London: 'The evolution of man', *Discovery* 25 (August): 49.

Oakley, K. P., and Hoskins, C. R. 1950 London: 'New evidence on the antiquity of Piltdown man', *Nature* 165: 379–82.

Oakley, K. P., and Leakey, M. D. 1937 London: 'Report on excavations at Jaywick Sands, Essex (1934)', *Proceedings of the Prehistoric Society*, 1937, 3: 217–60.

Oakley, K. P., and Montagu, M. F. A. 1949 London: 'A reconsideration of the Galley Hill skeleton', *Bulletin of the British Museum* (*Natural History*), Geology, 1, 2: 27–46.

Olsen, J. W. 1986 New York: Comment on Binford and Stone: 'Zkoukoudian: A closer look', *Current Anthropology* 27: 453–75.

Olson, T. R. 1985 New York: 'Cranial morphology and systematics of the Hadar Formation hominids and *Australopithecus africanus*', pp. 102–19 in: Delson, E. (editor) New York: *Ancestors: The Hard Evidence*.

Osborn, H. F. 1922 New York: Quoted in: 'Hesperopithecus, the first anthropoid primate found in America', *American Museum Novitates* (1925), 37: 1–5.

Osborn, H. F. 1925 New York: *American Museum of Natural History Bulletin*, February 1925: Quoted in *The Times*, London, 25 February 1928.

Osborn, H. F. 1927 Princeton, N. J.: *Man Rises to Parnassus*.

Ottaway, D. B. 1974a Paris: '3-million-year-old human fossils found', *Herald Tribune*, 28 October.

Ottaway, D. B. 1974b Paris: 'Oldest partial skeleton of "man" is found', *Herald Tribune*, 27 December.

Owen, R. 1849 London: *On the Nature of Limbs*.

Owen, R. 1855 London: 'Of the anthropoid apes and their relation to Man', *Proceedings of the Royal Institution of Great Britain* 1854–1858, 3.

Oxnard, C. E. 1972 Chicago: 'Functional morphology of primates: some mathematical and physical methods', in: Tuttle, R. (editor) 1972 Chicago: *The Functional and Evolutionary Biology of Primates*.

Partridge, T. C. 1973 London: 'Geomorphological dating of cave opening at Makapansgat, Sterkfontein, Swartkrans and Taung', *Nature* 246: 75–9.

Patterson, C., Forey, P. L., Greenwood, P. H., Miles, R. S., and Jefferies, R. P. S. 1979 London: 'The salmon, the lungfish and the cow: A reply', *Nature* 277: 175–6.

Payne, M. 1978 Washington: Personal communication. Interview with author.

Pei, W. C. 1929 Peking: 'An account of the discovery of an adult Sinanthropus skull in the Chou-K'ou-tien deposit', *Geological Society of China Bulletin* 8 (3).

Pengelly, W. 1869: 'The literature of Kent's Cavern', *Trans. Devon Ass.* 16: 189–434.

Pilbeam, D. 1972 New York: *The Ascent of Man*.

Pilbeam, D. 1977 New York: Quoted in: 'Puzzling out man's ascent', *Time*, 7 November: 53, 54.

Pilbeam, D. 1982 London: 'New hominoid skull material from the Miocene of Pakistan', *Nature* 295: 232–4.

Pilbeam, D. 1987 New York: Quoted in: Lewin, R. 1987c New York: *Bones of Contention: Controversies in the Search for Human Origins.*

Potts, R. 1982 Cambridge, Mass.: 'Lower Pleistocene site formation and hominid activities at Olduvai Gorge, Tanzania', Ph.D diss. Harvard Univ.

Potts, R. 1984: 'Home bases and early hominids', *American Scientist* 72: 338–47.

Potts, R., and Shipman, P. 1981 London: 'Cutmarks made by stone tools on bones from Olduvai Gorge, Tanzania', *Nature* 291: 577–80.

Poulton, J. 1987 London: 'All about Eve', *New Scientist*, 14 May: 51–3.

Pryce, E. 1986 London: 'The Piltdown hoax reconsidered, a response', *Antiquity* 60: 59–60.

Quatrefages, A. de, and Hamy, E. T. 1882 Paris: *Crania ethnica: Les crânes des races humaines. Pt 1: Races humaines fossiles.*

Rak, Y. 1983 New York: *The Australopithecine Face.*

Reader, J. A. 1978 Nairobi: White, T. D., presents *Australopithecus afarensis*, Notes on seminar and discussion, 28 June.

Reck, H. 1914 London: Quoted in: 'A Man of 150,000 years ago?', *Illustrated London News*, 4 April: 563.

Rightmire, G. P. 1985 New York: 'The tempo of change in the evolution of Mid-Pleistocene *Homo*', pp. 255–64 in: Delson, E. (editor) 1985 New York: *Ancestors: The Hard Evidence.*

Rivière, E. 1887 Paris: *De l'Antiquité de l'Homme dans les Alpes-Maritimes.*

Robinson, J. T. 1959 London: 'An alternative interpretation of the supposed giant deciduous hominid tooth from Olduvai', *Nature* 185: 407.

Robinson, J. T. 1960 London: 'The affinities of the new Olduvai australopithecine', *Nature* 186: 456–7.

Robinson, J. T. 1961 Washington: 'Australopithecines and the origin of Man', *Ann. Rep. Smithsonian Institution*, 1961: 479–500.

Robinson, J. T. 1965 London: '*Homo "habilis"* and the australopithecines', *Nature* 205: 121–4.

Robinson, J. T. and Mason, R. 1957 London: 'Occurrence of stone artifacts with *Australopithecus* at Sterkfontein', *Nature* 180: 521.

Royal Anthropological Institute 1933 Cambridge: 'Early human remains in East Africa', *Man* 33: 66.

Sarich, V. M., and Wilson, A. C. 1967a New York: 'Rates of albumin evolution in primates', *Proceedings of the National Academy of Sciences of the U.S.A.* 58: 142–8.

Sarich, V. M., and Wilson, A. C. 1967b New York: 'Immunological time scale for hominid evolution', *Science* 158: 1200–203.

Schaaffhausen, H. 1858 Bonn: 'On the crania of the most ancient races of man', *Muller's Archiv* 1858, p. 453; translated by G. Busk 1861 with remarks and original figures, taken from a cast of the Neanderthal cranium, *Natural History Review*, April 1861: 155–75.

Schlosser, M. 1903 Munich: 'Die fossilen Säugethiere Chinas', *Abhandl. der Königl. bayerischen Akad. der Wissenschaften*, Band 22, Abteil. 1.

Schmerling, P. C. 1833–4 Liège: *Recherches sur les Ossements Fossiles découverts dans les Cavernes de la Province de Liège*.

Schwalbe, G. 1906 Stuttgart: *Studien zur Vorgeschichte des Menschen*.

Shapiro, H. L. 1974 London: *Peking Man*: Chapter one.

Shipman, P. 1981 Washington: quoted p. 124 in: Lewin, R. 1981 Washington: 'Protohuman activity etched in fossil bones', *Science* 213: 123–4.

Shipman, P. 1984a: 'The earliest bone tools: re-assessing the evidence from Olduvai Gorge', *Anthroquest* 29: 9–10.

Shipman, P. 1984b New York: 'Ancestors: scavenger hunt', *Natural History* 93 (4): 20–27.

Simons, E. L. 1965 London: 'New fossil apes from Egypt and the initial differentiation of Hominoidea', *Nature* 223: 687.

Smith, B. H. 1986 London: 'Dental development in *Australopithecus* and early *Homo*', *Nature* 323: 327–30.

Smith, F. H., and Spencer, F. (editors) 1984 New York: *The Origins of Modern Humans: A World Survey of the Fossil Evidence*.

Smith, G. E. 1912 Dundee: Presidential Address, Anthropology Section, *Report of the British Association*, 1912.

Smith, G. E. 1913a London: 'Preliminary report on the cranial cast [Piltdown skull]', *Quarterly Journal of the Geological Society* 69: 145–7.

Smith, G. E. 1913b London: 'The Piltdown skull and braincast', *Nature* 92: 267.

Smith, G. E. 1917 London: 'Fourth note on the Piltdown gravel, with evidence of a second skull of *Eoanthropus dawsoni*', *Quarterly Journal of the Geological Society* 73: 1–10.

Smith, G. E. 1927 London: *The Evolution of Man* (2nd edition).

Smith, G. E. 1929 Manchester: Report in the *Manchester Guardian*, 16 September.

Smith, W. 1816 London: *Strata Identified by Organized Fossils*.

Smith, W. 1817 London: *Stratagraphical System of Organized Fossils*.

Solecki, R. S. 1957 New York: 'Shanidar cave', *Scientific American* 197 (5): 58–66.

Solecki, R. S. 1960 Washington: 'Three adult Neanderthal skeletons from Shanidar cave, northern Iraq', *Ann. Rep. Smithsonian Institution*, 1959: 603–35.

Solecki, R. S. 1975 Washington: 'Shanidar IV, a Neanderthal flower burial in northern Iraq', *Science* 190: 880–81.

Sollas, W. 1924 London: *Ancient Hunters* (3rd edition).

Spencer, F. (editor) 1982 New York: *A History of American Physical Anthropology 1930–1980*.

Spencer, F. 1984 New York: 'The Neanderthals and their evolutionary significance: A brief historical survey', pp. 1–49 in: Smith, F. H., and Spencer, F. (editors) 1984 New York: *The Origins of Modern Humans: A World Survey of the Fossil Evidence*.

Spencer, F. (in prep.) London: *Piltdown*, British Museum (Natural History) publications.

Star 1925 Johannesburg: News report, 4 February.

Stoneking, M., Bhatia, K., and Wilson, A. C. 1986: 'Rate of sequence divergence estimated from restriction maps of mitochondrial DNA from Papua New Guinea', *Cold Spring Harbor Symposia in Quantitative Biology* 51: 433–9.

Stoneking, M., and Cann, R. L. (in prep.) Edinburgh: 'African origin of human mitochondrial DNA', in: Mellars, P., and Stringer, C. B. (in prep.) Edinburgh: *The Origin and Dispersal of Modern Humans: Behavioural and Biological Perspectives*.

Stringer, C. B. 1984 Frankfurt: 'The definition of *Homo erectus* and the existence of the species in Africa and Europe', pp. 131–44 in: Andrews, P., and Franzen, J. L. (editors) 1984 Frankfurt: 'The early evolution of man, with special emphasis on Southeast Asia and Africa', *Courier Forschungsinstitut Senckenberg* 69.

Stringer, C. B. 1988 London: 'Comment on relevance of Qafzeh dating to origin of modern humans', *Nature* 331: 565–6.

Stringer, C. B. (in prep.) Cambridge: 'Documenting the origin of modern humans', in: E. Trinkaus (editor) (in prep.) Cambridge: *Corridors, Cul-de-sacs and Coalescence: The Biocultural Foundations of Modern People*.

Stringer, C. B., and Andrews, P. 1988 Washington: 'The genetic and fossil evidence of human evolution', *Science* 239: 1263–8.

Stringer, C. B., Hublin, J. J., and Vandermeersch, B. V. 1984 New York: 'The origin of anatomically modern humans in Western Europe', pp. 51–136 in: Smith, F. H., and Spencer, F. (editors) 1984 New York: *The Origin of Modern Humans*.

Stringer, C. B., and Kruszynski, R. G. 1981 London: 'Allez Neanderthal', *Nature* 289: 823–4.

Susman, R. L., and Stern, J. T. 1982 Washington: 'Functional morphology of *Homo habilis*', *Nature* 209: 953–7.

Szalay, F. S. (editor) 1975 Basel: *Approaches to Primate Paleobiology*.

Tattersall, I., and Eldredge, N. 1977 New Haven: 'Fact, theory, and fantasy in human paleontology', *American Scientist* 65: 204–11.

Teleki, G. 1981 New York: 'The omnivorous diet and eclectic feeding habits of chimpanzees in Gombe National Park, Tanzania', pp. 303–43 in: Harding, R., and Teleki, G. (editors) 1981 New York: *Omnivorous Primates*.

Terry, R. 1974 Johannesburg: 'Raymond A. Dart: Taung 1924–1974', *The Museum of Man and Science*.

Time 1977 New York: 'Puzzling out man's ascent', 7 November.

Time 1978 New York: 'Leakey's find – Tracks of an ancient ancestor', 6 March.

Times, The 1914 London: News report, 19 April.

Times, The 1928 London: 'Hesperopithecus dethroned', Leader comment, 25 February.

Times, The 1953 London: Parliamentary report, 27 November.

Tobias, P. V. 1964 London: 'The Olduvai Bed I hominine with special reference to its cranial capacity', *Nature* 202: 3–4.

Tobias, P. V. 1967 Cambridge: *Olduvai Gorge vol 2. The Cranium and Maxillary Dentition of Australopithecus (Zinjanthropus) boisei*.

Tobias, P. V. 1968 New Delhi: 'The age of death among the australopithecines', *Anthropologist*, special volume.

Tobias, P. V. 1978 Johannesburg: Personal communication. Interview with author.

Tobias, P. V. T. 1981 London: 'The emergence of man in Africa and beyond', pp. 43–57 in: Young, J. Z., Jope, E. M., and Oakley, K. P. (editors) 1981 London: 'The emergence of man', *Phil. Trans. R. Soc.* B.292.

Tobias, P. V., and Napier, J. R. 1964 London: Letter to *The Times*, 29 May.

Toth, N. 1982 Berkeley: 'The stone technologies of early hominids at Koobi Fora, Kenya', Ph.D diss. Univ. of California.

Trinkaus, E. 1984 New York: 'Western Asia', pp. 251–94 in: Smith, F. H., and Spencer F. (editors) 1984 New York: *The Origin of Modern Humans.*

Trinkaus, E. (editor) (in prep.) Cambridge: *Corridors, Cul-de-sacs and Coalescence: The Biocultural Foundations of Modern People.*

Trinkaus, E., and Howells, W. W. 1979 New York: 'The Neanderthals', *Scientific American* 241 (6): 118–33.

Tuttle, R. (editor) 1972 Chicago: *The Functional and Evolutionary Biology of Primates.*

Tuttle, R. H. (editor) 1976 The Hague: *Primate Morphology and Evolution.*

Valladas, H., Reyss, J. L., Joron, J. L., Valladas, G., Bar-Yosef, O., and Vandermeersch, B. 1988 London: 'Thermoluminescence dating of Mousterian "Proto-Cro-Magnon" remains from Israel and the origin of modern man', *Nature* 331: 614–16.

Vallois, H. V. 1949. Philadelphia: 'The Fontéchevade fossil men', *Amer. J. Phys. Anthrop.* NS 7: 339–62.

Vallois, H. V. 1954 London: 'Neandertals and Praesapiens', *J. Roy. Anthrop. Inst.* 84: 111–30.

Virchow, R. 1872 Berlin: 'Untersuchung des Neanderthal-Schädels', *Zoo. Ethn.* 4.

Walker, A. C. 1973 Nairobi: 'Remains attributable to Australopithecus in the East Rudolf succession', pp. 484–9 in: Coppens, Y., Howell, F. C., Isaac, G. Ll., and Leakey, R. E. F. (editors) 1976 Chicago: *Earliest Man and Environments in the Lake Rudolf Basin.*

Walker, A. C. 1978 Cambridge, Mass.: Personal communication. Interview with author.

Walker, A. C. 1981 Oxford: 'Biological adaptations in the Koobi Fora hominids', in prep. for: Leakey, R. E. F., and Isaac, G. Ll. (editors) *Koobi Fora Research Project monograph series.*

Walker, A. C., and Leakey, R. E. F. 1978 New York: 'The hominids of East Turkana', *Scientific American* 239 (8): 54–66.

Walker, A. C., Leakey, R. E. F., Harris, J. M., and Brown, F. H. 1986 London: '2·5 Myr *Australopithecus boisei* from west of Lake Turkana, Kenya', *Nature* 322: 517–22.

Wang, Y., Xue, X., Yue, L., Zhao, J., and Liu, S. 1979: 'Discovery of Dali fossil man and its preliminary study', *Sci. Sin.* 24: 303–6.

Washburn, S. 1960 New York: 'Tools and human evolution', *Scientific American* 203 (3): 3–15.

Washburn, S. L. (editor) 1963 Chicago: *Social Life of Early Man.*

Washburn, S. L., and Jay, P. C. (editors) 1968 New York: *Perspectives on Human Evolution.*

Washburn, S. L., and Lancaster, J. 1968 New York: 'The evolution of hunting', pp. 293–303 in: Lee, R. B., and DeVore, I. 1968 New York: *Man the Hunter*.

Waterston, D. 1913a London: 'The human skull etc. from Piltdown; discussion', *Quarterly Journal of the Geological Society* 69.

Waterston, D. 1913b London: 'The Piltdown mandible', *Nature* 92: 319.

Weidenreich, F. 1936: 'The mandibles of *Sinanthropus pekinensis*: a comparative study', *Palaeont. sinica*, Ser. D.7, III: 1–163.

Weidenreich, F. 1937: 'The dentition of *Sinanthropus pekinensis*: a comparative odontography of the hominids', *Palaeont. sinica*, New Ser. D.I, 1–180: 1–121.

Weidenreich, F., 1941: 'The extremity bones of *Sinanthropus pekinensis*', *Palaeont. sinica*, New Ser. D.5: 1–150.

Weidenreich, F. 1943: 'The skull of *Sinanthropus pekinensis*: a comparative study on a primitive hominid skull', *Palaeont. sinica*, New Ser. D.10: 1–291.

Weiner, J. S. 1955 London: *The Piltdown Forgery*.

Wells, L. H. 1966 Johannesburg: 'The Robert Broom memorial lecture', *South African Journal of Science*, September 1967: 364.

White, H. J. O. 1926 London: 'The geology of the country near Lewes, with map by Edmunds, F. H.', *Memoir Geological Survey of England and Wales*, Expl. sheet 319.

White, T. D. 1977 Philadelphia: 'New fossil hominids from Laetoli, Tanzania', *American Journal of Physical Anthropology* 46: 197–230.

White, T. D. 1985 New York: 'The hominids of Hadar and Laetoli: an element-by-element comparison of the dental samples', pp. 138–52 in: Delson, E. (editor) 1985 New York: *Ancestors: The Hard Evidence*.

White, T. D. 1987 Washington: Quoted in: Lewin, R. 1987b Washington: 'The earliest "humans" were more like apes', *Science* 236: 1061–3.

White, T. D., and Harris, J. M. 1977 Washington: 'Suid evolution and correlation of African hominid localities', *Science* 198: 13–21.

Wilson, A. C., Cann, R. L., Carr, S. M., George, M., Gyllensten, U. B., Helm-Bychowski, K. M., Higuchi, R. G., Palumbi, S. R., Prager, E. M., Sage, R. D., and Stoneking, M. 1985 London: 'Mitochondrial DNA and two perspectives of evolutionary genetics', *Biological Journal of the Linnean Society* 26: 375–400.

Wilson, A. C., Stoneking, M., Cann, R. L., Prager, E. M., Ferris, S. D., Wrischnik, L. A., and Higuchi, R. G. 1986 Berlin (in prep.): 'Mitochondrial clans and the age of our common mother', *Proceedings of the 7th International Congress of Human Genetics*.

Wolpoff, M. H. 1971 London: 'Competitive exclusion among Lower Pleistocene hominids: The single species hypothesis', *Man* 6: 601–14.

Wolpoff, M. H. 1980 New York: *Paleoanthropology*.

Wolpoff, M. H. 1981 London: 'Allez Neanderthal', *Nature* 289: 823–4.

Wolpoff, M. H., 1985: 'Evolution in *Homo erectus*: The question of stasis', *Paleobiology* 10: 389–406.

Wolpoff, M. H., Wu, X., and Thorne, A. G. 1984: 'Modern *Homo sapiens* origins: a general theory of hominid evolution involving the fossil evidence from East Asia', pp. 411–83 in: Smith, F. H., and Spencer, F. (editors) 1984 New York: *The Origins of Modern Humans: A World Survey of the Fossil Evidence*.

Woo, J. K. 1966 New York: 'The skull of Lantian Man', *Current Anthropology* 7: 83–6.

Woo, J. K. and Peng R. C. 1959: 'Fossil human skull of Early Palaeoanthropic stage found at Mapa, Shaoquan, Kwantung Province', *Vert. Palasiat.* 3: 176–82.

Wood, B. A. 1984 London: 'The origin of *Homo erectus*', pp. 99–111 in: Andrews, P., and Franzen, J. L. (editors) 1984 Frankfurt: 'The early evolution of man, with special emphasis on Southeast Asia and Africa', *Courier Forschungsinstitut Senckenberg* 69.

Wood, B. A. 1987 London: 'Who is the "real" *Homo habilis*?', *Nature* 327: 187–8.

Wood, B. A., Martin, L., and Andrews, P. (editors) 1986 Cambridge: *Major Topics in Primate and Human Evolution*.

Woodward, A. S. 1885 Macclesfield: 'Modern ideas of the Creation', *Macclesfield Courier and Herald*, 28 March.

Woodward, A. S. 1913 Birmingham: 'Missing links among extinct animals', *Report of the British Association*.

Woodward, A. S. W. 1916 London: 'Charles Dawson – An obituary', *Geological Magazine* (6) 3: 477–9.

Woodward, A. S. 1917 London: 'Fourth note on the Piltdown gravel, with evidence of a second skull of *Eoanthropus dawsoni*', *Quarterly Journal of the Geological Society* 73: 1–10.

Woodward, A. S. 1922 London: Letter to *The Times*, 22 May.

Woodward, A. S. 1933 London: 'Early human remains in East Africa', *Man* 33: 210.

Woodward, A. S. 1948 London: *The Earliest Englishman*.

Wu, R. 1982 Hong Kong: 'Recent advances of Chinese palaeoanthropology', *Occ. Pap. Ser. II* Univ. Hong Kong.

Wu, R., and Lin, S. 1983 New York: 'Peking Man', *Sci. Am.* 248: 78–86.

Wu, R., and Lin, S. 1985: *Chinese Palaeoanthropology: Retrospect and Prospect*.

Wu, R., and Olsen, J. W. (editors) 1985 Orlando: *Palaeoanthropology and Palaeolithic Archaeology in the People's Republic of China*.

Yates, F., and Healy, M. J. R. 1951 London: 'Statistical methods in anthropology', *Nature* 168: 1116.

Young, J. Z., Jope, E. M., and Oakley, K. P. (editors) 1981 London: 'The emergence of man', *Phil. Trans. R. Soc.* B.292: 3–5.

Zdansky, O. 1923 Peking: 'Uber ein Saungerknockenlager in Chou K'ou Tien', *Geological Survey of China Bulletin* 5: 83–9.

Zdansky, O. 1927 Peking: 'Preliminary notice on two teeth of a hominid from a cave in Chihli (China)', *Geological Society of China Bulletin* 5: 281–4.

Zdansky, O. 1928 Peking: 'Die Saugetiere der Quartarfauna von Chou K'ou Tien', *Palaeontologia Sinica*, Series C, 5 (4).

Zdansky, O. 1978 Uppsala: Personal communication. Interview with author.

Zuckerman, S. 1966 Edinburgh: 'Myths and methods in anatomy', *Journal of the Royal College of Surgeons of Edinburgh* 11: 87–114.

CHRONOLOGICAL TABLE

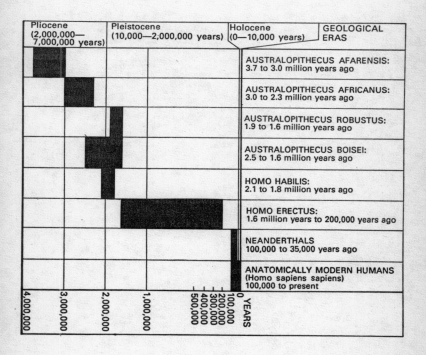

Pliocene (2,000,000—7,000,000 years)	Pleistocene (10,000—2,000,000 years)	Holocene (0—10,000 years)	GEOLOGICAL ERAS
			AUSTRALOPITHECUS AFARENSIS: 3.7 to 3.0 million years ago
			AUSTRALOPITHECUS AFRICANUS: 3.0 to 2.3 million years ago
			AUSTRALOPITHECUS ROBUSTUS: 1.9 to 1.6 million years ago
			AUSTRALOPITHECUS BOISEI: 2.5 to 1.6 million years ago
			HOMO HABILIS: 2.1 to 1.8 million years ago
			HOMO ERECTUS: 1.6 million years to 200,000 years ago
			NEANDERTHALS 100,000 to 35,000 years ago
			ANATOMICALLY MODERN HUMANS (Homo sapiens sapiens) 100,000 to present

4,000,000 3,000,000 2,000,000 1,000,000 500,000 400,000 300,000 200,000 100,000 0 YEARS

INDEX